KU-246-774

UNDERSTANDING EARLY YEARS INEQUALITY

Understanding Early Years Inequality uses critical sociological perspectives to examine the impact of changing assessment policy on primary school classrooms, with a particular focus on issues of inequality. Drawing on accounts of life in early years classrooms, Alice Bradbury suggests that a specific model of the 'good learner' operates, and that this model works to exclude some groups of pupils from positions of educational success.

Key themes examined throughout this book relate to:

- the relationship between assessment policy and children's identities as learners;
- the complexity of classroom life;
- the power of assessment to shape definitions of 'learning' and 'learners';
- the impact of discourses of class, race, religion and the 'inner city' on how children are assessed, and how assumptions about inner city schools and low attainment can put pressure on teachers to assess children in particular ways.

In this important text, the author argues that assessment policies can have a huge impact on classrooms and teachers, as well as having potentially damaging effects for young children, particularly those from minoritised and economically disadvantaged backgrounds. The book explores in detail the complex interaction of education policies with discourses of attainment and expectation, and the resulting reproduction of patterns of inequality.

Understanding Early Years Inequality will have an immediate impact on current debates about educational policy and practice in early years education, and will be of particular interest to academics and students in educational studies, sociology of

20 17004 373

NEW COLLEGE, SWINDON

te of Education, University of London,

UNDERSTANDING EARLY YEARS INEQUALITY

Policy, assessment and young children's identities

Alice Bradbury

Routledge
Taylor & Francis Group

LONDON AND NEW YORK

First published 2013
by Routledge
2 Park Square, Milton Park, Abingdon, Oxon OX14 4RN

Simultaneously published in the USA and Canada
by Routledge
711 Third Avenue, New York, NY 10017

Routledge is an imprint of the Taylor & Francis Group, an informa business

2017004373

© 2013 Alice Bradbury

The right of Alice Bradbury to be identified as author of this work has been asserted by her in accordance with sections 77 and 78 of the Copyright, Designs and Patents Act 1988.

All rights reserved. No part of this book may be reprinted or reproduced or utilised in any form or by any electronic, mechanical, or other means, now known or hereafter invented, including photocopying and recording, or in any information storage or retrieval system, without permission in writing from the publishers.

Trademark notice: Product or corporate names may be trademarks or registered trademarks, and are used only for identification and explanation without intent to infringe.

British Library Cataloguing in Publication Data
A catalogue record for this book is available from the British Library

Library of Congress Cataloging in Publication Data
    Bradbury, Alice, author.
Understanding early years inequality : policy, assessment and young children's identities / by Alice Bradbury.
pages cm
Includes index.
ISBN 978-0-415-63976-7 (hardback) – ISBN 978-0-415-63977-4 – 978-0-203-08318-5 1. Early childhood education–Social aspects–Great Britain. 2. Educational equalization–Great Britain. I. Title.
LB1139.3.G7B73 2012
372.21–dc23

                                                                                           2012039019

ISBN: 978-0-415-63976-7 (hbk)
ISBN: 978-0-415-63977-4 (pbk)
ISBN: 978-0-203-08318-5 (ebk)

Typeset in Bembo
by Fakenham Prepress Solutions, Fakenham, Norfolk NR21 8NN

CONTENTS

FIGURES AND TABLES

Figures

Tables

ACKNOWLEDGEMENTS

This book would not have been possible without the support of several people, all of whom I wish to thank. The empirical data was collected during a research study funded by the Economic and Social Research Council (Grant no. ES/G018987/1) with the support of the Institute of Education, University of London. Although they remain anonymous, I am enormously indebted to the teachers and children at the two schools in this study for making me feel so welcome and for putting up with my constant note-taking. I am especially grateful to the class teachers for allowing me access to their classrooms and giving up their time to be interviewed.

There are a number of people at the Institute of Education I need to thank for their help with this book, though any errors are, of course, my own. In particular, I am grateful for the support and guidance of Deborah Youdell and David Gillborn, who inspired me to research this area and have helped me throughout the process, from initial idea, through months of fieldwork, to writing up and book publication. They have pushed me to think and to write in different ways, and convinced me that the story this book tells is worth writing. I also wish to thank Michael Apple for his advice and particularly for inviting me to spend time at the University of Wisconsin-Madison, a trip which provided me with an international perspective on these issues. I am grateful to a number of colleagues at the Institute and elsewhere who have provided advice and comments on this work along the way, particularly Mindy Blaise, Paul Connolly, Beth Graue, Stephen Ball, Jon Swain and Carol Vincent. I am also grateful for the support of my colleagues in the Department of Education at Roehampton for their support during the writing of this book, and everyone from Routledge who has helped during the publication process.

On a more personal note, I wish to thank my husband Alistair for his unstinting support over the last few years, from the sympathy provided when the fieldwork was difficult, to sharing in the celebrations of each small success. I wish to extend my thanks to my family and friends, all of whom have encouraged me in this work, especially my mum Jenny and my sister Katy, and my friends at the Institute who have been there throughout the research process.

Finally, I dedicate this book to my father, Graham Bradbury, who has been immensely supportive of my work and also so helpful with his knowledge of publishing. My Dad brought me up to believe in a principle that is central to this work – that everyone should have an equal chance in education – and I will be for ever grateful.

1

POLICY AND INEQUALITY IN PRIMARY EDUCATION

Introduction

This book examines the relationship between education policy and inequalities in education, in the early years of primary education. Drawing on ethnographic accounts of two Reception classes of children aged four and five, I explore the relationships between assessment practices, children's identities as learners and the reproduction of disparities in attainment in terms of 'race', class and gender. It is a story, to put it simply, of how policy changes what teachers do, what they think is important and how they judge children as 'good' or 'bad' learners. It is a story of how some children, aged four or five, will spend their first year in school being talked about and assessed as having become successful learners and some will not, and of how *who* they are – in terms of 'race', class and gender, among others – will affect this. It is also a story of the inner city school, where government schemes and media representations encourage low expectations, and where teachers feel they have to change children's results so that they make sense within these ideas about urban schools.

In this book, critical sociological perspectives are used to examine the impact of changing assessment policy on primary school classrooms. Central themes include the complexity of classroom life and the power of assessment to shape definitions of 'learning' and 'learners'. The aim is to increase our understanding of how inequalities are produced and reproduced in the early years, through an examination of the impact of discourses of class, 'race', religion and the 'inner city' on how children are assessed. The focus of much of the ethnographic data here is on the impact of an assessment policy, introduced in 2003, for children in Reception, the first compulsory year of school. This assessment, the Early Years Foundation Stage Profile (EYFS Profile), was the first statutory assessment for children of this age in England and is one of the most formal systems worldwide (note that alternative systems operate in other parts of the UK). It is conducted through teacher assessment throughout the school year, and is based on teachers' observations of children in all areas of classroom life. The EYFS Profile includes social, physical and emotional development as well as more academic skills, and is explained in detail below. These assessments play a crucial role in shaping children's schooling and yet there has been virtually no research on the impact on the EYFS Profile on classroom practices. The Profile was reviewed and reformed in 2012 by the Conservative–Liberal Democrat coalition government, and, in the final chapter, I consider the impact of these changes to the assessment.

I begin this introductory chapter with a discussion of the wider context of education policy in the 2000s under New Labour, before explaining reform of the early years and the introduction of the EYFS Profile. These changes are then placed in an international context of increased standardisation in early childhood education. Final sections of the chapter explore reactions to the EYFS in the press and in government, and the patterns of inequalities the assessment has revealed, before I set out the structure of the rest of the book.

Education policy under New Labour

The introduction of a statutory assessment system for children aged five, comparable with Standard Assessment Tasks (Sats) for children aged seven and 11, has to be considered within the wider context of education policy under the New Labour governments of the late 1990s and 2000s. Increased regulation of the early years was consistent with a wider trend towards systems of accountability in schools in England (Ball, 2008). Policies such as high-stakes tests for children aged seven, 11, 14 and 16 at the end of each 'Key Stage', the use of league tables to compare results between schools, and school choice policies became embedded in the education system through the 1990s and 2000s, as Labour governments built upon the neoliberal market-based education policies of the Conservative governments in the 1990s. Under Labour, more detail was introduced to league tables, including 'value added' measures, and there were increased sanctions for schools deemed to be failing. Diversification of school types continued with the expansion of faith schools and the introduction of Academies, independent of control from local government. The wealth of new initiatives and reforms in education was accompanied by a huge investment in the sector, with a £33 billion increase in total spending on education during the first ten years of Labour governments (DCSF, 2009a: 3). In common with a worldwide trend of increased focus and investment in early years education, this included an 84 per cent increase in spending on education for the under fives in England between 1997 and 2009 (Institute for Fiscal Studies, 2009: 24).

In 2003, the Department for Education and Skills[1] introduced the term 'Foundation Stage' for provision for children from three to five years old, suggesting equal status with Key Stage 1 (ages 5–7) and Key Stage 2 (ages 7–11), which had existed for several years. Curriculum guidance was provided for the

Foundation Stage, and 'Early Learning Goals' were set. In 2008, this increased status was solidified when all educational provision from birth to five was brought together under the unwieldy term 'Early Years Foundation Stage' (EYFS). The intention was to create some consistency in provision across preschools, nursery schools, home childcare and school classes for three-to-five-year-olds, with the identification of key themes and principles. The EYFS was described as providing a 'regulatory and quality framework for the provision of learning, development and care' from birth to five years (DfE, 2010d). The framework set out objectives for children across different age groups using expected developmental points, including statements such as 'Learns by observation about actions and their effects' and 'Are logical thinkers from birth' (DfE, 2010a). These staged developmental points reach their conclusion in an assessment conducted at the end of the 'stage' – the Early Years Foundation Stage Profile, which is compiled in Reception in primary schools. Previously, systems of assessment for this age group varied widely and there was no statutory requirement to report the results to the government. 'Baseline' assessments were the main method used for assessing pupils when they first entered school, and these varied widely between different areas (Kirkup et al., 2003). The EYFS Profile was the first system to be consistent across different regions in England, allowing results from different areas to be compared and an analysis of patterns of attainment by pupil characteristics to be conducted for the first time.

The introduction of the Foundation Stage Framework and then the Early Years Foundation Stage reflected the government's concerns to 'raise standards' and increase accountability in this sector. The EYFS Profile results are used to monitor standards of teaching in Reception classes; they function as an accountability measure of 'value for money' in early years education. The introduction of a statutory assessment marked the spread of accountability mechanisms down into early years, and, as I discuss in later chapters, signalled the accompanying arrival of what Stephen Ball terms 'the terrors of performativity' into this sector (Ball, 2003b). Before I consider the detail of the EYFS Profile, I provide some background information on Early Years Foundation Stage classrooms.

The Early Years Foundation Stage

The Early Years Foundation Stage covers the wide variety of provision for children from birth to five that exists in England. Children under four attend a range of settings on a voluntary basis, including playgroups, preschools and care by childminders, all of which come under the EYFS framework. Children aged three and four may also attend Nursery classes located in primary schools. The government funds part-time childcare in a range of settings so that provision is free for all children of three and four; as a result, the majority of children are in some form of early years education at the age of four (DfE, 2010e). However, provision for children of four and five has a different status: attendance at school is compulsory by law from the term (semester) after a child's fifth birthday.[2] The vast majority of children begin to attend a 'Reception' class in the September or January before they turn five.[3] Reception classes cater for these four- and five-year-olds until they begin Year 1 in the following September. Thus compulsory education begins earlier than in many other countries and this is a constant source of debate in the sector (Alexander, 2009; DfE, 2010c). Reception classes, although located in primary schools, are the final year of the Early Years Foundation Stage, and thus are bound by its statutory requirements rather than the National Curriculum which applies to Key Stages 1 and 2. Before the Foundation Stage and the EYFS, Reception classes had not been part of a designated stage and were loosely linked to Key Stage 1 (Nutbrown, 2006), and the new designation has been regarded by many in the sector as an 'asset to status' (Hargreaves and Hopper, 2006). However, Reception remains an important part of the primary school: Reception children and staff participate in whole-school activities, use school facilities such as sports grounds and the lunch hall, and may also join in with assemblies. The headteacher of the school is responsible for the Reception class, although it may be managed on a day-to-day basis by an EYFS Coordinator. The Reception classes and Nursery classes for younger children are commonly known as the 'early years' in schools in England, and this is a term I use throughout this book to distinguish Reception from other 'early childhood' settings.

In England practices in Reception classes are guided, as part of the EYFS, by four main principles:

A Unique Child
- Every child is a competent learner from birth who can be resilient, capable, confident and self-assured.

Positive Relationships
- Children learn to be strong and independent from a base of loving and secure relationships with parents and/or a key person.

Enabling Environments
- The environment plays a key role in supporting and extending children's development and learning.

Learning and Development
- Children develop and learn in different ways and at different rates, and all areas of Learning and Development are equally important and inter-connected.

(from DCSF, 2008b)

As shown from these principles, the idea of 'development' is embedded in the EYFS. The importance of 'enabling environments' is a key consideration in the case of Reception classes, which provide a wide range of different activities to

TABLE 1.1 Examples of indoor and outdoor activities in Reception

Indoor activities	Outdoor activities
• Role-play, for example in the 'home corner' which may be set up as a kitchen, a café, a doctors' surgery, a school • Writing area with a range of implements and surfaces, plus writing on small whiteboards or the class whiteboard • Construction, for example wooden blocks • 'Small world' play, for example toy animals in a farm setting, cars on road mats, train sets, dinosaurs • Painting • Sand tray and water tray with containers and toys • Music area, for example tapes/CDs with player and instruments to play • Light box with different objects • Craft, for example making objects from old containers • Puzzle table with different jigsaws, word games, dominoes, maths games • Reading corner • Cooking with an adult	• Climbing frames, slides • Riding bikes, tricycles or scooters • Drawing in chalk on a board or the tarmac • Balance beams • Hoops and skipping ropes • Football/ball games • Dressing up outfits • Giant construction toys, for example giant building blocks • Toy cars and spaceships

enable 'learning and development' in all areas of the curriculum. Children spend the majority of the day in 'free play', where they can select what they want to do from a range of both indoor and outdoor activities and move freely between them. Some examples are given in Table 1.1.

Reception classes usually have one main class teacher and one or two 'teaching assistants' (TAs), who are not qualified teachers. During 'free play', the adults either supervise and support a specific activity, sometimes working with a pre-selected group of children, or move between activities observing children. Alongside this play-based curriculum there are some formal lessons conducted by the teacher, usually lasting less than 30 minutes, where children sit on an area of carpet and the teacher directs from the whiteboard. There are usually 'lessons' like this in mathematics, literacy and phonics each day, plus additional sessions on other topics. There are several other times when children sit together for 'story time' or to play a class game. The government provides free fruit for schools, so most Reception classes also have a mid-morning 'fruit time', sitting on the carpet. There may be no formal 'play times' because children move in and out of the classroom as they choose (when the weather allows). This structure and play-based curriculum is quite different from other classrooms in primary schools, and has very different physical requirements in terms of space and access.

The activities and lessons provided in Reception are based on the EYFS framework, which divide the play-based curriculum into six 'Areas of Learning'; these form the basis for the EYFS Profile:

- personal, social and emotional development
- communication, language and literacy
- problem solving, reasoning and numeracy
- knowledge and understanding of the world
- physical development
- creative development.

How the EYFS Profile works

The EYFS Profile is assessed throughout the year by the class teacher, who collects 'evidence' relating to the six areas of learning. These areas of learning are broken down into 13 smaller sections known as 'scales', which are spread unevenly across the six areas:

- Three Personal, Social and Emotional Development (PSED) scales:
  - Dispositions and Attitudes
  - Social Development
  - Emotional Development
- Four Communication, Language and Literacy (CLL) scales:
  - Language for Communicating and Thinking
  - Linking Sounds and Letters
  - Reading
  - Writing
- Three Problem Solving, Reasoning and Numeracy (PSRN) scales:
  - Numbers as Labels and for Counting
  - Calculating
  - Shape, Space and Measures
- One Knowledge and Understanding of the World (KUW) scale
  - One Physical Development (PD) scale
  - One Creative Development (CD) scale

(QCA, 2008)

Each of these 13 scales is made up of nine developmental statements or points, making a total of 117 points altogether. (A complete list of all the points is provided in Appendix 1.) Teachers make observations of children in the classroom, take photographs and collect children's work as evidence of their attainment of these points. The points vary in difficulty, but do not have to be achieved strictly in order. Table 1.2 shows some examples of EYFS Profile points, with examples of the kind of observations that would demonstrate them, taken from the EYFS Profile Handbook (QCA, 2008).

TABLE 1.2 Examples of observations and related Profile points from EYFS Profile Handbook

EYFS Profile point	Example of observation that would demonstrate the point
The child is confident to explore new experiences and talk about them with adults and peers. (PSED – Dispositions and Attitudes point 7)	Jack and Ellie are playing outside with the cars. Ellie decides to get the blocks to build a garage.
The child communicates needs, views and feelings, explaining his or her own needs. (PSED – Emotional Development point 5)	At circle time during Ramadan some of the children talk about their parents fasting. Colin looks very concerned. 'That must be very hard – I would miss my chips.'
During a range of activities, the child uses language to imagine, act out or develop experiences. (CLL – Language for Communication and Thinking point 5)	Marcel makes a ringing sound for a telephone. He picks up the phone in the hospital role-play area and says 'Hello,' and passes it to his friend saying 'It's for you, the ambulance is coming.'
The child attempts to read more complex words. (CLL – Linking Sounds and Letters point 8)	Walking round the sea life centre Jack notices the sign 'crabs' and says 'We haven't seen the crabs yet.'
The child consistently recognises numerals in a range of contexts. (PSRN – Numbers as Labels and for Counting point 5)	Keith walks past the Year 5 classroom. He notices the year group sign and says 'Oh look, a 5. I'm five.'
The child knows about technology and its use in his or her life and local environment. The child exploits the technological opportunities around him- or herself to enhance his or her learning. (KUW – point 7)	Tamsin picks up a tin of beans in the 'shop'. She holds a wooden block against the bar code and makes a beeping noise. 'That's 20p,' she says.
The child reacts to stories, music and rhythm, copying gestures and movements. (PD – point 1)	Sean hears a plane flying overhead and looks up to watch it. He puts out his arms and moves around, making engine noises.
The child recalls and sings songs independently, often as he or she engages with other activities. (CD – point 4)	Jack and Max are making a puzzle. Max begins to sing 'The Wheels on the Bus'. He sings it accurately. Jack joins in; they sing the song and make all the actions to match the song.

Source: Adapted from QCA, 2008

Towards the end of the academic year, teachers make a final decision on which points to award to each child. They are advised in the Handbook: 'Judgements against these scales should be made from observation of consistent and independent behaviour, predominantly from children's self-initiated activities' (QCA, 2008: 5). A positive or negative is recorded for each point, giving each child an overall total figure out of 117. This data is collected by the Local Authority. Unlike results from tests for older children, EYFS Profile data is not published at a school level so that different institutions can be compared; instead, the government publishes data for all schools in England with breakdowns by area, gender, ethnic group and other pupil characteristics. Results are also used in internal 'performance management' processes which assess teachers, and externally by government school inspectors and Local Authority advisers known as 'school improvement partners'. The data also forms an important part of the assessment of a school's performance conducted by Ofsted, the school inspection service. While there is no official 'expected level' in the EYFS Profile, unlike with Sats, the government uses benchmarks such as a 'good level of development', which is calculated as getting six or more in each of the seven PSED and CLL scales, as well as achieving a total of 78 or more out of 117 (DCSF, 2008a). These benchmarks are used in the reporting of national and regional EYFS Profile results each year, and allow for the scrutiny of results by pupil characteristics demonstrated later in this chapter.

International trends in early childhood education

Early Childhood Education (or ECE, as provision for children under eight is known internationally) has become increasingly prominent in education policy agendas across the world. In particular, the idea that investment in early childhood education has benefits beyond the sector has become commonplace in discussions of public spending priorities: the US Budget statement of 2010 was typical in its claims that 'Quality early education is an investment that pays off for years to come by preparing the youngest children for a lifetime of learning' (White House, 2010). 'Quality' early childhood education is touted as the solution to social problems, attainment gaps and economic decline. But, while many in the sector who have felt that their efforts have not been appreciated may welcome this increased focus, it has brought with it particular ideas and discourses – of 'quality', 'standards' and 'accountability' – which have had implications for both early childhood settings and the children who attend them.

The EYFS and its predecessor the Foundation Stage reflect an international trend towards increased standardisation and regulation of early childhood settings (Yelland, 2010b). Across the developed world, governments have focused on the need for provision across the early childhood sector to be consistent in its aims and to reach certain 'quality' standards (Dahlberg and Moss, 2005; Farquhar and Fitzsimons, 2008; Hultqvist and Dahlberg, 2001). In Australia, an Early Years Learning Framework was introduced in 2009 and linked with the National Quality Standard 'in order to ensure nationally consistent and quality early childhood education across sectors and jurisdictions' (DEEWR, 2010). In the United States, early childhood education was included in the Obama government's stimulus package; according to a White House website statement on education, 'The President supports a seamless and comprehensive set of services and support for children, from birth through age 5 [...] he will urge states to impose high standards across all publicly funded early learning settings' (White House, 2010). His predecessor's early childhood initiative, 'Good Start, Grow Smart', had already asked states to develop early learning standards, aligned with their standards for elementary schools (Brown, 2007). However, this trend towards standardisation prompts many questions from practitioners, researchers and academics – about the nature of 'quality' in ECE and how can it be measured, and about what standards should be expected and who is capable of assessing against them (Dahlberg, Moss and Pence, 2007; Yelland, 2010a). As Nicola Yelland has commented in relation to the EYFS in England:

> Teachers and carers are expected to assume and absorb the general defini-
> tions and observable behaviours as representative with little or no discussion
> about what constitutes "quality", the most effective, or best (for example)
> taking place. *(Yelland, 2010b: 6)*

In some ways, the EYFS is at the vanguard of this drive towards standardisation and accountability in early childhood education: a government review described it as 'an international exemplar' (Tickell, 2011). But the EYFS also mirrors the dominance of ideas about development, childhood and the importance of measurement seen in much ECE policy worldwide. Some of these ideas have a long history, while others have come to prominence more recently with the influence of neoliberal values of accountability. For decades, ECE policy has been dominated by discourses of 'development' and 'developmentally appro-priate practice' (DAP) which are based on developmental psychology and scientific 'reason' (Dahlberg and Moss, 2005). DAP is a powerful discourse because it works as 'an authoritative stamp that policy-makers recognize' due to its 'scientific' foundation (Brown, 2007: 656). According to Moss (2008), this is linked to:

> a particular form of modernity … [which is] highly regulatory, foregrounding
> order, control and certitude and privileging a particular concept of reason
> and knowledge: an instrumental, calculating and totalising reason and a
> scientific knowledge that is unified and claims to reveal an objective and
> universal truth about humanity, history and nature. *(Moss, 2008: 8)*

In the following chapters, I explore how this need for regulation and order is apparent in the EYFS; how it demands a specific form of 'knowledge' to be accumulated, and used to measure children in a particular way. In this sense, the EYFS is not a break from the past: discourses of development have been powerful in early years education in England for some time. However, I argue that the *statutory* nature of the EYFS does solidify specific discourses about the purpose of the early years, and in turn, some particular notions of childhood. In order to understand the power of policies such as the EYFS in shaping these ideas, there needs to be a recognition that

> there is no natural or evolutionary child, only the historically produced discourses and power relations that constitute the child as an object and subject of knowledge, practice and political intervention. *(Hultqvist and Dahlberg, 2001: 2)*

The EYFS is an example of the child as the subject of political intervention. Throughout this book, I argue that the EYFS has a powerful impact on the way in which early years educators understand how a child should be in the Reception classroom. This understanding of a 'learner' is shaped by the values that are implicit in the EYFS Profile points. Children are understood in relation to an idealised model of the 'learner', and the use of development statements as EYFS Profile points makes this process appear objective and scientific. The EYFS defines what is normal and what is not; like all developmental statements, they are transformed 'from a mythic norm ... to statements of how people should be' (Dahlberg and Moss, 2005: 7). Burman (2001) comments:

> whether milestones, gender types, reading ages, cognitive strategies, stages or skills ... they become enshrined within an apparatus of collective measurement and evaluation that constructs its own world of abstract autonomous babies; of norms, deviation from which is typically only acknowledged in the form of a deficit or 'problem'. *(Burman, 2001: 6, cited in Dahlberg and Moss, 2005: 7)*

With its designation of pupils as reaching or failing to reach a 'good level of development', the EYFS clearly defines some children as problematic at the very beginning of their education careers. This is a major concern of this book. The EYFS Profile represents an important baseline for children, a starting point for all further assessment. As I have argued elsewhere, the education system in England prioritises 'progress' and 'adding value' (Bradbury, 2011a), and thus these results have the potential to establish differences between children that, even if children all make progress at the same rate, will continue throughout their schooling. It is these differences in attainment in the EYFS Profile, which have the potential to set children on paths of educational success or failure, to which I now turn.

Inequality and the EYFS Profile

Over the last two decades, the government's publication of educational attainment levels has allowed a greater scrutiny of inequalities at all stages of education: overviews such as Gillborn and Mirza (2000) and Bhattacharyya, Ison and Blair (2003) analysed the complex and overlapping patterns of inequality that persist in the education system in England. At the same time, extensive research in schools has focused on the reproduction of unequal outcomes and experiences (Archer and Francis, 2007; Gillborn, 2008; Gillborn and Youdell, 2000; Rollock, 2007). However, other than Paul Connolly's study of infant classrooms (Connolly, 1998) conducted in the late 1990s, there had been little consideration of inequalities in early years or primary education until David Gillborn's 2006 discussion of the results arising from the new Foundation Stage Profile (Gillborn, 2006c; 2008). He pointed out that the new FSP results showed patterns of attainment by ethnic group (the government's term) that were broadly similar to those at Key Stages 2 and 4, while the previous local 'baseline' assessments showed far more variation between groups, with data from one large Local Authority area indicating that Black children were significantly more likely to reach the expected levels (Gillborn, 2006c: 327). Yet, there was no outcry or debate over this reversal of fortunes: 'the unnoticed, literally unremarkable changes in an assessment system [...] appear to have erased, virtually overnight, the only part of the education system where black children had out-performed their white counterparts' (p. 335). This article raised several important questions regarding inequalities and assessment in early years and was the direct inspiration for my research into classroom practices associated with the Profile.

Since 2003, the publication of the EYFS Profile results (and previously the Foundation Stage Profile results) by pupil characteristics has allowed greater scrutiny of differences in attainment in early years than ever before. In this analysis, I use data from three cohorts: the results from 2009, when this research was conducted in schools; and the results from 2010 and 2011. The results from 2012 show similar trends.[4] The aim is to show the persistence of disparities in attainment, by gender, 'race' and class indicators. The statistics focus on the differences in the proportions of students who gain the government's benchmark of a 'good level of development' on the EYFS Profile (hereafter also referred to as 'the benchmark').[5] In 2011 the Department also started using the term 'working securely' to mean gaining six or more points on the Literacy and Personal, Social and Emotional Development scales; some data is only available in this format, so it is used on occasion. It is important to note here that these data are taken as indicators of what children attain in the EYFS Profile, which may or may not equate to other assessments of their attainment; these are not taken as absolute indicators of 'ability' or potential. I intertwine my discussion of these statistics with examples of the press and political reaction to these results, to illustrate the discourses surrounding the Profile in the public arena.

The national picture

The benchmark of 'good level of development' is set quite high in comparison with the 'expected levels of attainment' at older key stages. In 2009, across England, 52 per cent of pupils reached the benchmark (DCSF, 2010a), and this was broadly consistent with previous years' results. This compares with 80 per cent of 11-year-olds gaining the expected Level 4 in English (and 79 per cent in Mathematics) in England in the same year (DCSF, 2010b). For several years, these low figures led to newspaper headlines bemoaning 'declining standards' and 'failing schools'; for example:

'One in five children unable to write their name or say alphabet' – *Daily Mail (Clark, 2006)*

'Under-fives struggle with writing' – *Guardian (Glendinning, 2007)*

'Under-fives too slow to catch on' – *TES (Ross, 2006)*

These articles often included examples of the EYFS Profile points (often incorrectly) which attempted to show the decline in standards. For example, a 2006 BBC News article titled 'Fewer children able to write name', began,

> More children than previously thought cannot write their names or recognise words like 'dog' and 'hat' by the age of five, according to new figures.
>
> *(BBC News, 2006)*

Such press coverage reflects a long tradition of concern over declining standards, which is part of a 'discourse of derision' (Ball, 1990) in education in the UK. This alarm at the results from EYFS was accompanied, however, by criticism of the provision of a curriculum and assessment system for early years, with the EYFS inappropriately termed the 'nappy curriculum' in many newspapers (for example, see Cassidy, 2010; Curtis, 2009; Paton, 2011).

Under the newly renamed but largely unchanged Early Years Foundation Stage Profile from 2008, there were some improvements in results, with 56 per cent of children gaining the benchmark in 2010 and 59 per cent in 2011 (DfE, 2011). This was perhaps due to increased confidence in the system following a period of 'bedding in', or indeed, as I discuss in Chapters Six and Seven, the pressure for improved results from local authorities and the government. Nevertheless, the press continued to react to results with headlines such as 'One in six boys of five can't write their name after year of school' (Loveys, 2010), and when the coalition government came to power in 2010, it announced a review of the entire EYFS (detailed below). This review did not, however, consider the wide disparities in attainment by different groups of pupils, which are my concern here and throughout this book.

Gender

Since the introduction of the Foundation Stage Profile in 2003, results have shown marked differences between levels of attainment between boys and girls (DCSF, 2007; 2008a; 2010a).[6] This has continued since the EYFS profile was introduced in 2008, as shown in Figure 1.1.

The 'gender gap' has frequently been cited as a concern in the government reports accompanying the statistics (DfE, 2011), and this lead to headlines such as:

'Girls beat the boys under "nappy curriculum" Early Years results – *Times*, 2010

'Boys of five "falling behind girls in writing skills"' – *Daily Mail*, 2010

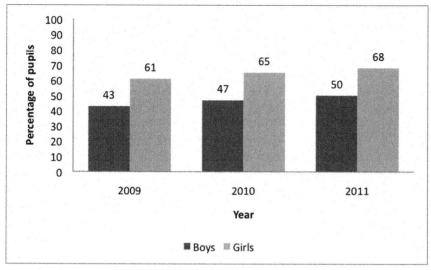

FIGURE 1.1 Percentage of pupils attaining a 'good level of development' by gender, 2009–2011

Source: DCSF, 2010a; DfE, 2010b; DfE, 2012b

This pattern is consistent with the wider education system in England: girls have outperformed boys in most statutory exams in the last decade. As a result, debates over gender have shifted (Skelton and Francis, 2009), and a 'poor boys' discourse of male students as 'victims' of schooling has come to dominate (Epstein et al., 1998).

However, attainment by gender is not consistent across the EYFS areas of learning: the report on the 2009 results notes that, although girls score higher than boys in 11 of the 13 EYFS Profile scales, more boys get the maximum number of points on the Knowledge and Understanding of the World scale, and the 'Calculating' scale in Problem Solving, Reasoning and Numeracy (DCSF, 2010a). The greatest differences between genders are on the Literacy scales, with 77 per cent of girls, compared with only 58 per cent of boys, gaining six or more points on the 'Writing' scale in 2011 (DfE 2011). These patterns mirror historical trends of higher male attainment in maths and science at all levels of education. These trends are connected, I would argue, to discourses of gendered attainment which, as Francis and Skelton (2005) comment position boys as 'naturally' intelligent and girls as 'plodding' hard-workers. Research in early childhood classrooms has suggested that long-standing discourses of gender difference and gendered accounts of 'development' have been linked to different expectations and assessments of students (Blaise, 2005; Connolly, 2004; Dyson, 1997; Skelton, Francis and Reiss, 2003), and it is important to consider the complexity of this issue rather than the simplistic analysis of 'girls beating boys'.

Class

The majority of discussions of class inequalities in England are based around analysis of children in receipt of Free School Meals (FSM), a crude proxy for 'lower' or 'working' class. In the case of the EYFS Profile, the differences in attainment between pupils on FSM and those not remain significant (see Figure 1.2).

These data, though revealing, can also be misleading in terms of pupil numbers: as Gillborn (2009) argues, while only 13 per cent of school students are eligible for FSM, 57 per cent of the population consider themselves 'working class', a term which is often used as synonymous with receiving FSM. Thus results which apply to only a small proportion of the population are inflated through a discursive slippage so that they apply to the majority. This has been particularly apparent in recent years with the frequent citing of 'white working-class boys' as the lowest attaining group (other than groups with very small numbers, such as Traveller and Gypsy/Roma pupils) when the statistics are actually based on FSM status. In the EFYS, the low percentage of boys receiving FSM reaching the government's benchmark has meant the Profile results have been brought into this debate; for example the *Guardian* newspaper titled its report on the publication of the 2009 results 'At five, a third of poor boys cannot write their names, report says' (*Guardian*, 2010).

This is not to say, however, that class (and class and gender) effects are not apparent: indeed, a more sophisticated measure provides further and more substantial evidence that the effects of income levels are present in early years.

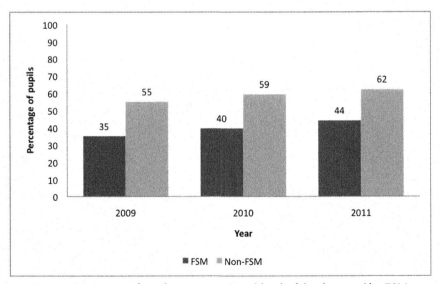

FIGURE 1.2   Percentage of pupils attaining a 'good level of development' by FSM status, 2009–2011

Source: DCSF, 2010a; DfE, 2010b; DfE, 2012b

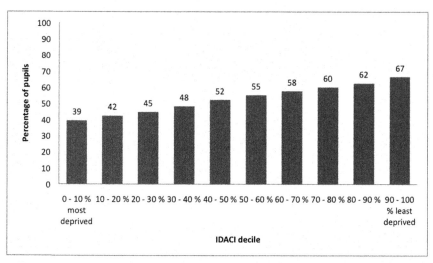

FIGURE 1.3   Percentage of pupils attaining a 'good level of development' by IDACI decile, 2009

Source: DCSF, 2010a

The government also publishes data relating to the Income Deprivation Affecting Children Index (IDACI), which measures deprivation in comparison with all other areas. IDACI scores allocate schools into groups of similar deprivation levels, each of which make up 10 per cent of the total. EYFS Profile results based on this Index for 2009 are shown in Figure 1.3. The pattern remained the same in 2010 (shown in Appendix 2). (Data was not published in this form for 2011.)

It is clear there is a strong correlation between deprivation and attainment of the benchmark in the EYFS Profile, at all levels, not only between pupils receiving FSM and those not. Since the coalition government came to power there has been much rhetoric around 'narrowing the gap' between lower income pupils and their more affluent counterparts, and when the 2011 EYFS Profile figures were released, a measure focusing on the 30 per cent most deprived children was also used. This included retrospective analysis of 2009 and 2010, and showed that, while only 42 per cent of children in the 30 per cent most deprived areas were deemed to be 'working securely' in 2009, this figure had risen to 51 per cent by 2011, an increase of nine points. During the same period, the percentage of children from the other 70 per cent of less deprived areas 'working securely' only rose six points, from 57 per cent to 63 per cent. The production of these figures in this form allowed the Department to claim some progress in 'narrowing the gap', although clear disparities between children at different levels of deprivation remain.

Previous research in this area has long argued that teachers' differential expectations of pupils due to class-based perceptions have an effect on their attainment in schools (Archer, Halsall and Hollingworth, 2007; Gillborn and Youdell, 2000). This is an important issue in this book, as both schools in this study were located in areas of socio-economic deprivation in inner London. Furthermore, as teachers in Reception collect information about children's families when they start school and often visit them at home, they gather more information about a child's perceived socio-economic status and home life than in other phases of education; this kind of information has previously been found to affect assumptions about pupils' attitudes and attainment (Gewirtz, 2001; Nayak, 2009; Wright, 2000).

Ethnic group

Despite the recent focus on White working-class boys as the 'victims' of education in England, there remain significant disparities in attainment by ethnic group[7] in statutory tests throughout the school system (Gillborn, 2009). The EYFS is no exception, with raced patterns of attainment broadly consistent since results began to be published by student characteristics (DCSF, 2010a; DfE, 2010b; DfE, 2012b). Figure 1.4 summarises the pattern for the results from 2009, using the larger ethnic groups for clarity (and presented in the order provided by the DCSF). (The data for 2010 and 2011, and the full data for all ethnic groups are reproduced in Appendix 2.[8])

In 2009, there were differences of over 15 percentage points between the proportions of higher attaining groups (Chinese, Mixed White and Asian, Indian, and White British) and the lower attaining groups (Pakistani, Bangladeshi, Any

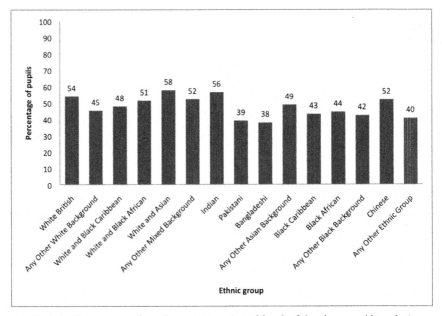

FIGURE 1.4   Percentage of pupils attaining a 'good level of development' by ethnic group, 2009

Source: DCSF, 2010a

Other Ethnic Group). A similar pattern was apparent in 2010 and in 2011; despite improvements from all groups, a distinct pattern remained.

As mentioned, results from the EYFS Profile have been used by David Gillborn (2006c; 2008) as an example of institutional racism. He argues that the lack of concern over the reversal of patterns of attainment by ethnic group in some areas is evidence that the 'normal workings' of the education system discriminate against children from minoritised communities. This viewpoint is influenced by Critical Race Theory (CRT), a body of scholarship originating in legal studies in the United States, which views racism as endemic in society; this work has increasing influence in studies of 'race' and education worldwide (Gillborn, 2006a; Ladson-Billings, 2004). I take Gillborn's argument as a starting point for my detailed analysis of how the EYFS Profile operates in classrooms and its complex relationship with the reproduction of race and other inequalities, and I return to reflect on how this data relates to his analysis in the concluding chapter. Issues of 'race' are very relevant in my research as the majority of pupils in the study schools were from minoritised communities[9], and issues of inequality by 'race' have been a long-standing concern in ECE (Connolly, 1998; Siraj-Blatchford, 1994; Wright, 1992). However, although this is an important element of the analysis, this is not a book only about 'race' in early years classrooms; I take an approach to identity informed by intersectionality.

Intersectional inequalities

Intersectionality is the idea that individual identity positions need to be understood as the intersections between different axes of identity. This framing has emerged from literature which has focused on the particular experiences of Black women, in contrast to work which has focused on gender or 'race' alone, and assumed that all women or all Black people have the same experience (Crenshaw, 1991; Phoenix and Pattynama, 2006). An intersectional analysis is crucial to any attempt at understanding how inequalities in education are produced and maintained. As we have seen with the EYFS statistics above, there are several significant axes of identity that impact on attainment, but to attempt to explore them one by one would mean ignoring the other significant differences. This argument is illustrated by Table 1.3, which uses data relating to gender, ethnic group and FSM status from the EYFS Profile results from 2009 (unfortunately, including IDACI here would produce an unreadable table). The darker shaded boxes indicate the five lowest attaining groups, and the lighter shaded boxes the five highest attaining groups.

The differences in attainment between, for example, White British FSM boys and White British non-FSM girls, suggest that simple analyses using one category can be misleading. Although all of the five lowest attaining groups are FSM boys, if we look at the Chinese FSM boys, we see that a higher proportion of these pupils reach the benchmark than some groups of *non*-FSM boys. The wide variance in results within ethnic groups, within genders and within FSM status illustrates the importance of using an intersectional approach to examination of these issues of

TABLE 1.3 Percentage of students attaining a 'good level of development' by ethnic group, gender and FSM status, 2009

	Boys, Non-FSM	Girls, Non-FSM	Boys, FSM	Girls, FSM
White British	47.8	67.2	24.9	42.2
Any Other White Background	39.0	54.5	28.6	41.2
White and Black Caribbean	41.8	62.1	30.5	47.5
White and Black African	44.1	65.3	28.8	47.9
White and Asian	52.4	70.8	26.6	48.0
Any Other Mixed Background	47.5	64.7	31.1	46.8
Indian	49.3	66.1	30.9	52.6
Pakistani	33.5	47.6	26.6	40.6
Bangladeshi	30.0	48.8	25.3	42.2
Any Other Asian Background	42.8	58.2	27.8	47.1
Black Caribbean	36.2	56.6	27.4	45.9
Black African	38.6	57.2	28.4	47.9
Any Other Black Background	36.3	56.1	25.0	45.1
Chinese	45.6	60.2	36.4	42.9
Any Other Ethnic Group	36.3	49.7	26.7	42.1

Source: DCSF, 2010a

identity. Furthermore, this data shows that although it is the low attainment of White British boys on FSM that has dominated debate relating to educational inequalities in recent years, the issues in early years education are complex. The debate often fails to consider other groups of pupils with such specificity. After all, only a tenth of a percentage more 'Any other Black background' FSM boys attain the benchmark, but this group rarely features in press reports. This book aims to address this imbalance by considering the attainment and experiences of several groups of pupils in detail.

Intersectional analysis also allows for an examination of other aspects of identity beyond the 'big three' of gender, class and race. In the case of this research, these other aspects include language, religion and location (particularly urban/rural divisions). The results for children with English as an additional language (EAL) are relevant here as many children in the schools in this study spoke a language other than English at home. These data show persistent disparities in attainment (see Figure 1.5).

There are no statistics based on religion, but the 2010 results do include some indication of another relevant issue, the geographical variations in results. Particularly relevant to this study, which was conducted in inner London, are statistics which show that the percentage of children gaining a 'good level of

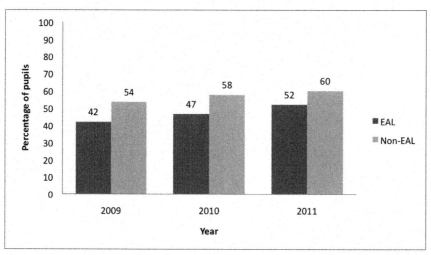

FIGURE 1.5 Percentage of pupils attaining a 'good level of development' by EAL status 2009–2011

Source: DCSF, 2010a; DfE, 2010b; DfE, 2012b

development' in London overall was 55 per cent (compared to 59 per cent across England), and in inner London the percentage was lower at 52 per cent (DfE, 2010b). In 2011, the percentages for London and inner London (at 60 per cent and 58 per cent) were closer to the national figure of 59 per cent, but the percentage of children 'working securely' in inner London was 46 per cent, compared to 50 per cent for the whole of London and 52 per cent in England (DfE, 2012b). These figures reflect long-standing concerns over the 'inner city' and education (Gulson, 2006; Leonardo and Hunter, 2009; Lupton and Tunstall, 2008), which I explore in detail in this book.

Before I set out how this book examines all of these disparities in attainment and the interaction with classroom practices, it is important to take note of the changes that happened to the EYFS in the early 2010s.

The coalition government's review and reform of the EYFS

In July 2010, following the formation of the Conservative–Liberal Democrat coalition government in May, the renamed Department for Education ordered a review of the EYFS which aimed to make it 'less bureaucratic and more focused on young children's learning and development' (DfE, 2010f). The Department's press release noted concerns not dissimilar to those in this book:

> Ministers are concerned that the EYFS framework is currently too rigid and puts too many burdens on the Early Years workforce, which has led to some

of the workforce saying they are spending less time with children, and more time ticking boxes. *(DfE, 2010f)*

The review was led by Dame Clare Tickell, the Chief Executive of Action for Children, and involved a consultation on the EYFS profile. Tickell's report, published in March 2011, called the EYFS 'cumbersome, repetitive and unnecessarily bureaucratic' (Tickell, 2011), and suggested it should be simplified and the number of goals to be attained by the end of the stage should be dramatically reduced. Alongside other recommendations relating to younger children, in relation to the EYFS Profile, Tickell recommended that there be a shift in focus to three 'prime areas of learning' and 'the basic social, emotional communication and language skills they need to learn and thrive at school' (Tickell, 2011). The Profile should be reduced, she argued, from 117 points to just '20 pieces of information that capture a child's level of development in a much less burdensome way' (Tickell, 2011: 6). These changes were introduced to schools from September 2012. The reforms were described as aiming to 'smooth the transition' from Reception to Year 1, and '[make] sure children start school ready and able to learn' (DfE, 2012c). Under the revised system, still called the EYFS Profile, teachers need to make a decision on 17 new early learning goals, each of which is made up of two to three sentences. Instead of a binary yes/no decision on these, they designate each child as 'meeting expected levels of development', 'exceeding expected levels', or 'not yet reaching expected levels' (DfE, 2012e).

The research discussed here was conducted in 2008 and 2009 and so is based on the old EYFS Profile (though I refer to it simply as the EYFS Profile throughout), and the impact of the new system is not yet known. As I discuss further in the concluding chapter, the Tickell review has left many of the fundamentals of the EYFS Profile system intact (the reliance on observations, the summative manner of assessment, and the use of decisions by teachers working with Local Authority moderation, among others). Furthermore, the reduction in the number of points to be assessed, while welcome in terms of the burden on teachers, has the potential to exacerbate the consequences of the EYFS Profile for some groups of children that I discuss here. The questions this book raises regarding the suitability of statutory assessment conducted by teachers and moderated by the local authority in early years education are as relevant to the coalition's version of the EYFS Profile as to New Labour's.

Understanding inequalities in the early years

The scale of differences in attainment in the EYFS Profile outlined in this chapter warrant serious consideration. They raise important questions regarding the causes of inequalities in education because they indicate that differences in attainment are present from the very beginning of formal education. They do not show, however, that the disparities in attainment apparent at age 11 and 16 are always present and therefore not the fault of the education system. Instead, they suggest, I would argue, that the processes and practices which work to create the disparities in attainment in later phases of schooling also operate in similar ways in early years, and in fact may be the result of what happens in the first years of school. It is important to remember, nonetheless, that these results cannot be taken as factual indications of 'real' attainment, for reasons that the research detailed in this book suggests. *They appear to be a record of inequalities, but are as much a product of inequalities in education, because they are produced in an environment which has certain expectations of different groups of pupils.* They play an important part in the reproduction of these expectations, year by year, and may play a role in the production of wider disparities in later key stages. In the later chapters of this book, I emphasise that the consistency in patterns of attainment by gender, 'race' and class is not a natural phenomenon, but the result of a system which demands that teachers grade children in particular ways, in order to make their results acceptable.

Attainment based on expectation is particularly powerful and concerning in early years education because these results appear to show that children come to school with these differences already in place, and there is little the education system can do about them. The EYFS Profile scores also provide a baseline for all future progress to be measured against, and, therefore, children with low EYFS Profile scores who make what is deemed to be adequate progress through their school careers can still end up with lower than expected levels of attainment. It is how these processes of expectation, judgement and assessment work in real classrooms that is the focus of this book.

Structure of the book

Chapter 2, 'Understanding learner identities in the early years classroom', sets out the theoretical tools used in this study and their relevance to the research. It focuses on how conceptualising some discourses as dominant in a setting helps us to see what is made common sense and inevitable, and what is made unintelligible. I explain how unpacking the way in which discourses operate to limit what is possible enables the researcher to consider *who* can be understood as a 'good learner'. I also explain further how I use the concept of intersectionality, which has its origins in Critical Race Theory and other literature, to examine children's identities in terms of 'race', class, gender and religion in combination. In thinking about identities, I explain how Judith Butler's ideas about performativity and intelligible subjects can be used, as in Deborah Youdell's work (2006b; 2011), to examine who is a recognisable subject and recognisable as a success in school. Finally, I discuss how conceptualisations of inequality in terms of 'race', class, gender and location offer useful tools to understand how patterns of attainment are reproduced. The chapter concludes with an explanation of the methodological approach taken in this research, a discussion of how the data was analysed and some brief information on the schools involved.

Chapter 3 is titled 'Assessing learners in the first year of school'. Here I argue that the EYFS Profile provides a model for 'learning' and the 'learner' that encompasses all aspects of classroom life, including emotions, physical deportment and social interaction. Becoming a 'learner' in this setting means performing a complex identity involving enthusiasm, submission, rationality and the capacity to make 'good choices'; this is a subjectivity infused with neoliberal values. This model of the 'learner' is given solidity and permanence through the EYFS Profile. Examples of classroom observations made for the Profile are used to demonstrate how this model of the ideal 'learner' is made real in Reception. I also examine how children have different 'learner identities' in the classroom, and how they are constituted in relation to this model of the learner. I go on to explain how teachers build up knowledge of pupils, which the EYFS Profile as a policy reinforces. I argue that teachers' belief in the veracity of this 'knowledge', which is given physical manifestation by the collection of evidence for the EYFS Profile, allows them to reject contradictory information and gives children's learner identities further solidity. In the final section, I set out another element of the discourse of what it means to be a success in school – the idea of 'authenticity'. This builds upon work on minority attainment and authenticity in relation to Chinese pupils (Archer and Francis, 2007). In these Reception classes, the discourse of the authentic learner is intimately connected to ideas about 'development' which dominate early years documents, but also to discourses of 'ability' which are common throughout the education sector. These two ideas, both of which are associated with the notion of innate natural difference (some children develop faster than others, some children are more intelligent than others), are confused in ways which reinforce their legitimacy as a means of describing children. This forms the basis for the idea that some children attain highly through authentic means because they are naturally 'able', while some do well merely through external pressures such as 'pushy parents'. However, as the good subject of schooling is an all-round learner, this idea is extended to all aspects of classroom life, and some children are constituted as merely performing the 'good learner' identity, while others are understood as *authentically* 'good learners'.

In Chapter 4, 'Assessing a "difficult intake": "Race", religion, class and gender in reception', I examine how teachers' knowledge is used in relation to the model of the ideal learner that operates in these classrooms to constitute some children as 'good learners'. It is argued that this 'good learner' discourse works actively to exclude some children from educational success, because the successful pupil is discursively constructed as the 'White middle-class' child, and also associated with girls. Discourses of the 'inner city' involving 'race', religion, parenting and class are invoked by teachers to constitute the majority of the students in these urban schools as distant from positive learner identities. This notion that these schools have a 'difficult intake' which is more challenging than other schools is strong enough to result in the rejection of the EYFS Profile (in spirit if not in practice), on the basis that it is only applicable to 'White middle-class' schools. This chapter concludes with a discussion of gender specifically in relation to ideal learner identities in Reception. I argue that girls are more intelligible as 'good learners' in these classrooms.

In Chapter 5, ' "Good" and "bad" learners in the classroom', detailed accounts of classroom life are used to demonstrate how individual children are constituted as 'good' or 'bad' learners, and the ways in which these identities are maintained. It is argued that only children in very specific intersectional positions – in this case Afghan and Kosovan girls who are perceived to come from aspiring 'good migrant' families – are intelligible as 'good' learners within the circulating discourse. For these children, there is 'intelligible space' to be constituted as successful which is not open to children from other backgrounds. Some children – mainly boys from lower income Bangladeshi and African-Caribbean families – are only intelligible as 'bad' learners. However, the performances required to remain within this intelligible space are sophisticated; I provide examples of how children's use of their discursive agency to unknowingly challenge how they are constituted has an impact on their learner identity. Within this analysis, I consider how discourses of authenticity can be used to delegitimise any student's attainment, rendering positive learner identities in need of constant maintenance.

In Chapter 6, 'Playing with numbers: Learner identities and assessment', I discuss how the micro-practices of the classroom interact with wider policy trends, including the spread of accountability into early years and the policy focus on reducing attainment gaps. I explain how the final EYFS Profile results are produced in ways that make them intelligible in terms of the 'difficult intake' discourse and individual children's learner identities. A final section discusses how the national policy which aims to reduce attainment gaps of schools in low income areas by introducing such schemes as 'Education Action Zones' and giving additional funding, may also give legitimacy to discourses which position 'inner city' children as inevitably low attaining. I also discuss the impact of 'value added' measures of attainment on teacher assessments. Data from one school shows how EYFS Profile results which were above average were lowered in response to concerns from local government education officials, who designated them 'too high' for a school in a deprived area, thus labelling more of these children as 'behind' at the very beginning of their school careers.

Finally, in Chapter 7, 'Policy, equality and "learning"', I examine the implication of these findings for primary and early years education both in England and internationally. I focus on three main issues, relating to notions of 'learning', policy effects and the reproduction of inequalities. First, I argue that extensive detailed assessments like the EYFS Profile limit how teachers can envisage 'good learning', and close down opportunities to think more freely about what is important in early years education, in ways which can be harmful to children. Second, in relation to policy, I argue that lessons can be learnt from this case study regarding the impact of standardised curricula and assessment in the early years. The case of Reception classes in England indicates that the problems associated with standardised testing in terms of inequalities are also found when statutory assessment is introduced into the early years. This results in some children being assessed as 'bad' learners, exempt from the possibility of educational success, at age four or five.

Lastly, I explain how the implications in terms of inequality of these processes are deeply concerning: in these schools, the EYFS Profile system appears to encourage the systematic reproduction of results which are lower for certain groups of pupils. I conclude by arguing that assessment policies can have a huge impact on classrooms and teachers; in this case, the use of assessment to monitor early years settings has damaging effects for young children, particularly those from minoritised and economically disadvantaged backgrounds. The remainder of this final chapter examines how we can use the detail of the data from Reception classrooms to explore possibilities for interruption in practice and policy, and the implications of the coalition government's reforms.

2

UNDERSTANDING LEARNER IDENTITIES IN THE EARLY YEARS CLASSROOM

Introduction

This chapter sets out the theoretical tools I use to examine issues of inequality in early years education. These tools are useful in thinking about power, identity, subjectivity, agency, discourse, 'race', class and gender, all of which are important facets of the complex data I discuss in this book. I begin by setting out the framework, influenced by Michel Foucault, which I use to explore power and discourse, locating this in the wider poststructural field. I explain how Judith Butler's notion of performativity can be helpful in examining issues of identity, and gender in particular, and how this can be used to consider what it means to be a learner in classrooms, and to engage with 'performative politics'. Further tools from postcolonial studies and Critical Race Theory are explained, with reference in particular to the use of intersectionality in making sense of issues of identity in education. I also set out how I use ideas from 'policy sociology' to consider the impact of policy on school practices and teachers. There are some tensions between these broadly critical approaches, which I acknowledge; however, I would argue that this range of tools is needed to make sense of the complexity of the issue of inequality in early years education. A final section of this chapter provides some information on the study on which this book is based and the schools involved.

Dominant discourses and 'good learners'

A central theme of the book is the power of dominant discourses to define a 'good learner' in Reception classrooms, and the way in which this excludes some identity positions. Like much of the work that I draw upon, the analysis is framed within a particular understanding of 'discourse' as productive, and as concerned with power, which is influenced by the work of Michel Foucault. Discourse is described by

Archer and Francis as 'referring to the socially organised patterns/frameworks of language knowledge and meaning' (2007: 26). These bodies of knowledge have the power to govern the way that individuals act, think and can be understood: they can operate as 'regimes of truth' (Foucault, 1980). In this study, these ideas are useful in thinking about the status of ideas about particular groups of children. Youdell argues:

> [We can] identify discourses of race or gender that set out what it means to be a gender or a race, but do this *as if* these were natural and/or self-evident. This is a crucial aspect of Foucault's account of discourse: while the terms of discourses may well be taken as reflecting 'truth', the ways things are, for Foucault these are not reflections but the very moment and means of the *production* of these truths. *(Youdell, 2006b: 35, emphasis in original)*

Thus discourse is productive as well as descriptive. This perspective recognises the power of discourses about 'race', gender or 'ability', for example, in constituting individuals' identities.

Analyses of discourse influenced by Foucault are helpful in education because they illuminate our understanding of the operation of power within the education sector. Ball argues that a focus on discourse provides 'different ways of looking at and beyond the obvious and puts different sorts of questions on the agenda for change' (1994: 2). I am interested in the 'truths' that emerge from a specific policy – the EYFS Profile – because of their power within classrooms to constitute children in different ways and to regulate practices:

> Discourses mobilise truth claims and constitute rather than simply reflect social reality […] Policies are very specific and practical regimes of truth and value and the ways in which policies are spoken and spoken about, their vocabularies, are part of the creation of the conditions of their acceptance and enactment. *(Ball, 2008: 5)*

In this study, I am concerned with how the ideas in the EYFS Profile and its related documents become a regime of truth within these classrooms through the enactment of this policy. This use of Foucault's argument that '"Truth" is linked in circular relations with systems of power which produce and sustain it, and to effects of power which it induces and which extend it' (Foucault, 1980: 133, in MacNaughton, 2005: 19), has similarities with MacNaughton's (2005) argument that early years education in Australia is governed and regulated by the dominant discourse of 'development'. I am interested in the way in which this specific assessment policy works with and against discourses – such as those relating to the nature of learning and to 'ability' and 'development' – which dominate in the early years in England, and the implications of this for children in Reception classrooms.

There is a political implication to this theorisation: these ways of thinking about the operation of power through discourse open up possibilities to question what is constituted as 'truth'. This view of the politics of knowledge challenges the Enlightenment notion of the 'rational and coherent individual telling a rational and coherent story about themselves' (MacNaughton, 2005: 4). Which of the many possible stories are told, and who gets to tell them and when, depends on the political situation of the time; therefore 'identifying the stories that are silenced or marginalised and then sharing them is a political act' (MacNaughton, 2005: 4). For Youdell (2006b), the historicity of meaning – that meaning is historically contingent, different at different times – and the fact that one discourse is not intrinsically more powerful than another reveal the potential for discourses which position certain identities negatively to be challenged. A conception of discourse as operating on and through institutions is useful in any research on schools or classrooms because it allows for an analysis of what possibilities are *foreclosed* by the dominance of certain discourses – what it is possible to say, and be, in a particular context. It also allows us to consider other discourses – those which 'might be characterised as subjugated, disavowed, alternative, marginal, counter or oppositional' (Youdell, 2006b: 176) – and how these operate and offer different possibilities. Thus there is optimism inherent in this approach, as well as a recognition of the limits of possibility of any situation.

These tools relating to power, discourse and identity are among those offered by poststructural theory[1]; a development in the social sciences which is part of what St.Pierre and Pillow characterise as a 'restless "post" period that troubles all those things we assumed were solid, substantial, and whole' (2000: 1). Poststructural ideas are an attempt to move on from positivist, modernist approaches that prioritise science, rationality and objectivity. Differences of approach within poststructural work should not be ignored, however: Peters argues that the term 'homogenises the differences among poststructural thinkers' (Peters, 1996 in St.Pierre and Pillow, 2000: 16). Poststructural ideas are increasingly used in analyses of early childhood education worldwide, though less frequently in the UK (see Blaise, 2005; Cannella and Viruru, 2004; MacNaughton, 2005; Yelland et al., 2008, among others). Yelland argues that 'early childhood education is coming to be known for its openness to new ideas; the multidisciplinary nature of the field has facilitated the process of reconceptualisation' (2005b: 5). This development owes much to feminist poststructuralists such as Walkerdine and Davies, whose work challenged the patriarchal element of early education (Davies, 1989; Davies, 1993; Walkerdine, 1990), and influenced the current generation of poststructural scholars in early years. Much of the poststructural work in early childhood has focused on the operation of 'development' and 'developmentally appropriate practice' (DAP) as a 'regime of truth' (Foucault, 1980). DAP is regarded as a modernist, 'scientifically' justified discourse; its origins lie in developmental psychology. This discourse has determined the ways in which children can be understood, and therefore the practices of early childhood education. Blaise refers to work that questions the dominant DAP discourse as 'post-developmentalism': 'a broad term used to define alternative theoretical perspectives that question modernist assumptions of truth, universality, and certainty' (2005: 3). Similarly, this work examines how these modernist assumptions continue to operate in Reception classrooms and how they are both disrupted and reinforced by policies such as the EYFS Profile.

Performativity and intelligible subjects

This study utilises the idea that circulating dominant discourses related to class, 'race', religion, gender and other axes of identity have an impact on how children are constituted as learners in schools. Research for several decades has found that teachers use stereotypes, assumptions and prejudices to inform their understandings of pupil's identities. Following Deborah Youdell's work in this field (2006a; 2006b; 2006c), I attempt to examine how children's learner identities are established and maintained through everyday classroom practices and interactions. This approach is based on a conception of identity as *performative,* following Butler (1990; 1997): the subject is 'understood not as pre-existing, self-knowing, and continuous, but as subjectivated through her/his ongoing constitution in and by discourse (Youdell, 2006a: 35). Here, the performative is a 'discursive practice that enacts or produces what it names' (Butler, 1993: 241); it is through performatives that subjection occurs, although the subject appears to prefigure discourse. No elements of identity are fixed, including gender; instead identity is performatively constituted through those very things that appear to be proof of it. Performatives may be verbal but also corporeal, through gesture, dress and action; in Butler's words, 'what the body says and does (or does not say and does not do) as well as how the body appears' (Butler, 2006: 533). Ways of 'doing boy' or 'being a proper girl' are only approximations, however – Butler writes 'against proper objects' (1994: 1). Nayak and Kehily summarise this argument:

> Being a 'proper boy' or 'proper girl' is, then, a fantasy that is both hankered after and embodied through an approximation of its norms. ... [Butler] has remarked upon the everyday violence committed through the imposition of such normative phantasms. To this extent identity is also always an act of exclusion, a point of closure, the feverish demarcation of a boundary that elides the mercurial qualities of subjectivity itself. *(Nayak and Kehily, 2006: 465)*

Conceptualising gender as performative reveals 'the apparently pre-existing subject is an artefact of its performative constitution' (Youdell, 2006c: 515) and thus as inherently unstable, requiring constant maintenance. It is through this instability that there is the possibility of disruption and the deployment of discursive agency.

Butler's work on performativity focused initially on gender and sexuality, but has been broadened out by Butler herself and others to consider how 'race', class and other identities are performatively constituted (Butler, 2004a; Youdell, 2003).

Butler's work is also useful in considering how individuals are subjectivated within hierarchies, such as in Renold's work on friendship groups based on heteronormative practices (Renold, 2006) and in Youdell's description of the 'hierarchy within the other' (Youdell, 2003). Research in schools has provided empirical evidence of not only how identity is performed, but also how individuals can use their 'discursive agency' to bring their subjectivation into question. Within poststructural theory, agency is not inherently held by a 'knowing' subject, but both produced and constrained by circulating discourses. The concept of 'discursive agency' and possibility of 'troubling' hegemonic discourses through performatives has meant that Butler's work has been linked to political projects of destabilising hierarchical relations, in terms of gender, 'race' and sexuality. Youdell argues the case for:

> [A] politics in subjectivation, in which discursively constituted and constrained subjects deploy discursive agency and act within and at the borders of the constraints of their subjectivation. By interrogating and rendering visible the subjectivating practices that constitute particular sorts of students tied to particular subjectivities and, by extension, particular educational (and wider) trajectories, we begin to uncover the potential of Butler's performative politics or a politics in subjectivation [...] discursive interventions might enable new discourses to be rendered intelligible or enduring discourse to be unsettled within school contexts. *(Youdell, 2006c: 526)*

Thus the alterability of identity can be used to challenge accepted hierarchies and the range of possible subject positions. Butler has written, in response to the use of her work in education, that it is through the analysis of 'the activities through which gender is instituted', that gender 'stands a chance of being de-instituted or instituted differently' (2006: 529).

However, this optimism is tempered by recognition of the enduring power of dominant discourses and the need to remain 'intelligible'. This concept of intelligibility is particularly useful in this study as it relates to how children come to be seen as different types of learner, or what Youdell (2006c) terms 'viable studenthood'. Butler (2004a) describes 'variable orders of intelligibility' and the consequence of being unintelligible as rendering an individual as 'non-human'. Youdell has taken on these concepts to explore the issue of what it means to become a 'student' and a 'learner' (the former being an assessment of the pupil as a whole, and the latter only relating to academic achievement) and how some students can take on subject positions that position them as unintelligible within the school context and outside 'learner' status (2006b; 2007):

> 'who' a student is – in terms of gender, sexuality, social class, ability, disability, race, ethnicity and religion as well as popular and sub-cultural belongings – is inextricably linked with the 'sort' of student and learner that s/he gets to

be, and the educational inclusions s/he enjoys, and/or the exclusions s/he faces. *(Youdell, 2006b: 2)*

Youdell argues that discourses can combine to create 'truths' about students' identities as learners. She uses Butler's idea of performative identity to examine how students may be constituted as 'impossible' and 'ideal' learners. Certain identity positions come to be synonymous with the 'ideal learner', set up for educational success. For others, their identity markers all but foreclose the possibility of success, as they are seen as 'impossible learners'. Furthermore, Youdell argues that discourses of 'ability', which are linked to assessment, are crucial for the constitution of the 'good/bad student' and 'ideal/impossible learner' dichotomies. However, other discourses about conduct and effort interact with 'ability' and gender, class and ethnicity to constitute these learner identities. Other ethnographic work in schools, and particularly Connolly's study of Year 1 classrooms (1998), have similarly used an analysis based on children's identities as learners (Archer, 2003; Rollock, 2007; Shain, 2010; Wright, 1992).

In this study, I disregard the division between student and learner because I argue that within early years education, the elision of academic and personal, emotional and social skills in formal assessments blurs the distinction between the student and learner; thus, learning encompasses all elements of classroom life in Reception. Nonetheless, Youdell's argument remains useful here: I explore how some subject positions are unintelligible as learners in Reception, and extend this to consider how entire classes of children can be rendered outside educational success through discourses relating to class, 'race' and the inner city. I also use the concept of recognisability to consider how some profiles of EYFS results (specifically those that are higher than the national average) become unacceptable for schools in inner city areas. As in Youdell's work, I make use of the concept of an 'ideal' learner, an idea which is related to an older concept of the 'ideal client' of education (Becker, 1952 in Gillborn, 1990), and was used by Gillborn to consider how this 'ideal' contributes to institutional racism in schools. Youdell argues that a focus on the unspoken ideal 'allows us to identify the proliferation of discourses of the educational Other' (2006b: 97). Traditionally, researchers have identified teachers' 'ideal learner' as White, middle class and male (Gillborn, 1990; Walkerdine, 1990). The identification of boys as ideal learners has been linked to discourses which associated rationality and intelligence with masculinity, while the feminine subject of schooling was associated with passivity and irrationality (Walkerdine, 1990). However, in more recent years, this ideal male pupil has been questioned with the advent of girls' consistent educational success in statutory exams and the emergence of the discourse of boys' underachievement (Archer and Francis, 2007; Epstein et al., 1998).

To summarise, I understand 'learner identities' as particular subject positions which are framed by dominant discourses of what it means to be a learner.

Learner identities are the way in which teachers constitute pupils as successful or unsuccessful, well behaved or badly behaved, teachable or not teachable, through the deployment of discourses. These identities are inherently linked to children's intersectional positions, another key concept to which I now turn.

Intersectional learner identities

Intersectionality is the idea that we should consider an individual's position in terms of multiple axes of difference, rather than with one single axis, such as 'race' or gender. Brah and Phoenix provide this definition:

> We regard the concept of 'intersectionality' as signifying the complex, irreducible, varied, and variable effects which ensure when multiple axis of differentiation – economic, political, cultural, psychic, subjective and experiential – intersect in historically specific contexts. The concept emphasizes that the different dimensions of social life cannot be separated into discrete and pure strands. *(Brah and Phoenix, 2004: 76)*

An approach informed by intersectionality avoids the problem of regarding ethnic groups or classes as homogenous and essentialising the differences between them. It recognises what Yuval-Davis has called the 'inadequacy of analysing various social divisions, but especially "race" and gender, as separate, internally homogenous, social categories' (Yuval-Davis, 2006: 206). Thus, in this book, I explore the learner identities of children in relation to their intersectional positions in terms of 'race', gender and class, and other axes, including religion and location.

Intersectionality is a concept which, although linked in some cases to Critical Race Theory, has wider academic origins. It is increasingly popular in many areas of research (Phoenix and Pattynama, 2006) and has been described as 'the most important contribution that women's studies have made so far' (McCall, 2005: 1771). The term itself was first used by Kimberlé Crenshaw (1989; 1991), but the concept relates to a long-standing concern with the different experiences of women from different ethnic groups and social classes. Work which has engaged with Butler's notion of performativity has increasingly focused on interconnecting performatives of 'race', class, gender and sexuality (such as Rasmussen and Harwood, 2003; Youdell, 2006b). Intersectionality offers the opportunity to decentre the normative centre, which has been, in the case of feminist scholarship, White women (Brah and Phoenix, 2004). It allows for the great complexity of human experience, while avoiding the simplicity of 'additive' understandings of disadvantage, which were concerned with 'double' and 'triple oppression', as if disadvantage could be mathematically calculated. Crenshaw's 1991 article, for example, argues that the experiences of violence against women of colour can be explored only through an understanding of their experiences as women and as people of colour together, not as separate axes of disadvantage (Crenshaw, 1991). It is this invitation to understand the complexity of lived experience, Davis argues, that makes intersectionality such a useful concept:

> 'Intersectionality initiates a process of discovery, alerting us to the fact that the world around us is always more complicated and contradictory than we ever could have anticipated ... it encourages complexity, stimulates creativity, and avoids premature closure. *(Davis, 2008: 79)*

Intersectionality also allows for an appreciation of historical, social and political context in examining how individuals experience discrimination, and as such has been an important concept in postcolonial studies (McClintock, 1995). It has also been used to consider contemporary concerns about globalisation and 'postmodern imperialisms' (Brah and Phoenix, 2004: 83). As I discuss in further detail below, the context of this study – London in the late 2000s – is significant in thinking about the discourses through which the learner identities of pupils are constituted.

Intersectionality has been criticised for its lack of absolute, universal definition (Verloo, 2006) and the absence of an accompanying set of rigid methodological guidelines (McCall, 2005). There are debates over whether intersectionality should be understood as a crossroads, as axes of difference, or as a process, and the extent to which it is a 'theory' (Davis, 2008). Yuval-Davis, for example, has rejected Crenshaw's metaphor of intersectionality as a crossroads on the grounds that it remains an 'additive model' (Yuval-Davis, 2006). There is also some debate over the nature and extent of the categories that can be used in intersectional analysis; a problem that has been called 'the Achilles heel of intersectionality' (Ludwig, 2006: 247, in Davis, 2008: 76). Butler criticised the 'etc.' used by many writers after listing 'race', class and gender as indicating 'exhaustion' and the 'illimitable process of signification' (Butler, 1990), and there is continued debate over the number of categories that should be, and can be, taken into account in any intersectional analysis, and their relative importance. Yuval-Davis contends that all categories of difference are not equal: 'in specific historical situations and in relation to specific people there are some social divisions that are more important than others in constructing specific positionings' (2006: 203). Furthermore, she argues, categories have different 'organising logics' which affect how they can be analysed. Davis cites what she calls an 'interesting compromise' on this issue from Leiprecht and Lutz (2006) whereby 'race', class and gender are taken as the 'minimum standard' of analysis, with other categories added depending on the context and research problem (cited in Davis, 2008: 81). I recognise that this tension is apparent in my work, where the analysis of children's intersectional positions can be limited by a reliance on official information and visual interpretations, and there is an overall temptation to focus on the 'big three' of race, class and gender. However, the analysis here is written with the intention, at least, of exploring the complexity of children's identities in all relevant respects, even though some of my theoretical tools (such as those relating to 'race' discussed below) are more usually applied to a single category. I agree with Davis's contention that 'the vagueness and open-endedness of "intersectionality" may be the very secret to its success' (2008: 69). Intersectionality allows for the complexity of lived experience: it does not expect analysis to be simple or straightforward, or indeed to apply the same rules in different places and at different times. For a study based in the incredibly complex world of school classrooms, I would argue that this is a distinct advantage. The children in these inner city Reception classes are constituted through complicated webs of discourse, and it is through a specifically intersectional analysis that we can be open to appreciating this complexity. The analysis is also informed by Youdell's contention that simply talking about multiple categories 'is not necessarily to move past these categories in any fundamental way', but that intersectionality is useful as an 'orientating notion that points us towards particular sorts of questions and substantive concerns' (Youdell, 2011: 40). In this case, it points towards questions relating to how children in particular intersectional positions are intelligible as 'good learners', and for whom this position is impossible.

Inequalities in education

This study is concerned with the complexity of inequalities in early years education, and the detailed learner identities of individual children, in terms of their class, gender and race positions, and the interaction of these with other discourses of religion, language, migration and the urban. However, the visibility of 'race' as a category of difference in the schools in which the study was conducted foregrounds this issue throughout, and requires that I deal seriously with the complexity of 'race' as a concept. In this section, I explain my uses of the terms 'race' and 'racism' before discussing the theoretical tools employed from Critical Race Theory and postcolonial feminism.

The concept of 'race'

An awareness of the complexity and significance of the language of 'race' and 'racism' is important for this study; as Gillborn writes: 'Language not only describes an issue, it helps to define the issue: it can make certain understandings seem natural and commonsensical, while others are presented as outrageous or unworkable' (2008: 2). Thus it is imperative that the terms I use are fully explained; the result being not that these terms are made unproblematic, rather that their problematic nature is fully illustrated. 'Race' is a contested term which has been understood in different ways in different times (Omi and Winant, 2004). Historically, 'race' has been used to refer to essentialist, deterministic conceptions of biological differences between groups: a scientific discourse linked to racial subjugation, colonisation and White superiority. In the early twenty-first century, however, this biological definition has been largely rejected, and 'the socially constructed status of the concept of race … is widely recognised' (Omi and Winant, 2004: 7). The conception of 'race' as socially constructed includes an awareness of the different meanings of the term throughout history and the continued role of human interaction in reworking and changing the meaning of racial categories. This involves a rejection of the significance of physical 'racial markers' such as skin tone as denoting fundamental biological differences between people, alongside an awareness that some people's perception of these racial markers and the attributes associated with that 'racial identity' have significant impacts on the lived experiences of minoritised people, and that these impacts vary by location and time. This understanding of 'race' intends to find a position for the concept which, in Omi and Winant's phrase, 'steer[s] between the Scylla of "race as illusionary" and the Charybdis of "racial objectivism"' (2004: 11). I concur that 'race' cannot be understood either as an ideological construct (for this ignores the level of experience), nor as an objective condition (for the categories used are historically contingent and incoherent in terms of everyday life). Therefore, I use the term to refer to 'race' as a social construct, constantly remade and re-inscribed by discourses. The idea of 'race' as a social construct is central to Critical Race Theory; Carbado explains:

> Importantly, race does not exist 'out there', ontologically prior to its production and instantiation in discourses. Instead, the social processes of race are constituted by discourses – in, for example, law, politics, science, and education. These racialised discourses are deployed against, enacted upon, and given meaning through their associations with human bodies. *(Carbado, 2002: 181)*

Regarding 'race' as socially constructed does not imply that it is fixed or understood in the same way; it is a complex and contingent social construct. This can be related to Butler's use of performativity: Carbado and Gulati (2000) attempt this when they discuss 'identity performance' in the workplace, whereby minoritised employees attempt to engage in performatives that bring up positive discourses related to their identities. I find this combination of poststructural perspectives with Critical Race Theory productive in considering the agency of children in the processes by which they are constituted as different types of learner.

Since the term 'race' is problematic, 'ethnicity' is occasionally used to indicate a broader understanding of difference, and the terms 'ethnicity' and 'ethnic group' are frequently used in governmental reports and statistics, and in research. I use the term 'race' (and 'ethnicity' or 'ethnic group' when referring to government statistics), but with an awareness of the complexity of these terms, particularly with regard to their role in making racial differences appear normal, natural and common sense. In line with many scholars influenced by CRT, I also use the term 'minoritised' to refer to groups who are not White, as the White population forms the majority overall in the UK; 'minoritised' is used to show that the 'minority' status of these groups is dependent on context and not inherent. The terms used to categorise different groups are also problematic: Omi and Winant describe racial categories as 'patently absurd reductions of human variation' (2004: 10), yet they may engender some sense of belonging. Gunaratnam refers to what Radhakrishnan called the 'treacherous bind': the problem of the reliance on 'racial categories that are complicit with racial typologies and thinking' (2003: 23). However, for ease of reading, some categories are necessary. I use the term 'Black' to refer to those who identify their family heritage as African or Caribbean. Where it is necessary to group ethnic groups together, I use the term 'Asian' to refer to people who would identify their heritage as Pakistani, Indian or Bangladeshi; otherwise more specific terms are used where possible in recognition of the need to disrupt notions of groups as based solely around nationalities or geographical areas. Where possible, I refer to individuals' own self-identifications of category.

'Racism'

'Racism' is also a complex term, with multiple meanings in terms of how it operates, how it can be identified, and what constitutes 'racism'. Most commonly, 'racism' is regarded as conscious and explicit, often based on scientific conceptions of biologically different 'races' organised in a hierarchy. In popular discourse, the term is associated with bigoted comments and offensive language from individuals – the 'rotten apple' conception of racism (Gillborn, 2002). However, research on racism in education and elsewhere has focused on a more subtle conception of racism as unconscious, implicit and more widespread. Discourses of 'culture' and 'difference' can operate as proxies for 'race' in a less obvious form of racism: 'the presence or absence of 'racial' terms … is not necessary to define a discourse as racist' (Gillborn and Youdell, 2000: 5). Racism is identified by its effects, such as disadvantaging one group in a setting. The term 'institutional racism' describes processes by which groups of people can be systematically affected by processes and practices which are implicitly and unintentionally racist. Although the term has a longer history, the definition of 'institutional racism' most commonly used is from the Macpherson report into the police investigation into the murder of Stephen Lawrence, a Black teenager, in 1993:

> The collective failure of an organisation to provide an appropriate and professional service to people because of their colour, culture or ethnic origin. It can be seen or detected in processes, attitudes and behaviour which amount to discrimination through unwitting prejudice, ignorance, thought-lessness and racist stereotyping which disadvantage minority ethnic people.
> *(Macpherson et al., 1999: 28)*

This definition expands 'racism' to include all actions and processes – however well-intentioned and however seemingly innocuous – that result in minorities being disadvantaged. This is particularly useful in the case of schools, where several studies have shown how well-intentioned teachers can operate in racist ways (for example, Archer and Francis, 2007; Mirza, 1992; Wright, 1992). A more sophisticated view of 'racism' is necessary because, although people are broadly sympathetic to criticisms of racism, it is such a strong word that it engenders a defensiveness when issues of everyday racism are discussed (Gillborn, 2008).

Critical Race Theory

CRT is a body of ideas originating in legal scholarship in the United States and growing in influence in many other social science disciplines, including education, worldwide (Dixson and Rousseau, 2006; Gillborn, 2006b; Ladson-Billings, 2004; Ladson-Billings and Tate, 1995). CRT arose in response to Critial Legal Studies (CLS), a legal movement which rejected traditional legal scholarship 'in favor of a form of law that spoke to the specificity of individuals and groups in social and cultural contexts' (Ladson-Billings, 2004: 52). CLS focused on the legitimising effects of legal discourses in terms of social inequalities, but failed to focus on the issue of 'race'. CRT was thus born out of a concern to consider the centrality of 'race' to the ordering of society. CRT literature goes further than discussions of unintentional racism, to describe racism as endemic, 'deeply ingrained legally, culturally, and even psychologically' (Tate, 1997: 234).

This is of the central tenets of CRT: that racism is endemic in society, present in everyday interactions and processes that appear neutral and benign. Racism is not limited to explicit acts of racist prejudice, but widespread and often unintentional; it is 'normal, not aberrant' (Delgado, 1995: 14). CRT is concerned with how everyday 'business as usual' forms of racism (Delgado, 1995) operate within a system of 'White supremacy' (Crenshaw et al., 1995). This term refers not to extreme political groupings, but to 'the operation of forces that saturate the everyday mundane actions and policies that shape the world in the interests of White people' (Gillborn, 2008: 35). In the UK, this viewpoint has been seen as an extension of 'the long history of antiracist struggle and the attempt to broaden the approach to examine institutional racism that operates through subtle, sometimes unintended processes, explanations, assumptions and practices' (Gillborn, 2008: 27).

CRT and other similar scholarship uses a conception of 'race' as socially constructed, as already discussed. 'Race' is also seen as a highly contingent concept, different at different times and locations; who gets to be 'White', for example, has been shown to be a moveable issue over time (Ignatiev, 1995). Connected to this socially constructed notion of 'race' are the critiques within CRT of 'Whiteness' and its consequences (although some have questioned whether this repositions Whiteness at the centre, for example Apple, 1998; Leonardo, 2009). As Gillborn argues, 'Whiteness exists forcefully and is constantly re-enacted and reinforced; through endless, overlapping racialised and racist actions and discourses' (2008: 170–1). One focus has been on the advantages of Whiteness (Leonardo, 2004b; McIntosh, 1992). This work has considered the complex and unseen ways in which Whiteness accords privileges in society; McIntosh's account of these advantages throughout a typical day shows powerfully how simple but significant many of these privileges are. Leonardo has argued, however, that a focus on the privileges of Whiteness 'obscures the subject of domination, or the agent of actions, because the situation is described as happening almost without the knowledge of Whites' (2004a: 138). Instead he argues that a focus on White supremacy would result in greater progress than the current situation where 'racial understanding proceeds at the snail's pace of the White imaginary' (2004a: 138, 141). Although there are sections of this book that focus on the learner identities of White pupils, I heed Leonardo's concerns and make a conscious effort to focus in the main on the exclusionary practices affecting minoritised pupils, rather than the advantages given to White pupils.

CRT scholarship has, at times, departed from mainstream academic conventions in its use of chronicles and storytelling (see, for example, Bell, 1992; Gillborn, 2008; Ladson-Billings, 2006). This technique aims to examine the 'myths, presuppositions, and received wisdoms that make up the common culture about race' (Delgado, 1995: 14) through a focus on the experiences of individuals from minoritised groups. The intention is to 'add necessary contextual contours to the seeming "objectivity" of positivist perspectives' (Ladson-Billings, 2004: 53). The influence of this tendency can be seen in this book in the final chapter, which takes up a story written relating to early years assessment by Gillborn, and updates it in line with my findings here.

Postcolonial feminism

Postcolonial studies have been concerned with the legacy of colonialism and particularly how colonialism legitimises discourses which support the hegemony of those who colonised and a constructed inferiority of those who were colonised. While Franz Fanon's work first considered the racialisation of and relationships between the colonisers and colonised (Fanon, 1967), it is Edward Said's 'Orientalism' (1978) which is often regarded as the origin of postcolonial studies. Said argued that colonial rule was justified by the construction of an Oriental/Western binary which contrasted the rational Westerners with the emotional/irrational 'Orientals', through the representation of the Other as deviant, deficient and exotic. 'Orientalism' remains in contemporary societies as a derogatory discourse which constructs those previously colonised as inferior.

Postcolonial feminists' work (such as Brah, 1996; Mohanty, 1988; Spivak, 1988) has addressed the absence of minoritised women in postcolonial studies, emphasising the importance of these women's intersectional positions in societies formed through complex racial, sexual and class discourses. Ann Phoenix comments '[s]uch work has rendered visible the power relations through which minoritised women are positioned and how their treatment frequently fits with a normalised absence/pathologised presence couplet' (Phoenix, 2009: 102). Postcolonial studies have made significant contributions to the field of education (Subedi and Daza, 2008). For example, postcolonial work has included a focus on the experiences of individuals from ex-colonies in the British education system. Phoenix's work on the Caribbean women's memories of schooling in the UK considers how postcolonial ideas of 'diaspora space' (Brah, 1996) can contribute to our understanding of minoritised children's experiences of school (Phoenix, 2009). She argues that Caribbean girls suffered 'epistemic violence' in that attending school 'involved learning that they were constructed as inadequate learners and undesirable femininities' (Phoenix, 2009: 101), but that they also demonstrated agency in resisting their subjection as inferior – what she calls 'de-colonising practices'. In early childhood education, the contribution of postcolonial studies has been limited, perhaps because, as Viruru argues, 'dominant discourses in early childhood education are not open to dialogue with perspectives that question fundamental realities' such as 'development'. She continues, 'Postcolonial theory's insistence on and acceptance of multiplicities and ambiguities thus stands in stark contrast to commonly accepted ideas of how children grow and develop' (Viruru, 2005: 12). Where it has been used, in work such as Cannella and Viruru's (2004) study of childhood and colonisation, the focus has been on deconstructing Western notions of childhood, Enlightenment conceptions of 'progress', and early childhood pedagogy. As such, this body of work is aligned with the poststructural literature on 'development' discussed earlier in this chapter.

This postcolonial literature is relevant for this study's focus on the intersectional positions of minoritised children, both those whose families have been in the UK for several generations and more recent arrivals. In particular, this body of work informs the focus on specific local and historical contexts when considering identity, for example in discussions of Muslim identities in Britain in the late 2000s.

Reconciling theoretical tensions

It is important to acknowledge at this point that there are contradictions involved in combining some of the conceptual tools I have discussed. One issue relates to the relative importance of different aspects of identity. CRT literature often focuses on the unique importance of racism in shaping the lives of individuals: racism is not simply analogous to other oppressions, such as those based on class, but is *uniquely* important. There is some tension between this position and the idea of intersectionality as dealing equally with multiple categories of identity, which needs to be reconciled in this study. Instead of conceptualising 'race' as uniquely important in all situations, I adhere to the principle that intersectional analysis should deal with the categories of relevance in any given context together, rather than prioritising one axis of identity. This approach coheres with CRT perspectives as there are a variety of approaches within some CRT literature, including work which focuses on issues of class and 'race' (Allen, 2009; Leonardo, 2009; Roediger, 1991). Although 'race' is foregrounded in some of the analysis, this is due to the greater relevance of this category in the context, not a theoretical position where 'race' is conceived as more important.

A second issue relates to the tensions between using CRT and poststructural approaches. This is a productive combination in my view, not least because, as

Gillborn and Youdell have argued, 'notions of the performative and subjectivation to explain how "race" continues to appear as "natural" or "self-evident"' (Gillborn and Youdell, 2009: 183). This study requires a subtle and detailed understanding of how identities are made through discourse, within a context of a racialised (and classed and gendered) society. An understanding of how certain dominant discourses operate as regimes of truth allows for a greater understanding of how everyday discourses and practices in schools systematically disadvantage minoritised pupils. Furthermore, contributions from legal CRT scholars such as Carbado and Gulati to understandings of identity and performance (following on from and in combination with Butler's work on intelligibility and recognisability and Youdell's work on school subjectivities) can be usefully applied to complex classroom contexts. What a poststructural politics of the performative and CRT share is a desire to uncover the taken for granted, the unsaid, and through this recognition, to disrupt patterns of inequality. While CRT uses 'White supremacy' to describe the hidden hegemonic assumptions about 'race' and their impact on the lived experiences of minoritised people, those who use Foucault and Butler might see the same as a series of regulatory discourses which constrain who and what minoritised people can be, while still remaining, to paraphrase Butler, 'intelligible minorities'. I would argue that a combination of CRT and poststructural theory opens up opportunities for thinking about issues of inequality and policy in schools in new and productive ways, and hope that this study demonstrates some of these opportunities.

Policy and policy technologies

A final set of theoretical tools is used in this work relating to the formation, enactment and impact of education policy – those from 'policy sociology' (Ball, 1997), where 'sociological concepts, ideas and research are used as tools for making sense of policy' (Ball, 2008: 4). An individual policy can only be understood in terms of its context, and particularly the language and rhetoric that, at the time, prioritises some ideas about how education should be organised over others. As Ball argues, 'Policy discourses also organise their own specific rationalities, making particular sets of ideas obvious, commonsense and "true"' (2008: 5). Here, I make use of Ball's work, which uses Lyotard's work on performativity in relation to the marketisation of education (Ball, 2003b), and his alternative use of performativity as the production of knowledge as knowledge (Youdell, 2010). In Ball's work, performativity is a set of practices of disciplinary power, including performance management systems and the publication of assessment scores, which can affect how schools function and who teachers and pupils can be within them. I argue that the introduction of statutory assessment arrangements in early years is made possible by the establishment of neoliberal discourses of performativity, managerialism and competition between schools, and that these discourses have an impact on inequalities in education.

The introduction of statutory assessment has brought with it an increase in what Ball calls, after Lyotard, 'the terrors of performativity' (Ball, 2003b). Performativity,

Ball argues, is a neoliberal mode of state regulation which requires teachers to respond to targets and indicators and discard personal beliefs and values:

> Performativity is a technology, a culture and a mode of regulation that employs judgements, comparisons and displays as means of incentive, control, attrition and change – based on rewards and sanctions (both material and symbolic). The performances (of individual subjects or organizations) serve as measures of productivity or output, or displays of 'quality', or 'moments' of promotion or inspection. As such they stand for, encapsulate or represent the worth, quality or value of an individual or organization within a field of judgement. *(Ball, 2003b: 216)*

In recent decades, education policy in the UK and elsewhere has been influenced by neoliberal principles (Apple, 2006; Ball, 2008). This 'policy epidemic' (Levin, 1998 cited in Ball, 2003b: 215) has led to policy changes affecting assessment practices in particular. Ball argues that neoliberal education reform is novel in that it 'does not simply change what we, as educators, scholars and researchers do, it changes who we are' (2003b: 215). This is done through 'policy technologies', which Ball defines as involving 'the calculated deployment of techniques and artefacts to organise human forces and capabilities into functioning networks of power' (2003b: 216). Three interrelated 'policy technologies' – the market, managerialism and performativity – work to change practices and identities in schools. They may vary in emphasis in different countries and localities, but all involve the alignment of public sector organisations with private sector values and methods (Ball, 2003b). There has been much critical literature on the impact of neoliberalism on education systems in the UK and elsewhere (Adnett and Davies, 2002; Apple, 2006; Labaree, 2007; Lauder and Hughes, 1999 among many others), and work specifically focused on the impact of neoliberal assessment policy (Booher-Jennings, 2008; Gillborn and Youdell, 2000). Much of this work has focused on the changed role of assessment in schools: tests are no longer simply a judge of an individual pupil's attainment, but simultaneously a judge of the teacher's performance, and the school's performance (Stobart, 2008). This, as I demonstrate in this book, has great implications for classroom practices and for teachers.

Research in schools has shown that the use of 'expected levels' and benchmarks, such as the five A*–C GCSE benchmark in secondary school league tables, creates a focus on borderline candidates who can have a disproportionate effect on the school's statistics (Booher-Jennings, 2005; Gillborn and Youdell, 2000). Gillborn and Youdell's study (2000) of two secondary schools in England found that the GCSE benchmark led to an 'A–C economy' where teachers focused upon 'D–C conversion' in order to increase the school's percentages in league tables. This caused practices which they describe as 'educational triage', where education is 'rationed' in that help is only given to pupils deemed 'suitable cases for treatment'. Those who were seen as having little chance of getting a C grade were deemed 'hopeless cases'. Booher-Jennings' study (2005) in the American school system found a disproportionate emphasis on the 'bubble kids' who were seen as having the potential to pass the state test. Stobart (2008) argues that this targeting of resources has become institutionalised with the establishment of government-funded 'booster classes' for primary pupils taking national Sats tests in the UK. He goes on to argue that testing adheres to 'Goodhart's Law', which states that 'when a measure becomes a target, it ceases to be a good measure' (2008: 125); thus, if the stakes are high enough and the measure narrow enough, distortions and corruptions of the system result. This, he argues, can be seen in changing classroom practices, such as 'teaching to the test' where the curriculum is halted or narrowed in order to prepare for the assessment. Similar arguments have been made in relation to early years education; for example, Graue and Johnson's research in US early elementary classrooms concluded that 'a focus on accountability without attention to instructional and assessment resources quality is inherently flawed' (2011: 1859).

Assessment policy has also been significant in producing cultures of assessing teachers' 'performance' which have questioned the professionalism of teachers (Ball, 2008; Osgood, 2006). In the UK system, assessment is often the main way in which a teacher's individual performance is judged in the performance management process, and may affect teachers' pay or decisions on promotions (Teachernet, 2009). Research has suggested that this shift towards performativity can reduce the time spent by teachers on other activities (Lyotard's 'law of contradiction' as discussed by Ball, 2003b) and that it has psychological 'costs', where teachers struggle between the requirements of the accountability system and what they feel is best for the students (Ball, 2003b; Jeffrey and Woods, 1998; Stobart, 2008). As I have argued elsewhere, the EYFS Profile as enacted in some Reception classrooms has a contradictory impact on teachers' views of their own professionalism (Bradbury, 2012); thus it can be seen as further evidence of the process by which teachers are 'de-professionalised' and then 're-professionalised' (Seddon, 1997 cited in Ball, 2003b). In early years education internationally, there has been particular concern over the impact of recent policy on teachers' professional status and practice:

> Conservative forces have constructed and implemented an agenda that attempts to reduce educational outcomes to the minutiae of observable outcomes that can be demonstrated in simple tasks that require routine responses rather than consider the educational experience as engagement with people and ideas. *(Yelland, 2007: 9)*

Dahlberg and Moss see this development as part of a rationality that has become hegemonic in early years education, where schools (and therefore teachers) can only be evaluated through 'objective and universally valid' measurement techniques (2005: 5). It is with an awareness of how policies such as the EYFS Profile can produce hegemonic ideas through the operation of certain discourses as regimes of truth, that I analyse the data from this study.

Researching inequality in the early years

The data used in this book were collected during a study conducted between 2008 and 2009 in two schools in an inner London borough, funded by the Economic and Social Research Council (Grant no. ES/G018987/1). The study aimed to explore the practices associated with the EYFS Profile in Reception classrooms and their relationship to disparities in attainment by class, 'race' and other categories. Over the course of one academic year, fieldwork focused on one Reception class in each of the two schools, which I refer to as Gatehouse Primary School and St Mary's Church of England Primary School. Fieldwork involved the collection of a range of qualitative data through interviews, document collection and observation in the classroom and during meetings. All names have been changed throughout.

Access to the two research sites was made through existing contacts, though I had not previously conducted any research in either school, nor had contact with them professionally. A third school, which had a different population of pupils as the majority of children were from a White British background, withdrew from the research at an early stage. However, I decided that the two remaining schools were sufficiently different in terms of size, organisation and church/community status to offer alternative perspectives. Conducting research in two schools also allowed me to spend more time in each classroom, engage more with the participants and collect in-depth data.

Fieldwork began with interviews with the main class teachers in Reception (Paul at St Mary's and Jim at Gatehouse) in June and July 2008, in order to establish the form of the research project and explore their initial thoughts on the EYFS Profile. Classroom observation then began at the beginning of the autumn term, allowing me to observe some children's first week in school. I spent one day each week for most of the academic year from September to July in each classroom, depending on the requests of the teacher and external events; for example, at St Mary's, observation was suspended for a brief period while a student teacher taught the class. During observation days, I would spend some time with the teacher before the school day discussing what had happened in the past week, then observe the class throughout their time in the classroom, and often have informal conversations with the class teacher and other staff throughout the day. I also observed key meetings, including the weekly Profile meetings at St Mary's where observations were discussed. Field notes were taken at the time and then written up with other comments on the research process as soon as possible after the event. Observations were conducted as a non-participant, where possible given the age of the children involved, although I did intervene in situations where the safety of a child was at stake. Also, in order to build a relationship with the teacher, I took part in school trips, sports days and other events where an additional adult was useful. On these occasions, I did not take field notes.

Semi-structured interviews with the class teachers took place throughout the school year, including at key points such as the formalisation of the EYFS Profile results in June. Additional teachers were interviewed at Gatehouse, where there was a more flexible approach to staffing than at St Mary's. The EYFS Coordinator (Lynn), who was responsible for Nursery and Reception, was interviewed, along with the Reception support teacher (Susan); both these teachers regularly taught Jim's Reception class.

Documents were also collected from both schools, including school policies and the final EYFS results. During the fieldwork, I also made notes on the children's EYFS Profile folders, where observations and photographs are collected, and on other classroom documents such as weekly plans, handover reports from Nursery classes and grouping systems. All of this information was provided with my reassurance that it would be kept anonymous. Data were also collected on the children in each class: at St Mary's I was provided with a class list detailing the children's ethnic groups with the EYFS Profile data, and at Gatehouse this information was displayed in the classroom. It was not possible to collect information on whether children were in receipt of free school meals (FSM) at either school, but I was able to use whole school FSM percentages from the Families of Schools Data (DCSF, 2008c) to gain an overall figure.

The classroom observations and the interviews generated a large volume of data to be processed. Field notes were typed up in their entirety as soon as possible after the school visit and names were changed to pseudonyms at this point to protect the participants' anonymity. Interviews were also transcribed without omissions and with pseudonyms, and notes taken before and after the interview process were also typed up. A key to the transcripts is provided in Appendix 3. Direct quotes from the interviews or field notes are indicated by double quotation marks, to distinguish them from quotes from literature or indications of the complexity of terms (where single quotation marks are used).

All of the observation data was then transferred into the NVivo qualitative data analysis program, to allow for systematic coding using a range of emerging themes. Interviews were initially coded separately along the same themes, outside of NVivo, and then coded with the software at the end of the data collection for ease of reference. Documents were mainly paper-based and were coded outside NVivo. As discussed further below, this processing was done with an awareness of the constraints of my own 'discursive repertoire' (Youdell, 2006b: 56); throughout, I acknowledge that there may have been many discourses operating in these classrooms that I took for granted as normal in a primary school and therefore paid little attention to.

The ethical considerations involved in this project were fully examined before the fieldwork took place; the research was carried out within ESRC and BERA guidelines (BERA, 2004). and was informed by literature on the particular issues involved in researching issues of 'race' and identity (Connolly and Troyna, 1998; Gunaratnam, 2003; Troyna, 1995) and by the literature on research involving young children (Hatch, 2007; Wood et al., 2008). The teachers were assured that the data would be made anonymous, with all names of the Local Authority, schools, teachers and children being changed. Identifying features of the schools have also been omitted where necessary, and the participants were not informed of the name of the other school involved (nor were any of my colleagues or personal contacts).

Gatehouse Primary School

Gatehouse Primary is a large two-form entry community primary school in inner London with over 400 pupils. There is a Nursery class which takes children from three and a half years, and there are several out-of-hours activities at the school, such as breakfast and after-school clubs. The school is situated near a large housing estate with a mixture of high-rise blocks and some low-rise housing, and there are two other schools nearby. According to 'Families of Schools' data, in 2008 approximately 60 per cent of pupils were eligible for Free School Meals (FSM), and fewer than 5 per cent of the children were registered as 'White British'. Significant other ethnic groups were 'Other White background' (approximately 20 per cent), Bangladeshi (15 per cent) and 'Any other ethnic group' (40 per cent) (DCSF, 2008c). Approximately 90 per cent of pupils had English as an additional language (EAL). The two Reception classes at Gatehouse occupied a large triple classroom with dividing doors in between that remained open, with a carpet area and whiteboard at each end. There were doors which opened straight onto the outside playground, which was large and contained climbing frames and goalposts. During free play time, children were allowed to move around between the three rooms which were set up with several activities, and could move outside when the weather allowed. There were several adults present at different times in the classroom, including: Jim, the class teacher; Lynn, the EYFS Coordinator; Susan, the support teacher; and Laura, Becky and Anne, teaching assistants.[2] The parallel Reception class shared the space with Jim's class and all of the children were taught by both teachers at different times. The class teacher of this parallel class (Liz) was newly qualified and was not involved in the research, but is referred to by other teachers in the data.

In Jim's Reception class, there were 12 children in the autumn term and 27 for the rest of the year (13 boys and 14 girls), as some children joined the class in January. Information on the children's ethnic groups was displayed in the classroom for both Reception classes. According to this display, across both classes the larger groups were Bangladeshi (9 children), Iraqi (8), Lebanese (8), Kosovan (7), Moroccan (6), Afghan (6) and White British (4). There were also children in the year group who were listed as Black Caribbean, Somali, Mongolian and Algerian.

St Mary's Church of England Primary School

St Mary's is a small Church of England voluntary aided primary in inner London, in an area of mixed housing and commercial properties. It is located next to the church in a small building which is quite cramped. The school is one-form entry, and the total number of children enrolled is approximately 140. According to the Families of Schools Data (DCSF, 2008c), at the time of the fieldwork approximately 50 per cent of pupils were eligible for FSM. About 10 per cent of pupils were White British, 20 per cent Other White background, 20 per cent Bangladeshi, 25 per cent Black groups, and 20 per cent Any other ethnic group. Approximately 70 per cent of pupils were registered as EAL. The Reception classroom at St Mary's was a single small classroom with a carpet, and areas set out for activities. Doors opened from the classroom onto a small outside area which was used for outside play by the class. The resources at St Mary's were far less numerous than at Gatehouse and there was less variety in what was on offer apart from the adult-led activities. At St Mary's, the free play activities remained constant, consisting of a writing area, home corner, painting, train sets, and outside play. The children also attended assembly every day after the morning register. There was just one class teacher involved in Reception (Paul), and three teachings assistants and one learning support assistant. One of the teaching assistants, Kelly, was involved in the EYFS Profile meetings with Paul, and thus features in the data more than the other staff.

In the Reception class at St Mary's there were 23 pupils – 9 boys and 14 girls. According to the official data on ethnic groups in the class, there were 5 Bangladeshi children, 4 Black African children, 2 Black other and 2 White British children in the class. Other children came from Chinese, Kosovan, Moroccan, Mixed other, Pakistani, and Other ethnic groups.

Reflections on the research process

My theoretical approaches influence the way I conceive of the research that I conduct, and my place within it. In conducting ethnographic studies of these Reception classrooms, I am aware of the need for reflexivity; it would be unwise to assume that my constitution as a White, middle-class British woman in my late 20s/early 30s (and the discourses surrounding these identity positions) does not have an impact on the research process (Archer, 2002; Phoenix, 1996). However, it is important to make clear that I do not conceive of myself as a neutral researcher who can understand fully a rational, coherent respondent, or that I can understand the impact of the 'readable' elements of my identity on the research. In engaging with reflexivity I do not intend to oversimplify the nature of identity categories as fixed. In line with my theoretical position regarding the constitution of the subject, I regard neither the researcher nor the researched as having 'ascribed' characteristics which can simply be 'read' and considered (Youdell, 2006b: 63). Nonetheless, given what Youdell calls 'the centrality of visual economies to discourses of gender and race' (2006b: 65), it is possible to speculate on the impact of the 'visible' aspects of my identity. For example, I think that being recognisable as a White woman, an identity which is obviously very common among primary teachers, may have helped me to seem less 'other'; my past career as a primary teacher also contributed to this. My age may also have helped when acting the *faux naïf*, especially with older participants; in terms of power relations it may have also balanced out my position as the 'expert' visitor from a university.

As argued in relation to women researchers (Oakley, 2005), issues of power are always significant in the research situation, which is inherently power-imbalanced from the start (Phoenix, 1996). This is the case nowhere more than in research on minoritised groups by White researchers; some of this work has been criticised as 'objectifying, voyeuristic, and blunt' (Youdell, 2006b: 61). I am well aware that, as suggested in CRT literature (Harris, 1993; McIntosh, 1992), I am the beneficiary of White privilege in the research situation as much as in all other aspects of daily life. Following the traditions of CRT, I would argue that my work is affected by and part of racist society; as Gillborn argues, 'We are all captured, to some degree, by the very machinery of racism and White Supremacy that we seek to criticize in our work' (Gillborn, 2008: 203). The issue of White researchers engaging in projects concerned with 'race' and minoritised groups is the subject of much debate (Archer, 2002; Gillborn, 2008), and CRT literature has been concerned with the different 'standing' of anti-racist arguments by White and minoritised scholars (Bell, 1992). White researchers need to be aware of the limits of their understanding of the lived experiences of minoritised people, without this preventing them from engaging in research concerned with 'race'. Indeed, Gillborn argues that Whiteness can be used in anti-racist work (2008: 201); this argument is summarised in his use of Stuart Hall's advice that 'we must struggle where we are' (2008: 202). After all, as Leonardo argues, 'White guilt can be a paralysing sentiment that helps neither Whites nor people of color' (2004a: 140).

Throughout the project, I have been conscious of my own constituted subjectivity and how this affects the research that I undertake, the analysis I offer of the data and how I present that analysis. Exploring discourses in the study schools is, as Youdell explains: 'not the collection "real" or "actual" discourse but is wholly constrained by my own discursive repertoire – the discourses I see and name – and my capacity to represent these' (2006b: 56). My 'making sense' of the data I produce is constrained in the same ways as the teachers are in 'making sense' of their experiences; I too am involved in the ongoing constitution of the participants through discourse. However, I am also aware that, as Youdell argues, the individuals involved are capable of exercising discursive agency (Butler, 1997) – within limits, and both intentionally and unintentionally – and affect how they are constituted (2006: 64). It is with an awareness of all of these issues that I present my arguments in relation to the data in the following chapters.

3

ASSESSING LEARNERS IN THE FIRST YEAR OF SCHOOL

Introduction

In this chapter, I examine the impact of the EYFS Profile and the related discourses that operate in Reception classrooms. I set out how the EYFS Profile provides a model of 'good learning' that involves neoliberal values, including rational choices, flexibility and submission. The second section considers how the EYFS Profile reinforces the idea of objective 'teacher knowledge' and how this works to allow teachers to dismiss evidence that does not cohere with their 'knowledge' of a child. Finally in this chapter, I examine alternative discourses of success in the Reception classrooms, including the idea of authentic learning, and how these are deployed in relation to assessing children's status as learners.

Educational success

> In New Labour's Britain it seems impermissible for the citizen to be anything other than successful. In education there has been an unrelenting focus on successful pupils and students, successful teachers, and, of course, successful schools. (Bradford and Hey, 2007: 595)

Sociological research in education has long been interested in the articulation and definition of educational success in policy and in schools. Much of this literature focuses on a construction of the 'ideal' pupil or learner that operates in schools, following Becker's (1952) discussion of the 'ideal client' (Francis and Skelton, 2005; Gillborn, 1990; Youdell, 2006b). In recent years, it has been argued that the marketisation-driven prioritisation of high-stakes tests has redefined educational success as high attainment in statutory assessments, and that this has had an impact on classroom practices (Gillborn and Youdell, 2000; Keddie and Mills, 2007). In this chapter, I begin to unpack the model of educational success that is discursively produced by the EYFS Profile and how it operates within these Reception classrooms. I argue that central to this model is a specific notion of the 'learner' as an individualised subject of schooling. This learner identity is discursively produced within a framework of neoliberal values of flexibility, conformity, responsibility and choice. It goes beyond strictly educational success to encompass all aspects of schooling, including attitudes, behaviour and conduct, and this wider prescription of what it means to be a learner is discursively reinforced by the range of attributes covered by the EYFS Profile. Developmental discourses provide for a conception of Reception children as transforming themselves into learners; children are seen, at times, as arriving 'unmade' due to their young age, and by the end of the year they are assessed in terms of how they now function as a pupil. Furthermore, some children are constituted as occupying positions as 'good learners' with more *authenticity* than others; some children, especially children from minoritised groups, are constructed as *superficially* 'good' learners, in contrast to natural, *innately* 'good' learners.

The EYFS Profile and the ideal learner

It is important to consider how a 'learner' is defined in order to explore who is recognisable as a learner, and who is not. This chapter considers how the idea of the learner is articulated in the EYFS Profile and Reception classrooms, before later chapters explore how individual children are assessed through this framework. A central argument of this book is that, in their first year of school, children are constituted in different ways as having successfully or unsuccessfully become learners, within a historically specific, neoliberal conception of the learner. This is aided by the EYFS Profile, which provides a mechanism for assessing children's status as 'good' or 'bad' learners, but is also based on long-standing tendencies for teachers to view pupils as appropriate or inappropriate subjects of schooling (Allan, 1999; Walkerdine, 1990; Youdell, 2006b). The wide-ranging elements of the EYFS Profile work to produce a definition of the learner which encompasses all aspects of school life, and blurs the distinction between 'academic' and social/emotional elements of school. Thus the distinction made by Youdell (2006b) between individuals as 'learners' and as 'students' is blurred; 'academic' achievements remain important, but the early years learner has to be a flexible, 'all-rounder' in order to be constituted as having achieved a successful transition into a subject of schooling. The importance of assessment in account-ability cultures ensures that what is tested equates to what is valued; this is sometimes talked about as the principle of 'alignment' (Graue and Johnson, 2011), where the content of the classroom is aligned with and coheres with assessment demands. Just as in later key stages testing encourages a focus on 'core subjects' or A–C students, in Reception, the focus is on all of the aspects of life included in the EYFS Profile.

These definitions are important because different children are constituted as different types of learners based on their proximity to an idealised notion of the learner; a learner who is implicitly White and middle class. Furthermore, mechanisms such as the EYFS Profile close down the possibilities for a more flexible conception of learning and learners which might allow for recognisable and 'authentic' success for children from other ethnic groups and social class positions.

In the Reception classrooms at Gatehouse and St Mary's, learning and being a learner had very specific meanings: these involved being enthusiastic and motivated to learn, able to choose activities appropriately, and able to display this learning at the correct times and in the correct ways. These values, as I have argued elsewhere (Bradbury, 2013), are based on neoliberal discourses of individual responsibility, flexibility and self-regulation which pervade policy, and are given solidity through the points of the EYFS Profile. Like Dahlberg and Moss, I argue that this is part of a 'new normality of the child', where the ideal is 'a child who will be flexible, who is developmentally ready for the uncertainties and opportunities of the twenty-first century' (2005: 7). The learner as described in the EYFS Profile encompasses many of these characteristics, and is prescribed a specific subjectivity which includes a wide range of attributes, which children must embody in order to be recognisable as having successfully become a learner. These are based on becoming a rational, self-knowing subject, able to access 'learning' in all its forms, process it, and reproduce it for the purposes of assessment. It is important to note that this is not an explicit discourse of the learner; rather it is an implicit and taken-for-granted notion which has developed over many decades of teaching, and is currently framed by neoliberal values. In the past, this discussion might have concentrated on what it means to be a pupil, but my focus here is on the particular construction of the learner, the term itself reflecting a move towards the individual as responsible for their own schooling. This focus on the individual also serves to obscure the role to the teacher in constituting children as different types of learner. Davies writes:

> So much is the autonomous individual constituted as central to the educational enterprise that teachers can feel quite upset if their power to constitute their students becomes visible to themselves and those around them. The responsibility and power to shape students inside the range of possible subjectivities, subjectivities that are recognisable as viable ways of being, are thus papered over in this emphasis on the freedom of the subject who is actively shaping itself through engagement with the syllabus. *(Davies, 2006: 430)*

As in Davies's description, I would argue that the EYFS Profile works to obscure the teachers' role by providing a mechanism which is notionally separate from the teacher, because the EYFS Profile is constructed as a neutral and objective assessment system. The Profile system also legitimises this wider conception of learning by assessing children on their emotions and attitudes as well as 'academic' subjects. The Profile covers almost everything that is done in the classroom: thus when a teacher reprimands a child for calling out and constitutes him or her in that moment as a 'bad learner', this is 'papered over' by the idea that learning to listen is part of the programme of learning in Reception. The teacher's role in constituting children as learners is further obscured by the breadth of the EYFS Profile and the detail required; their teacher assessments are discussed in terms of objectivity and neutrality as assessments of individual EYFS Profile points, not in terms of how they constitute the pupils as learners.

At the same time, however, the EYFS Profile also reduces the possibilities of what being a learner might mean: it is inflexible in its requirements, and absolute in terms of success or failure. This reduction means there is less opportunity for children to be successful as learners in different ways, and this has implications for groups of pupils who do not fit with idealised notions of the learner predicated on an implicit White middle-class ideal, as I discuss later. However, children are not powerless in the face of their constitution as 'good' or 'bad' learners, nor are identities fixed and solid: learner identities are provisional and fragile in that they are performatives which require constant maintenance. They are a part of recognis-ability as a subject in school; Butler comments:

> The student achieves precisely through mastering skills and this mundane practical appropriation of norms and rules culminates in 'excellent work' and fine marks that can be recognised publicly as such. The acts of skill acquisition are thus modes of subject formation, and this formation takes place within a set of norms that confer or withdraw recognition [...] The conferral of recognition, however, does not just happen once, if it happens at all, so a certain anxiety is built into the norm. *(Butler, 2006: 532)*

Being recognisable as a learner is a performance that needs to be sustained. Children unknowingly invest in these performances; they seem to recognise the fragility of their identities as learners in a situation where positive identities can be altered or withdrawn. Furthermore, the 'conferral of recognition' has to be intelligible within circulating discourses: it has to be thinkable that this child (with their gender, class and 'race' identity) can be a 'good' learner, or indeed a learner at all. These issues are discussed in depth in the following chapters.

The Reception child as neoliberal subject

I argue that the Reception child as learner has clearly defined character-istics which are in keeping with neoliberal values. This argument is linked to Walkerdine's discussion of the 'neoliberal subject' (Walkerdine, 2003; also Francis and Skelton, 2005; Walkerdine and Ringrose, 2006). Walkerdine describes the characteristics associated with the neoliberal subject; Francis and Skelton summarise these as:

Industrious
Diligent
Responsible and self-regulating (and self-blaming)
Introspective
Flexible and self-transforming
Reflective
Caring *(Francis and Skelton, 2005: 124)*

Although not all of these characteristics are present in the EYFS Profile, there are distinct similarities. According to the points included in the EYFS Profile, one of the most important facets of being a learner is being independent and enthusiastic, and able to make rational choices about what activities to engage in and how.; These points from the Personal, Social and Emotional Development scales demonstrate this:

> Displays high levels of involvement in self-chosen activities *(PSED 1, point 3)*
> Selects and uses activities and resources independently *(PSED 1, point 5)*
> Continues to be interested, motivated and excited to learn *(PSED 1, point 6)*

Here we see the importance of choosing in itself, and being motivated. Enthusiasm is valued in conjunction with rationality. The 'free play' organisation of the classroom in Reception provides the opportunity for children to be these motivated, rational choosers who engage purposefully in 'learning' in all its forms. As Tobin has noted in relation to other early childhood settings, this process of choice mirrors practices of consumption (Tobin, 1995). In this context, children are assessed on their 'motivation' and 'excitement' in engaging with these forms of learning, encouraged to select one and show 'involvement'. In the Reception classrooms I observed, children were frequently described by the teachers as 'with it' or 'on the ball', suggesting a required level of engagement. However, the practice of choosing was not simple, because the activities provided varied in status in the same way that different types of learning vary in status: the writing table, for instance, offers more opportunity to show 'learning' than the train set; the maths puzzles more than riding the tricycles. Like consumers, children must not simply choose, but choose *well* in order to be constituted as good learners. As Bauman argues, within neoliberal discourse, 'Freedom to choose does not mean that all choices are right – there are good and bad choices [...] the kind of choice made is the evidence of competence or its lack' (2005: 76).

In Reception, children may demonstrate this lack of competence through 'bad' choosing, such as being obsessive about one activity: at St Mary's the class teacher often complained that two boys always played with the train set, "doing exactly the bloody same thing every day". This was taken as indicative of a lack of imagination and a refusal to learn. Instead of demonstrating competence in choosing, they provided evidence of their lack of competence. They also failed to display self-regulation – choosing based on emotion (presuming they play with trains because they enjoy it) rather than rationally. This need for rationality is linked to neoliberal discourses of individual responsibility: ideally a learner takes responsibility for their learning by making rational choices about what they spend their time upon. 'Good' learners choose a variety of activities (ideally providing enough evidence for all of the 13 scales of the EYFS Profile), and engage fully with them: "moving about" was also seen negatively by staff at St Mary's.

This discourse of choice is linked to finding and taking up opportunities, 'having a go', and improving oneself, which are all linked to neoliberal values. Walkerdine uses Paul du Gay's term 'entrepreneur of the self' to encapsulate the individual responsibility to improve oneself required of a neoliberal subject (2003: 240); similarly, Woodrow and Press describe the model of the early years child as 'consumers-in-waiting' (2008: 96). Furthermore, those children who were not skilled choosers and were therefore constituted as 'bad' learners are much like Bauman's (2005) 'flawed consumers' or 'defective consumers' – not only missing out on a range of opportunities to provide evidence of themselves as 'good' learners, but also being positioned badly by their very act of choosing badly.

A further element of being a 'good' learner was a tendency to somehow *display* learning: engagement with activities needed to be followed up by some way of showing learning which could be observed, and preferably used for the EYFS Profile. This included taking work to show the teacher (so that it could be photographed or copied for the EYFS Profile folders) and, most commonly, answering questions on the carpet. This ability to display learning was a key part of being a learner. Here, Paul (class teacher at St Mary's) explains what he means by the term "bright" in relation to Parinda, a girl in his class:

> "Parinda's quite bright! [...] when I say bright, she's got a lot of knowledge and she knows how to express it – it's gone in, processed and she's showing it".

This display of learning constitutes effective functioning as a subject of schooling; it is the sort of 'learning' that the EYFS Profile is designed to recognise and value. Children who were quiet or reticent, despite being 'good' in many ways, could be exempt from being an all-round 'good' learner because they did not display their learning through speech or demonstration, or did so at the wrong time. Furthermore, learning that was displayed in particular contexts outside formal lesson times was sometimes ignored or discounted, while at other times being useful, and displaying learning was particularly powerful in constituting some children as 'good' learners. Most obviously, being able to answer questions on the carpet was highly valued, in part for its usefulness in moving the lesson on, as well as in showing what the child had learnt. This is also connected to the notions of the 'good teacher' engaging the learners and organising well-paced lessons. Jim, the class teacher at Gatehouse, described his reliance on his "bright sparks" to answer questions and get the lesson going, for example. Thus, in these classrooms, the learner was also required to be flexible and self-regulating. They needed to assess when enthusiasm and initiative were inappropriate, and when submission to authority was necessary. Although lesson times in Reception were based on free play, at other times the classes were expected to join in with many of the conventions of primary schooling, such as lining up before moving rooms, sitting cross-legged for assembly and on the carpet, and putting up your hand to request permission to speak. These times required a different facet of being a learner – being obedient and self-regulating, which involved understanding and joining in with all of these routines quickly and quietly. This need for 'docile bodies' (Foucault, 1991) was in direct contrast to the enthusiasm required when a teacher asked a question, sang a song or played a game; a 'good' learner was able to recognise these different requirements.

More formally, the value attached to following and respecting rules is indicated by EYFS Profile points on the Personal, Social and Emotional Development scales:

> Understands that there need to be agreed values and codes of behaviour for groups of people, including adults and children, to work together harmoniously. *(PSED 2, point 6)*

> Understands what is right, what is wrong, and why. *(PSED 3, point 8)*

This is *self*-regulation, where good behaviour arises from within the child rather than through instruction; this links to other discourses of individual responsibility. In particular, displays of emotion were discouraged: having a tantrum, shouting and being angry were all seen as evidence of immaturity. Paul described children in his class when they first arrived as "just crying every time they don't get their own way", the opposite of the EYFS Profile description of a child who 'Expresses needs and feelings in appropriate ways' (PSED 3, point 3). In the following section, I discuss how this model of a 'good' learner is made real and recognised in Reception classrooms through observation.

Observing the 'good' learner

The EYFS Profile provides a restricted model of what a learner 'looks like', and therefore how learners can be recognised in the classroom. This is illustrated by the collection and processing of observations made for the purposes of the EYFS Profile. The EYFS Profile narrows what counts as 'useful' information about a child, and informs the kinds of activities, comments and incidents that are recorded. First, observations are made (on sticky notes, labels and class lists) which relate to the skills and activities that are valued in the EYFS Profile. Second, observations are also sorted into 'useful' and 'not useful' in terms of the EYFS Profile. At St Mary's, this sorting was quite explicit – the main teacher and a teaching assistant would throw away observations made by other members of staff if they did not fit the EYFS Profile points. Thus only a small proportion of what a child says and does in the classroom is recognised and valued; this is an entirely subjective system of assessment which only allows for the skills and attributes of the EFYS Profile to be regarded as important.

In Table 3.1, I set out some examples of EYFS Profile observations from the Reception classrooms. These were noted down during my time in the classrooms at St Mary's and Gatehouse and collected from the official EYFS Profile folders, from collections of observations not yet stuck into folders, and from teachers' notes – all stages of the processing of the observations. These are organised loosely into the characteristics discussed above, to demonstrate the values imbedded within

TABLE 3.1 EYFS Profile observations from Gatehouse and St Mary's primary schools

Rationality, good choices, motivation	Parinda happily plays for long periods at activities of her choice.	Paige has excellent gross motor skills. She enjoys playing with the other children and her scooter.	Nasser joins in with the hunt for colours around the school.
Self-regulation and commitment	Karimah plays with the mosaics for 30 minutes. She does 3.	Naima played with the Tap Tap [game] for 10 mins. N did not talk. She made a house, choosing shapes appropriately.	Demi takes turns on the scooter and knows that it is fair to share.
Flexibility and recognising requirements, submission	Demi is very helpful when completing the jigsaw. She shows others how to complete the missing sections by looking for the colours.	Ahmed corrected Mr A when he counted 7 instead of 8. Ahmed shouted "Eight".	Suhan is joining in with class routines.
Enthusiasm	Rafeek really enjoyed the number search and is able to come to the front and correctly name #7. (Recognising numbers in context)	Iryna enjoys the home corner with her friends (engages in imaginative play)	Adiba took a photo and was very happy.
Displaying learning	Carl says "See you on the Wednesday" to an adult.	Khalid made a trumpet in the junk modelling area. He came to show me and 'play' it.	Malika says when wrapping something up "We only need a little bit 'cause that's small".
	Khadija recognised the picture of Barack Obama.	Demi chose the magnetic letter capital and lower case accurately to make her name [with photo].	Maira says "I am Muslim" when talking to Susan about Hajj. (Have an awareness of culture and religion)

the EYFS Profile process. I also separately set out some observations which show the importance of displaying learning, particularly through comments that can be quickly noted down.

These observations work at three different levels: first, they represent the teachers' selection of what to look at in the classroom and what to write down, and for whom (decisions that are affected by the EYFS Profile); second, they represent teachers' interpretation of what they see (who is happy, who understands) which is affected by children's identities as learners; and third, they provide examples of the model of the 'good' learner outlined above.

In later sections of the book, I examine the relationship between observations such as these and teachers' 'knowledge' of children – focusing on the first two levels above. My focus here instead is on the ways in which these observations reveal the model of the learner prescribed by the EYFS Profile, which values rationality, appropriate enthusiasm, submission and flexibility. The need to make good choices is shown throughout by the kind of activities that are noted down, most of which relate to specific EYFS Profile points (included by the teachers in brackets on occasion). Meanwhile, the need for flexibility is also apparent: being a 'good' learner requires doing different things at different times, with an understanding of what is valued in any given situation. In the examples above, we see how children are required to be adaptable in what they do: for example, Ahmed understands when rules are applicable – he realises that it is acceptable to shout out when the teacher has deliberately counted incorrectly – and that submission is not always important. The examples of displaying learning show how important children's comments were in demonstrating learning; thus what becomes valued is not understanding but the ability to articulate this understanding. For example, it is noted that Malika says 'We only need a little bit 'cause that's small' when wrapping something up, demonstrating an understanding of size and area. Another child might also understand this, but without a comment about it, this understanding is not recognised. Thus the EYFS Profile increases the significance of verbal communication, which has real implications in classrooms like these where many children do not speak English as their first language. However, displaying learning is not simply about talking; it is also important to show a teacher or other children what you have done (like Khalid showing off the trumpet he made). I return to this issue of agency in terms of learner identities in Chapter 5.

These examples of observations, just a few among many hundreds written down during the course of a year, illustrate the complexity of this learner identity and its contradictions. The use of observations such as these plays an important role in teachers' construction of their 'knowledge' of children.

The EYFS Profile and 'teacher knowledge'

The ideal 'good learner' identity discussed in this chapter was not an explicit or fixed model, and importantly, there was little recognition from the teachers of their responsibility in constituting children as 'good' or 'bad' learners, despite their roles as official assessors of the children's attainment and as collectors of evidence. Instead, the teachers engaged with a powerful discourse of 'teacher knowledge' which presented their constructed (and constituting) 'knowledge' of the pupils as neutral, factual and objective. Thus the picture they built up of each child, through official observations and daily classroom life, was constructed as factual and certain knowledge, rather than subjective opinion. This discourse dominated these classrooms in such a way that teachers dismissed information which did not correspond with their 'knowledge'. This was informed by development concepts which provided the idea that these young children needed to be 'discovered' and their true identities drawn out by skilful teachers. Thus 'teacher knowledge' was constructed as an important part of an early years teacher's skill and profession-alism, rather than as subjective and discursively constrained.

The idea of 'teacher knowledge' originates in EYFS policy documents which assert that long-term observation is the best method of assessing a child. This was also reinforced by advice the teachers at Gatehouse and St Mary's claimed they received from the Local Authority on how to conduct the EYFS Profile. Jim commented that "We were basically told that assessment is now almost 50 per cent teacher knowledge – you don't have to have a note, you don't have to have it written down, you just need to know". The teachers' reliance on 'knowledge' of the pupils is part of a counter discourse in early years education, where ideas that lost legitimacy in a results-driven culture – 'disqualified knowl-edges' (Foucault, 1980) regarding caring about children and the slow build up of knowledge about children's development – are re-legitimised. This links to ideas already discussed about developmental progress and the need to discover a child: what Paul at St Mary's called "trying to work out where they're at and who they are, as individuals [...] to kind of open them up and get a picture of what's going on". These ideas are reinforced by a previous Department for Education and Skills document called 'Creating the picture', which explains how early years teachers should gain this 'knowledge' of their pupils (DES, 2007). Unusually, in early years the counter discourse finds itself in alignment with assessment policy: notions of teaching as preparing children for tests are rejected in favour of teacher assessment through the accumulation of 'knowledge' as a less damaging assessment tool.

The collection of 'knowledge' in relation to the EYFS Profile points is implicitly an assessment of the child's proximity to the ideal learner, and thus of the normality of each child, within this framework. This is underpinned by wider conceptions of how normality can be assessed; as Foucault writes:

> The judges of normality are everywhere. We are in the society of the teacher-judge, the doctor-judge, the educator-judge, the social worker-judge; it is on them that the universal reign of the normative is based; and each individual, wherever he may find himself, subjects to it his body, his gestures, his behaviour, his aptitudes, his achievements. *(Foucault, 1991: 304)*

The omnipresence of 'judges of normality' more widely, I would argue, allows these 'teacher-judges' to place great emphasis on their 'knowledge' as factual and unquestionable. The veracity of teacher knowledge was rarely questioned, and this was in part due to the fact that part of their professional identity appeared to rely upon their ability to 'know' the children through observation. This 'knowing' was quite certain, despite the use of this romanticised vision of 'discovering' pupils. Paul commented that "My experience is they normally do [open up], by about March". Here, discourses of ability and development (discussed further in later parts of this chapter) – which construct ability as something which some children have innately, and some lack – remain powerful; the teachers are still able to find the 'true' child in the end because 'ability' is innate and fixed. It may not always be reflected in how children behave in the classroom, and so the teacher has to discover them and gradually come to gain an accurate understanding of them.

The idea of a supposedly objective process of observation was used in this discourse to lend teachers' knowledge a sense of scientific certainty, and allowed some observations to be rejected because they did not fit the teacher's view of the child. In the weekly EYFS Profile meetings at St Mary's, Paul and the teaching assistant, Kelly, would look through the observations and discuss them; observations were described as "100 per cent him" if they fitted well with their view of the child, while other observations were rejected and discarded. One incident which reveals how discussions were framed by the idea that the teachers 'knew' the children, and that this 'knowledge' was unquestionable, is described below.

Reece, Ryan and the supply teacher's observations

This episode took place during one of the weekly meetings between Paul and Kelly to "discuss the children" and update their EYFS Profile files. Each week they concentrated on four "focus children", and on this occasion, two of the four (organised alphabetically) were Reece and Ryan, two African-Caribbean boys. The learner identities constructed for these two boys are discussed in detail in the following chapter; it is sufficient to note here that neither was seen positively, and Paul often seemed to mix the two boys up (their names began with the same letter, and there was only one other Black boy in the class at the time). In the meeting, Paul and Kelly were looking at two 'long observations' (page-long detailed observations of a child over 10 to 15 minutes); one each of Reece and Ryan. These had been written by a supply teacher who had been in the class for a day while Paul was absent. First, they looked together at one for Reece, which described him playing with farm animals.

> Paul reads from the observation and makes a few notes about 'working relationships' in Reece's folder. He continues; the observation says that Reece was grouping the farm animals. He writes down 'grouping things'. Paul reads out: "Reece said 'Let's put all the pigs on the mud!' Reece would

never say that, that's bollocks!" They both laugh. He repeats, 'Let's put all the pigs on the mud!' in a posh voice, and says, "I'm not going to put that".

Kelly: "It was the supply teacher who wrote it".

Paul reads *[as Reece]*: "'Let's put all the cows …'. Uh-uh" *[as if to mean 'no way']*. He laughs again. "Why is she writing this?"

Kelly: "Maybe she mixed up Ryan and Reece?"

Paul: "How funny".

Kelly: "He's [Ryan's] much more likely to say that. She could easily have got the two mixed up".

Paul agrees: "Yes, this is bollocks". They cross out and swap over the names on the two observations made by the supply teacher. *(Field notes, St Mary's)*

In this episode, what is significant is the assumed impossibility, to Paul and Kelly, of Reece saying this sentence due to their prior 'knowledge' of Reece. The very idea of him saying full sentences and organising the farm animals logically is laughable to them, and rejected as simply untrue, literally impossible. Despite evidence to the contrary, Paul's previous 'knowledge' of Reece continues to constitute him outside the boundaries of being a 'good' learner (which is strongly associated with making statements like those listed in the observation – being logical, articulate and organised). The supply teacher, as an impartial outsider with little knowledge of the children, has no motive in making up what she observed, yet the possibility of her recording accurately what Reece said is not even entertained. The justification for this is that she does not 'know' the children like Paul and Kelly do, and therefore is a questionable source of information. The swapping over of Ryan and Reece's names provides Paul and Kelly with an explanation for what they perceive as impossible. Ryan was seen as more articulate in general and so Kelly says it is "much more likely" that Ryan is the boy in the observation. As they went through the observation, listing points for Ryan, Paul found further information which he felt supported the decision to swap. He read out a section about working independently and commented: "That again is Ryan; he will go and play on his own". Paul and Kelly's 'knowledge' of the children is the justification for this swap, used to reject the depiction of Reece and instigate the changeover to Ryan's name. Paul *knows* what 'is' Ryan and what 'isn't' Reece, and information that supports this is accepted, but that which questions it is rejected.[1]

The next stage of the meeting revealed more about Paul and Kelly's 'knowledge' of Reece. After discussing other matters and other children, Paul and Kelly looked at the second observation, now labelled as being about Reece.

Paul reads out the second observation (Kelly has changed the name on the sheet and throughout the observation). It is about the 'Fishing for numbers' game.[2]

Paul: "I still don't believe 100 per cent that he said that. She's turned it into sentences – it's no use to us". Paul continues to read, up to a part when Reece says he wants to have two fishing rods. Paul laughs: "Here comes the fight". As he reads, it becomes apparent that Reece just said "I need both", meaning he needed two rods to get the numbers; no fight happens. They list some more points for Reece. Kelly comments that the "disjointed speech" in the observation sounded like Reece so she knew they were mixed up. *(Field notes, St Mary's)*

When faced with further positive information about Reece, Paul again rejects it. He doesn't "believe" that the supply teacher noted down accurately what he said, and instead suggests that she embellished it. However, later Kelly uses the speech patterns in the observation to justify using it for Reece: their "disjointed" nature is indicative of Reece to her. Clearly, this information can be used both to reinforce what is already known about Reece, or simply rejected: "it's no use to us". It is "no use" to Paul because it does not fit with what he already knows about Reece. This shows how observations and evidence are used to back up what the teacher already 'knows', not as a collection of evidence on which to base judgements.

Furthermore, Paul feels able to predict what will happen in observations: "Here comes the fight" is his response to Reece asking for two sticks. In fact, it could be argued that Reece is acting quite logically (two rods means picking up more numbers), but this element of Reece's behaviour is ignored or goes unrecognised in favour of a prediction that sees him causing trouble. Later in the meeting, when looking at another observation for Reece which described him not letting other children play with some blocks, Kelly comments, "That is *so* him". Thus information which fits with the largely negative picture of Reece is accepted without question, and even that which isn't obviously negative, like Reece wanting to use two sticks, is interpreted as evidence that he is difficult.

In this example, we see how the adults' certainty in the veracity of their 'knowledge' of the children outweighs evidence to the contrary and taints their analysis of observations done by other people. This is what makes this discourse so powerful; it regards 'teacher knowledge', however changing, unreliable or subjective, as sacrosanct, objective truth.

How 'knowledge' relates to the EYFS Profile

In Chapter 6, I discuss how 'teacher knowledge' contributes to the production of the final EYFS Profile scores. However, as in the example above, the discourse of collecting and using 'knowledge' is implicated in the *entire processing of evidence* for the EYFS Profile. The observations contribute to the 'knowledge' of children but are also affected by 'knowledge', which defines which are useful and even recognised as realistic. At St Mary's, 'teacher knowledge' would be used in making sense of ambiguous observations, as in this example from another EYFS Profile meeting:

Paul and Kelly are looking at a long observation for Liam. They are trying to make sense of what it says about him filling a teapot with sand; they are remembering the incident as well as looking at what is written down. They have already found some points relating to literacy, and Paul says after writing down a PSED point, "He works well with other children – he always does". Paul says about the teapot: "He was good at filling it up, wasn't he? His fine motor skills are good". Kelly tries to remember, and says Liam was looking around. Paul says, "Making choices then. He is good anyway – our knowledge beyond this is that he good at choosing". They note it down.
(Field notes, St Mary's)

Here, Paul and Kelly use their 'knowledge' to determine what the observation about Liam represents in terms of EYFS Profile points. They use their "knowledge beyond this" to help them work out what the observations suggests Liam can do, sometimes making tenuous connections between what has been noted down and the EYFS Profile points. What is clear is that they rely on their acquired 'knowledge' of Liam as a 'good' learner in processing the observation, and in turn the observation comes to be evidence of this 'knowledge'.

How a child comes to be 'known'

In this section, I consider the sources of information used by teachers to 'discover' the children and build their 'knowledge' of them. The most significant of these was of course through daily interaction with the children in the classroom, dinner hall and playground. However, before the children even interacted with the teacher in school, there were two major sources of information – home visits and Nursery information – which contributed to how a child was understood as a learner. Although the teachers described the process of discovering children *in the classroom*, I would argue that these sources of information meant that children did not arrive in the classroom as 'blank slates' ready to be uncovered: some had already begun to be understood as 'good' or 'bad' learners before they had even started school.

Significantly, the teachers engaged with a discourse which sees educational success as linked to family background and children's characteristics as genetically determined. This meant that 'knowledge' about families provided a viable source of information about new pupils. This mirrors Mirza's argument that, despite the scientific establishment's dismissal of genetically determined characteristics, 'this new age of gene science appears to be able to accommodate a new popular version of biological determinism' (1998: 116). Most importantly in this case, the importance of genetic connections legitimises the idea that children can come to be 'known' through knowledge of their parents. Information about the families was collected both formally and informally, through a "parent questionnaire" at St Mary's and home visits at Gatehouse. At St Mary's, Paul commented that the questionnaire was "how we get a picture of them", and that he had constructed it so that he could "read through the lines to find out the set up". This suggests that this information, including the presence or absence of both parents, the number of siblings, and the parents' occupational status (all of which are entwined with class and race in popular discourses), helps him to understand the child. At Gatehouse, children who came from other preschools were visited at home, and a similar need to understand the home situation was mentioned:

> AB: What about information on the children from outside?
>
> Jim: We go to their homes and talk to their parents and ask them really awkward difficult questions.
>
> AB: Like what?
>
> Jim: Like "Where is dad? Is dad likely to turn up at school? Why are you in the UK?" Difficult questions that the school needs for their database, and actually does kind of – I've realised as the years have gone on, it is quite useful, useful information, although really really difficult to ask sometimes, awkward situations. *(Interview with Jim, Gatehouse)*

As above, Jim's questions suggest that information about the family composition and racial/cultural background of the family (including reasons for migrating to the UK) is important in Jim's understanding of the child. Similarly, another Gatehouse teacher (Lynn) returned from one home visit and made comments about the mother "answering the door in her underwear" and letting the children ride their bikes inside the house and over mattresses. In another case, a home visit provided a source of positive information:

> Jim is talking to the other staff about a home visit. Jim makes a point of saying that the new girl (Farah) is "one of seven, with another one on the way" – the women are shocked. The new girl is described as "quite bright, quite a bit of English". They hope the new girl will be a good model of English for Jim's children. She is described as Afghan, and Pashto speaking. They discuss if there are any other Afghan children. Jim mentions that older children in the family have gone to university and says "obviously they have high aspirations". The family is also described as very "with it" – Dad took time off work to meet Farah's new teacher. *(Field notes, Gatehouse)*

In this case, Farah is already constituted as a 'good' learner – she is a useful English speaker with parents who fit into positive models of parenting (aspiring, committed to education). Even though her family might be seen as too large (and this brings up many discourses of 'uncivilised' minority families), Farah is already seen positively within the classroom, before she has even arrived. Similarly, Jim also commented frequently on how he saw one pupil, Sophea, independently prepare and eat a bowl of cereal when he visited her home, and how mature this was. This information was repeated whenever Sophea did something sensible or independent in the classroom. Thus the information from home visits was not only crucial in *beginning* the constitution of some pupils as 'good' learners, but also in the ongoing maintenance of these identities in the classroom.

The other information which meant that the children did not start from a neutral position was that provided from their nurseries, both within the school and outside.[3] This information was often very detailed and made strong judgements about the child, and also included information about the parents and their occupations. The children coming up from the Nursery at Gatehouse in January were labelled as 'top', 'middle' or 'bottom' by their Nursery teacher. Handwritten notes from the handover meeting included comments such as "Jasmina – attention seeker" and "Zafir – stroppy and stubborn". Another child was listed as having a "reliable parent". The formal reports included detailed information on the children's experiences in Nursery, which constituted them as different types of learners:

> "Zafir […] does need reminding of expectations when sitting on the carpet".

> "Bethany is a visual learner".

> "Hakim […] likes to be the first to try activities suited to more able children. He can become disagreeable when asked to perform a task he deems easy or when he is tired. [His target is] to follow routines and behaviour expectations in the classroom […] Hakim is a quiet child […] Hakim is an active learner".

> "Ashlee […] is a good all-rounder […] considerate to those younger or less able […] has a big personality".

> "Jena [has had] extended time abroad […] is a quiet child".

It is clear from these examples that before any of these children arrive in Jim's Reception class, he will have begun to get to 'know' them. Jim will know that Jena's family have taken her abroad for a considerable time, a practice disapproved of by schools. Another child, Bilqis, is described with particularly feminine traits of being quiet and liking playing "with mummies and babies". Because this information is so specific and extensive (the reports last several pages and include samples of work), it forms a clear basis for the construction of the children's identities. It makes the children intelligible to Jim because it explains the pupils in a similar way to how he needs to understand them, dealing with the same six areas of the EYFS Profile. He commented, "The information from Nursery is useful, especially the kind of medical information, information about their parents". Thus, as with the home visits and parental interviews, the parents become proxies for understanding the child.

The potential effect of the Nursery information was also shown at St Mary's, where there were three new children in January. Paul received information about two of the new children soon to be starting in his class:

> Paul tells me that the information from the local nursery has arrived about the new children. He shows me their information packs and says, "We can see just from their pictures that Nalini is really on the ball and Dinesh not at all". He shows me the children's drawings on the front of the packs – Nalini's is of a recognisable house done in several colours; Dinesh's is a grid, all in orange felt tip. *(Field notes, St Mary's)*

Here we can see how Paul begins to construct Nalini's and Dinesh's learner identities very early on, perhaps before he has even met them, based on their drawings. The children may have been asked to do the same activity – perhaps to 'draw a house' – and Paul uses the information to make an impromptu assessment of their ability and/or development. Nalini is already "on the ball" while Dinesh is far from it; they already occupy opposite ends of the spectrum in terms of engagement with learning. These identities, while reinforced by classroom observations and further information, stayed with these two children throughout the year (Nalini scored 89 in the EYFS Profile, while Dinesh was the lowest in the class with 20 points). This incident reveals how the simplest of events can mark a child as a 'good' or 'bad' learner in this context: once seen, these pictures become part of Paul's 'knowledge' of Dinesh and Nalini and can be used as evidence; thus Paul's subjective reading of them is taken as fact, with no questions asked over the reliability of this information or its context.

Navigating assessment in Reception

It is worth noting here that, although the teachers constructed their 'knowledge' of the children as definite, neutral and objective, their responses to the EYFS Profile and assessment in general were contradictory and complex. The certainty of 'knowledge' contrasted with the ambivalence felt towards the EYFS Profile as a policy; in general, the Profile was described as impractical and an inadequate method of recording their 'knowledge' of the children. Paul was typical in his comment on the Profile points: "It's all rubbish, they're wide, they're broad, they're vague". The Profile was frequently discussed as a blunt instrument which failed to capture the intricacies of a child's attainment: Jim explained, "You're quantifying something that's not quantifiable. Some of it is quantifiable, but for the majority of it, it's not". Jim's comment on the use of numbers as results was also typical:

> "It's really hard because they're asking for a number. […] If you ask an open-ended question you're going to get an open-ended answer, but if you ask a

closed question you get a closed answer, but they are asking *an open-ended question, with a closed answer*, it's kind of, the two don't really go together". *(Jim, Gatehouse)*

However, at other times the EYFS Profile was also seen as a neutral, objective instrument which could be used in conjunction with teacher 'knowledge' if it were written better. At Gatehouse, Lynn commented that it was possible to assess maths points accurately: "Some of them are very clear and are very black and white – that a child *is* able to recognise up to number nine. They either are or they aren't; it's not a fuzzy situation".

The practical implications of the assessment were also a frequent source of frustration and seemed to put a limit on its accuracy:

"There's 117 profile points, you know, and you're supposed to have evidence, three pieces of evidence, for each. There is no way that you can do that. [...] If you look at the profile book, it's just, like, nonsense. You know there's no way you're going to see Johnny doing this or that because you've got 30 Johnnys. You can't find that on a daily basis". *(Paul, St Mary's)*

Thus there were contradictions within the teachers' views of the assessment and their use of a discourse of 'teacher knowledge' as certain.

Despite these complaints, there was some sympathy with the need for an official assessment. Jim commented:

"It's just government statistics really … you have to quantify something. I mean the way that it works at the moment is, if you're funding stuff and you're giving all these schools money, you need to know, the government need to know that they're getting their money back from it, that they are, the people who you're giving money to, are doing their work, so you need a figure, you need a percentage". *(Jim, Gatehouse)*

Similarly, the dominance of assessment as a method of accountability was shown by Paul's comment that "the school's totally about results". However, this discourse was also resisted; Jim continued:

"And I just think that it's like a hoop to jump though – you need to do this to get a figure and everyone's doing the same thing, you get a kind of average, and I suppose to a point that's quite useful, they know they're getting their money's worth, or not getting their money's worth, and where they need to put money into and things like that. But, they're *five* – it's just stupid". *(Jim, Gatehouse)*

At times, the Reception teachers attempted to argue against these priorities, positioning themselves alternatively as early years teachers who cared more about the children. Jim commented: "Well I find the whole thing a bit strange anyhow, assessing you know, five-year-olds, so strictly, you know, 117 points – it's just ridiculous". These comments reproduce what Osgood has described as a 'counter hegemony' in early years education, which rejects the hyper-rational judgment of teaching and replaces it with a more flexible understanding of what the children can do and achieve (Osgood, 2006). This counter discourse positions the teachers within their professional discourses as 'good teachers', who wish to re-engage with the 'disqualified knowledges' (Foucault, 1980) of early years education, which emphasised more than just the production of results. However, in the quote above we see how Jim cannot escape the neoliberal discourse of education as an economic transaction between the state (as funder) and the schools (as providers of a measurable service). All the Reception teachers engaged with and also rejected the policy discourses which display what Dahlberg and Moss describe as 'hegemonic rationality' in early years education:

> a rationality that cannot imagine any other way to justify and evaluate preschools except in terms of their ability to produce pre-specified outcomes and through the application of measurement techniques that are assumed to be objective and universally valid. *(Dahlberg and Moss, 2005: 5)*

As we have seen, the Reception teachers engage with this rationality in that they criticise the EYFS Profile for being vague and subjective, suggesting that they would prefer an objective and universally valid system, and that this would be a rational method of evaluation. Their comments on the need for the government to produce a number (and their occasional sympathy with this need) suggest that they are engaged in the maintenance of this hegemonic rationality: by accepting the need for a numerical judgement of their teaching, they reproduce a discourse of rational, objective evaluation of early years education. Fundamentally, they are also restricted by their statutory obligation to produce the EYFS Profile figures; as Jim put it: "I understand why it needs to be done, and I understand the reasons behind it, but it just seems, you know, it seems a bit irrelevant … but I still have to do it". This comment reflects what Osgood terms 'passive resistance', where teachers are 'overtly opposed' to policy reform 'yet feel powerless to resist' (2006: 189). These teachers are engaged in everyday processes of reworking and resisting policy, at the same time as they rely on policy discourses to justify and explain their practice. The teachers' contradictory responses – whereby the EYFS Profile is an inappropriate, vague assessment system and yet objective, factual assessment using observation is still something to be aimed for – are complicated by the deployment of discourses which both reject and coalesce with neoliberal values of accountability. These contradictions are relevant for the later discussion of how the final results are produced.

A final point about the teachers' responses to assessment policy is that they are connected to the teachers' views of their professionalism and status, as I have argued elsewhere (Bradbury, 2012). Some research has suggested that increasing formalisation of early years has been an 'asset to status' (Hargreaves and Hopper, 2006), and these teachers certainly appeared to feel pride in using their 'knowledge' in the EYFS Profile; however, the requirements of the Profile also appeared to result in feelings of stress and incompetence. Paul described the need to produce evidence as making him feel "absolutely incompetent, all the time, constantly"; while Jim described the Profile as "the Sats of the Foundation Stage" and "a lot of pressure". Furthermore, as I discuss in Chapter 6, the process of moderation was seen as an attack on the teachers' professionalism and judgement. All of these factors – the construction of 'knowledge' as objective, the link to professionalism, and the doubt and resentment felt in relation to the policy – played a part in the teachers' constitution of children as different types of learner.

The ideal learner in context: ability and development

As discussed, the model of the ideal learner was not explicit in these Reception classrooms, but it *was* present in assumptions about what is important in teachers' discussions, in the EYFS Profile documents and in classroom practices. However, it operated in competition with other longer-established discourses about how educational success might be understood: long-standing discourses of ability and development were deployed in these classrooms in ways which both coincided with and challenged the neoliberal values discussed above.

Ability and intelligence

Discourses of ability are well established in the education system in the UK (Gillborn and Youdell, 2000) and inform policy, including early years policy: the EYFS Profile handbook refers to 'children across the ability range', for example (QCA, 2008: 22). However, assumptions about ability 'are rarely voiced in any explicit or systematic way' (Gillborn and Youdell, 2000: 52). In the schools in this study, assumptions about ability and intelligence were similarly left unexplained but remained potent, especially in relation to the EYFS Profile, despite the lack of any scientific evidence that 'ability' is a single, measurable, innate phenomenon (Sternberg, 1996, in Gillborn and Youdell, 2000: 59). For instance, in my first interview with class teacher Jim at Gatehouse, when I asked about 'attainment' in his class he was confused and assumed that what I meant was, in his words, "ability". In my understanding, 'attainment' is what children score in tests, whereas 'ability' denotes an innate quality, or a level of intelligence. Jim described "a big range, there's right from still unable to write someone's name, to full sentences and full stops, capital letters", using points taken directly from the EYFS Profile, a measure of attainment in that it intends to measure what children can do. This confusion between two quite different ideas was typical of discourses of ability, which often included an assumption that ability as a phenomenon was common sense and widely understood, even though the terms were not always agreed upon. This was seen in comments such as one from Susan, another teacher at Gatehouse, who said some children were "brighter, or whatever word we should use".

Ability was a powerful organising concept in these classrooms, with a tripartite 'top-middle-bottom' or 'high-middle-lower' model often used. As mentioned, at Gatehouse, the notes on the new children coming up from Nursery (taken during a meeting of the old and new teachers) divided the children into 'top', 'middle' and 'bottom' groups before they even arrived; in the summer term children were organised into 'ability groups'. Thus during their first year of school, children were already being designated as successful, average or unsuccessful. However, the conflation of "potential" and "ability" in discussions at Gatehouse revealed the slipperiness of terms associated with ability: when Jim was explaining the ability groups to me, he told me that two pupils were in the highest group "not because they're there yet, but because I think they've got potential". This suggests that Jim views ability as more than what he can see in the classroom – as what he judges to be possible for that child because of their innate characteristics. This is an important distinction, which allows for disparities between how well a child attains in assessments and the teacher's assessment of them as a learner. The idea of potential suggests that there is something innate about these children which means that, although they might not be doing brilliantly now, they will do in the future. This is closely connected to the idea of being an 'authentic' learner I outline below, with the natural ability to learn in appropriate ways.

The use of terms such as "with it" and "sparky" by teachers in both schools, which were related to discourses of innate ability, indicated an assessment of children in terms of how alert or engaged they were. This demonstrates the link with the required enthusiasm for learning discussed earlier; here these two discourses overlap and work together to position some children as 'good' learners. This link between showing learning through language and being 'high ability' is particularly relevant here given the high proportion of EAL children in both Reception classes.

The fluidity of terms relating to notions of ability is important in how this discourse of fixed and measurable intelligence functions in the classroom: ability is constructed as a definable common-sense concept, yet it means different things at different times and to different people. Although it is used in policy and in the Local Authority's moderation process, the term is rarely officially defined, which allows the common-sense nature of ability to continue unchecked. In both schools, ability discourses operated as a regime of truth to define and organise pupils in the class; these designations operated as a central part of assessments of children as 'good' and 'bad' learners, alongside the neoliberal values discussed earlier in this chapter.

Developmental discourses

Early childhood researchers have long argued that development discourses based on developmental psychology and developmentally appropriate practice (DAP) operate as a regime of truth in early years education (Dahlberg and Moss, 2005; MacNaughton, 2005; Yelland, 2005a). Early years policy in England also uses development as a significant organising concept; nowhere more than in the EYFS Profile where four of the six areas of the EYFS Profile have titles including the term. The very first of the EYFS principles is 'Child development', where development is described thus:

> Development is a continuous, complex interaction of environmental and genetic factors in which the body, brain and behaviour become more complex. *(DCSF, 2009b)*

Thus the policy documents construct development as a scientific process of increasing complexity in body, mind and behaviour. The use of 'genetic factors' as an explanation for differences suggests fixity and inevitability, while the reference to 'environmental' factors reflects the connections made between home life and 'readiness' for school. Given the prominence of development in these documents, it is unsurprising that the teachers in my study also used the term 'development' in multiple ways. Both class teachers talked about development as an important part of their knowledge base as early years teachers: Paul complained about a lack of training during his PGCE on "developmental stuff, which is what a lot of it, most of it, is", suggesting the unique developmental knowledge required to teach young children. This idea of specific early years knowledge is based on the notion that development is a neutral and scientific body of knowledge, which can be used to organise children hierarchically (Yelland, 2005a). This was apparent in Paul's attempts to replace words like 'ability' or 'clever' with 'development', which suggested he regarded it as a more accurate and more neutral, scientific term which sufficiently described the complexity of children's progress. He even criticised other adults' use of the term 'clever'. Here he is referring to comments made by a student TA:

> "She was saying about 'the clever ones get it right away'. I mean that's just such the wrong attitude; it's nothing to do with if they're clever, it's not a term that should be used in [Reception] ... it really annoys me that attitude. It's all about development. It's all about what's going under the [surface?] – I always see that iceberg, with all that stuff that's going on [...] This clever/ not clever, it's just so unhelpful". *(Paul, St Mary's)*

Here Paul attempts to reject ability discourses in favour of 'development', which he seems to locate as an individual, intrinsic and sometimes hidden quality. For Paul, development is about more than being able to express learning and cleverness; it is more subtle and takes greater skill to uncover (something also apparent when Paul discussed his ability to 'discover' his pupils' hidden qualities). This intangible development of a child is both scientifically recognisable and also elusive: it is constructed as neutral without being defined. As with 'ability', there is a lack of specificity surrounding the term 'development', which allows this discourse to operate alongside others in the classroom.

Development and ability together

As has been apparent from the data on these two terms, development and ability were used without exact definition or discussion. This fluidity allowed the terms also to be used interchangeably, as seen in Paul's comments. Although I am not suggesting that the teachers believed the two terms to mean exactly the same concept, it was clear that since neither was defined, they were used as if it were just common sense to use them without any explanation of the distinction. Indeed, the EYFS Profile document refers to both development as a guiding principle and also to the 'ability range', without explanation of what the difference between them might be. This undefined concept is what Paul refers to when he says "whatever you want to call it", where "it" has some real meaning even without a name. When Susan says "whatever word we are meant to use", it reveals the strength of this common-sense idea, despite the continued debate over the concepts and their uses; because everyone knows what it is, the term used is irrelevant, merely changing with educational fashions. The slippage between these terms, however, is hugely significant in understanding how children in Reception are understood as learners: the pseudo-scientific overtones of 'development' give the term 'ability' a neutrality and inevitability that is usually only alluded to. It also allows for both the idea of ability/development as something that is neutral and scientific, and the idea of it as something that can be assessed or 'discovered' as part of a teacher's knowledge of the child.

An example of this confusion between the terms can be seen in Jim's discussion of one of his pupils, whom he has allocated to a higher group:

> "Carl is not the brightest child in the whole class; he's not somebody who can read and write and knows all his letters and numbers, but he is quite mature and he's really willing to learn, so I made the decision [to put him in a higher group] because I thought he could cope, and he can. Whether or not that was the right decision; whether or not he needs more developmental stuff before the stage he's at now, I don't know, I haven't really assessed him yet". *(Jim, Gatehouse)*

Here Jim appears to equate being "bright" with reading and writing and knowing numbers (using ability discourses), and balances this with maturity and a willingness to learn (using development discourses). He also involves "developmental stuff" alongside these. Carl's learner identity thus involves all of these elements, and will be discovered, Jim suggests, by assessment.

The idea of discovery was an important part of the entanglement of these two discourses: Paul argued that the children were too young to be affected by their ability yet, in comments which suggested that although he might be concerned with 'development', their 'abilities' would always be there under the surface:

> "I think at this stage it's not because their abilities are influencing their learning yet, if you like. 'Cause clearly some children pick things up much faster than others, just because their potential to learn is just different, in those subjects, and their skills and all that – some are brilliant athletes, they're born brilliant athletes, you know what I mean. Some of them can learn how to jump properly, and fair enough. So, to an extent, by Year 6 they do, they are showing their, you know, um [pauses, thinking of word] specialisations, their gifts if you want; their gifts are clearer; whereas at this stage I don't think they're clear at all". *(Paul, St Mary's)*

In this comment, Paul engages with the idea of innate qualities that children are born with, but which only 'show' (or perhaps can be discovered) as children get older. That these abilities exist is taken for granted – children's potential is "just different". In early years, Paul has to find these qualities while they are unclear, through his understanding of development. Paul uses terms such as "gifts" and "specialisations" which cloak the idea of ability with suggestions of sympathy with children's uniqueness and individuality, distant from ideas of ranking children or labelling them "high" or "low". However, Paul's shift from using "abilities" and "potential" to using "gifts" reveals the dangerous way in which these terms can come to mean inherited intelligence, even when they appear to mean something milder. Comments such as these have real implications for what a child can 'be' in the classroom: the idea of fixed ability remains.

These examples demonstrate how Reception is unique in that it is the location where two powerful discourses collide, are integrated and are reconciled: a discourse of development from early years practice and principles, and one of ability from primary education (and popular, 'common sense' discourse). Although the EYFS policy uses development as a guiding principle, discussions at both schools were dominated by a notion of differences between children that were wider than just development, though they borrowed assumed scientific legitimacy from the term. The result of this entwinement is a potent and dangerous conception of ability/development as measurable and neutral. Burman has criticised the dominance of development discourses in early years education, arguing that it is related to an 'apparatus of collective measurement and evaluation' (2001: 6, in Dahlberg and Moss, 2005) which defines what is appropriate and what is a 'problem'. A combination of ability and development has even more power to designate some children as appropriate and some as problematic because it confuses attainment and progress with a fixed ability that children have in different amounts, and borrows scientific legitimacy from developmental psychology. In combination with the idea that teachers can 'know' children (and thus 'know' their level of ability or development), these ideas are significant in the construction of children's learner identities.

Authenticity

As I have argued, Reception involves inauguration into schooling and into school subjectivities: children are judged and assessed on their relative success at *becoming* a learner, an idea itself legitimised by the strength of developmental discourses in early years education. However, as I discuss in the next section, becoming and being a learner can both be understood as being done with varying degrees of 'authenticity', a notion which is connected to long-standing discourses of ability and development. These concepts form part of an overarching discourse of 'authenticity' in being a learner. The learner displays all the elements of this identity, including enthusiasm for learning, rational choices, obedience when necessary and a tendency to display what they have learnt. But, some children are constituted as doing these things *because they are naturally inclined to*, and some are constituted as *merely performing* these attributes. Authentic learners are seen as having innate, natural tendencies to be a learner in all aspects, while inauthentic learners are merely emulating these qualities in school. In this discussion I am drawing on Archer and Francis's work on Chinese pupils' academic success (Archer and Francis, 2007). This work in turn owes much to previous work on discussions of girls' learning styles, particularly in 'masculine' subjects, as not the 'proper way' (Walkerdine, 1990). Archer and Francis argue that similarly some Chinese students are subject to racist discourses which suggest they are 'not achieving in the right way'; they conclude:

> The 'ideal learner' is an inherently embodied discourse which always excludes minority ethnic pupils and denies them from inhabiting positions or identities of 'success' with any sense of permanency or authenticity. *(Archer and Francis, 2007: 170)*

Although I would take issue with the argument that minoritised pupils are always excluded (as my analysis of some children's learner identities in later chapters suggests), this idea of authenticity is useful in that it adds subtlety to the analysis of who gets to be a 'success'. Archer and Francis's work also demonstrates that those children constituted as part of a 'model minority' may suffer the disadvantage of being understood as inauthentic. With regard to the 'permanency' of positions of success, I argue that no pupil ever has a permanent, unalterable position of success due to the need for constant acts of recognition as a viable subject, whether they are from a minoritised group or not. However, it may be that some pupils occupy positions as 'good' learners with more precariousness and fragility. Authenticity is part of this variance.

In these Reception classrooms, this discourse of authenticity was powerful in demarcating those who were genuinely successful, and those who might appear to be, but were not.

In this quote, Paul is discussing how he understands "thinking skills" (a term he introduced) in relation to Dylan, a boy in his class:

> "There are some children who are very good at repeating, and memorising, but in terms of real thinking skills: not really there. I mean Dylan's quite sprightly [?] and he's brilliant at rhymes and … his language is excellent and his ability to repeat things probably; repeat is the thing. He's been surrounded by a lot of high-level language and thinking and stuff … but actual understanding is not there. […] So, you get what I mean, there are a lot of children who have learnt a lot, but they haven't intellectually got that thinking skills and problem solving […] There are too many children coming out that are able to repeat things, like a parrot, or follow a writing frame … They'll do that, but ask them to really truly do something authentic and they can't do it and I think that's a major problem". *(Paul, St Mary's)*

In Paul's understanding, children such as Dylan display a great deal of learning through language and repetition, but this is not an indication of their "intellect" or "understanding"; it is simply a performance of learning. These children are unable to "really truly do something authentic"; they are unmasked as merely putting on a show of learning. This contention that some children "truly" do "real" things is at the heart of this discourse of authenticity.

Authenticity discourses are connected but not identical to ability/development discourses. Authenticity is similarly about innate qualities, but the wider conception of learning that operates in these Reception classrooms results in a broader conception of the innate qualities that are necessary to succeed at school. The authentic learner must not only be enthusiastic, make good choices and show learning, but *do these things naturally*, rather than because they have been encouraged to do so by 'pushy' parents. Thus being 'high ability' or 'more developed' is helpful in being constituted as authentic, but may not necessarily be enough because being a learner is a wider ideal. Like the Chinese pupils in Archer and Francis's study, some pupils in these Reception classrooms were seen as achieving in the 'wrong way' because of home pressures. However, the idea of authenticity goes wider than simply *learning* in the 'wrong way' it includes those children who for other reasons are seen as merely 'acting out' the learner identity, rather than truly embodying it. So, enthusiasm for learning must be natural, not superficial; rationality must be an inherent trait, not taught; and obedience must be due to a deep understanding of what is appropriate, not just a slavish adherence to the rules.

This discourse was deployed without any discussion of who is able to assess what is "truly" done or authentic, and this ambiguity allowed for the dismissal of some children's achievements as inauthentic. At Gatehouse, Jim made some comments regarding an Afghan girl in his class whom I thought he saw as a 'good' learner, when he placed her in the second-to-top ability group:

Jim is showing me the list for the ability groups for the first time. I ask about Khadija who is in the second-to-top group, and Jim says that she answers lots of questions. "She's very vocal, but she's there for consolidation. I'm not sure it's all there". *(Field notes, Gatehouse)*

Thus Khadija's skills as a learner are rendered inauthentic – she is merely "vocal", a superficial display of learning. Jim says, "I'm not sure it's all there", suggesting that the real innate intelligence is missing. On another occasion, a girl was put in a lower-ability group even though Jim accepted she has learnt all the required 'high-frequency words'; this was seen as being only achieved because "her mum has been working flat out since she joined Reception".

This discourse of authenticity could also be used to dismiss high attainment on the EYFS Profile, as in the case of Liri, a Kosovan pupil:

Jim and I are looking at the list of final EYFS Profile scores in rank order. He tells me he has been concerned about where some children are in the list. He says, "Like Liri – I wasn't sure because she's above Khadija and Khalid, but she's one of those children, you know, when you look in the booklet and there's all these examples, she says those things, so she scores highly on the EYFS Profile". *(Field notes, Gatehouse)*

Here we see how Liri's high placement on the EYFS Profile ranked scores is dismissed as being due to her merely saying the right things. Liri's mother was a teacher, which Jim mentioned several times, and the implication seemed to be that she had been taught (presumably not explicitly) to say the kind of things that the EYFS Profile recognises as part of being a 'good' learner. At a later interview, I asked Jim why Liri was in the middle-ability group even though she scored so highly in the EYFS Profile. He answered:

"Liri possibly was in the wrong group here, but she's not very confident at independently [working], so I think she needed something a little bit easier – like the work was a little bit easier, just to build her confidence". *(Jim, Gatehouse)*

Although Jim admits she may have been wrongly placed, he explains Liri's group in terms of the wider skills needed to be a 'good' learner. Liri is described as lacking confidence and independence, both of which are important learner skills. Thus, although she might contribute in class and be keen to learn, Jim assesses her as not really possessing the right skills to be a 'good' learner.

This issue of authenticity is important because it means a pupil may appear to be a 'good' learner, without ever gaining recognition as *authentically* so. It is also important because it can be deployed in ways which render a child's success as illegitimate. It suggests there is a right way and a wrong way to be a 'good' learner, to be close to the ideal, and this has particular relevance for some groups of pupils.

Discourses of authenticity are linked to 'race' and class in similar ways to that found in the literature on ability (Archer and Francis, 2007; Gillborn and Youdell, 2000). I extend these arguments to encompass a wider range of attributes associated with a 'good' learner. Raced, gendered and classed ideas about who can be authentic allow for apparent educational success, while simultaneously constituting some pupils negatively. However, it is important to note that the demands of performativity do not require authenticity, only results, and the teachers still value those children who are seen as inauthentic 'good' learners because they score highly on assessments like the EYFS Profile, and this is their priority.

The ideal learner identity inherent in the EYFS Profile, the power of 'teacher knowledge' and this discourse of authenticity all have important roles in understanding how inequalities in the early years are produced and maintained. In the following chapters, I examine how they operate on both group and individual levels to position children as successful or unsuccessful in the process of becoming a learner.

4

ASSESSING A 'DIFFICULT INTAKE'

'Race', religion, class and gender in reception

Introduction

In this chapter, I consider how the conception of the learner explored in the previous chapter operated in these classrooms to exclude some children from positions of education success. I argue that 'good' learner identities are implicitly and explicitly linked to Whiteness and middle-classness in prevailing educational discourse and practice, and this rendered the inner city, minoritised and lower socio-economic status children at Gatehouse and St Mary's as a 'difficult intake', unintelligible as 'good' learners. At both schools, the children were discussed (as a group) in ways which constituted them as incommensurate with 'good' learner identities. This included comments on class, parenting, religion, language and 'race', both in combination and separately. I use the phrase 'difficult intake' here to sum up these negative discourses; this comes from a comment from Jim about "a school like this, with a difficult intake".

Before discussing the data, it is worth noting that the two schools did have an unusually high proportion of children eligible for Free School Meals (FSM), with English as an additional language (EAL) and from minoritised communities in comparison with schools in England as a whole, but were not unusual in their Local Authority area or indeed London[1] (CMPO and ESRC, 2010; DCSF, 2008c).

The 'White middle-class' ideal

In these classrooms, an idealised learner identity was often linked to White middle-class children who were placed in contrast to the children at St Mary's and Gatehouse. Within this association, the links between middle-classness and Whiteness were often implicit. For example, Lynn (early years coordinator at Gatehouse) commented on the EYFS Profile:

"These goals are fair enough if you're an English-speaking middle-class child whose parents work with you at home, but our children are not like that – they're few and far between whose parents work with them – who will engage with them, who know what it means to develop a child's mind". *(Lynn, Gatehouse)*

Lynn appears to regard English-speaking middle-class children as the universal or normal child assumed by the EYFS Profile, making the Profile irrelevant to the Gatehouse children. Simultaneously, she engages in a deficit discourse about Gatehouse parents' knowledge and skills, based on their assumed lack of developmental knowledge. Although Lynn refers to "English-speaking" children, she does not name 'race' explicitly; non-English-speaking acts here as a proxy for non-White. Her comments powerfully locate lower income, non-English-speaking (minoritised) families as unknowing, uncommitted, and as failing their own children.

This deficit discourse was often used to compare the children at Gatehouse with an idealised White middle-class child. For example, Lynn described the families at high-attaining schools:

"They're middle-class, English parents who are involved in their children, who come and support the class teacher, who know to bring in their child's book bag every single day, who know the importance of not showing up in shorts and T-shirt on a day like today when it's freezing". *(Lynn, Gatehouse)*

Here, the "achieving" White middle-class school's parents are described as supportive, capable and caring, while the Gatehouse parents are positioned as incompetent. Again, "English" operates here as a proxy for silenced Whiteness. A contrast is set up between 'knowing' parents and the Gatehouse parents: Lynn continued by commenting on her expectations of parents who do not provide their child with an appropriate coat, saying, "If they can't even figure that out, do you think they're going to be spending any time, like, reading to them? If they can't even put a coat on their child, do you think they're going to spend the time?". As seen in the previous section, children's parents are seen as important in understanding the child and their attainment. Lynn's comments, such as, "These people can't even grasp this" and "This is what I'm working with" suggest that the parents are not intelligent enough to care for their children appropriately, and she has to cope with a poor quality of parent at Gatehouse. This is an individualised discourse; the issue of poverty (which may well be the reason why some children do not have a warm coat) is obscured and the individual failure of parents to act responsibly is emphasised. We see here how a 'difficult intake' discourse operates to make positions of educational success all but impossible for the Gatehouse children, but also how responsibility is located within individual families and their failures.

The operation of 'difficult intake' discourses

The deployment of discourses of a 'difficult intake' were complex, and had multiple forms with great slippage between them; teachers cited some discourses explicitly, but also cited one thing as a proxy for another. But what is left unsaid can work powerfully to constitute these children as Other. Apple (1999) comments in relation to 'race' that it acts as an 'absent presence' in education, powerful even when it is not explicitly cited. In this section we see how 'race', class and ideas about the exotic but dangerous inner city operate as 'absent presences' in these Reception classrooms.

When asked about their intakes, the teachers all described their schools in terms of how unusual they were for having large proportions of children with EAL, receiving FSM and from minority communities. The teachers' comments about intake were not merely descriptive, but drew on policy discourses which position minoritised and FSM pupils as needing extra support and sensitivity. Instantly, these pupils were positioned in contrast with 'normal' (White and middle-class) children as unusual and requiring particular provisions. Comments such as this, from Lynn, revealed how, within these descriptions, the teachers slip easily between discourses of language, nationality, assimilation and income when positioning the children negatively:

> "Pretty much everyone is English as an additional language. I mean the children were all born, the majority of the time, in England, but their parents weren't. So of course their home language is something other than English, so that's something they've got to work with as well. And our parents, as I said, a lot of them are on income support, a lot of them don't work, a lot of them have issues with assimilating into a different culture, and dealing with money issues and things like that". *(Lynn, Gatehouse)*

Here a number of different elements are cited, but 'race' is never explicitly mentioned. Nonetheless, the emphasis Lynn puts on the high proportion of EAL children resonates in a context where schools with a majority of pupils from minority communities are constituted as problematic through discourses of 'swamping' and 'tipping points' (the point when there are so many minoritised pupils that White families leave) (Gillborn, 2008: 78–81).

A central part of the 'difficult intake' discourse was the idea of the disadvantaged inner city, which linked the location of the school and the home lives of the pupils with inevitable low attainment. Assumptions were made about children's home lives, such as in Paul's comment: "With the social backgrounds they have, they don't see a lot of books, so they've got really into them here". This general discourse of social deficit was inextricably linked to ideas about the inner city which related, I would argue, to the policy context whereby 'urban' communities are constituted negatively, often in terms of segregation by 'race' and class (Gulson,

2006; Lupton and Tunstall, 2008). This was particularly the case in the 2000s when policy focused on community cohesion and areas such as this part of inner London were designated 'Education Action Zones'. At Gatehouse, comments relating to the urban locality were made during lessons: Jim told the children he had picked a particular book about two men who live in a tower block because "many of you live in flats". On another occasion, Lynn explained a washing line in a picture book saying, "I know it's not how you do your laundry, but if you lived somewhere with lots of space". The focus of these comments reveals the teachers' deficit perception of the inner city; they assumed that all the children lived in the local tower blocks, and commented on what was 'missing' in the children's experiences. These assumptions about the local community, linked to discourses of urban deprivation, the inner city and 'race', were also indicated in Lynn's comments on the role of the school:

> "In this school, as with many inner city London schools, we have to take on quite a bit of other issues that the parents are going through, beyond what their children's academic issues might be [...] A lot of the parents that we have, it might be the first time they have ever sent a child to school, it might be their first child, it might be their first experience with British school [...] A lot of these children don't have bikes at home; parents don't have the space to practice, parents don't take them to the park, parents don't, you know, ride that bike. And a lot of children have obesity issues, and health issues; and with a lot of them it's that they live in these tall flats, they don't get to go out, they don't get to do all the running around. Their parents a lot of the time come from very hot countries and get very concerned about the cold; they don't like to let their children go out".
> *(Lynn, Gatehouse)*

In this revealing quote, Lynn constitutes the Gatehouse pupils and their families as inherently lacking in terms of knowledge of the education system, material possessions and parenting attitudes. She again deploys the idea of the unknowing parent, which she contrasted with "English-speaking middle-class" parents in previous comments, and any recognition of the impact of poverty on what parents can do is only ever tacit ("they don't have bikes"). The entanglement of a range of discourses is very powerful: she is both critical of the parents (they "don't let" their children go out) and sympathetic ("they live in these tall flats, they don't get to go out"). The comments Lynn makes relating to poverty (including poor health, obesity, lack of space) reflect a conception of inner city populations as victims, similar to Leonardo and Hunter's comments on perceptions of urban communities of colour in the US:

> Even when they are viewed sympathetically, which is not often, they are seen rather as passive victims of larger social inequality, not agents or experts in their own lives. This image of urban residents portrays them utterly

without power, creativity, perseverance, or intelligence to fight back against an unfair system. *(Leonardo and Hunter, 2009: 153)*

This patronising construction of the inner city parents as lacking agency is significant in the 'difficult intake' discourse as it also positions the children as unable to help themselves to improve their lives; as lacking perseverance or intelligence. This is not dissimilar to constructions of the inner city population present in UK government policy on urban regeneration (Gulson, 2006), which has focused on the 'problems' of inner cities. In this discourse, the teachers' work becomes even more important: they not only need to teach the children, but also to persuade them that education will 'improve' them.

However, this discourse runs alongside and in tension with a discourse of individual failure, as seen in Lynn's comments about parents not knowing school routines, not taking their children to the park, and not letting children outside because the parents are "from very hot countries". This approach is also apparent in policy on urban areas; as Lupton and Tunstall argue, 'in a neoliberal analysis of the problems of low-income neighbourhoods [...] structural problems are individualised and spatialised' (2008: 114). Nonetheless, the link made between the inner city and the inevitability of problems is still made: 'disadvantaged neighbourhoods [...] are discursively repositioned as irredeemably problematic' (Lupton and Tunstall, 2008: 114). These two discourses of individual failure and structural inequality are deployed together to constitute the children at Gatehouse as unusually "difficult" and children from lower socio-economic groups as inevitably unsuccessful in school. In the following sections I focus on some specific facets of the 'difficult intake' discourse present in these schools.

'Race' and immigration

As seen in the previous comments, the 'difficult intake' discourse is racialised. This was sometimes explicit, such as when Jim contrasted Gatehouse with a school in "middle-class White England", but more frequently implicit, such as when Lynn talked about parents who "come from hot countries". This implicit citation of race is in keeping with the policy context, where issues of race are 'collapsed into' the issue of 'social exclusion' (Lewis, 2000). In the quote above, Lynn constructed the minoritised children as having failed to assimilate, as evidenced by their lack of engagement with 'British' cultural norms such as playing in the park or riding a bike. This takes on greater importance in a situation where assimilation and integration are valued through a discourse of 'cohesion' (Gillborn, 2008). Similarly, at St Mary's, Paul made comments which emphasised the Otherness of minority children and their families:

Paul starts to explain that the school is taking in some more children in January because it "is desperate for kids. They'll take anyone". He describes the families as coming from "who knows where" and says that their "social and educational values are . . ". and he pulls a face as if to say they are dubious. He says that they arrive in the country, can't get into the schools they want, come to St Mary's and then move when the schools they wanted can take them. *(Field notes, St Mary's)*

Here, Paul makes a clear link between what he sees as the 'poor quality' of pupils at St Mary's and their origins "who knows where", as well as associating this with poor "social and educational values". His comments on children moving school ignore the fact that this decision could be taken as evidence of a real commitment to education; neoliberal policy on schools is based, after all, on parents exercising their right to 'choose' (Gewirtz, Ball and Bowe, 1995), and choice advice is aimed specifically at disadvantaged parents (Exley, 2009). His comments suggest instead that they are abusing the system by transferring their children, and he does not take into account the complex problems of temporary housing and settling into a new country experienced by many new migrants in London, instead focusing on the disruptive effect to his classroom. This, and Paul's comment that the children come from "who knows where", bring up discourses of good and bad, acceptable and unacceptable migrants, defined by their assimilation into institutional structures. It positions the newly arrived children negatively as 'bad migrants', implicitly citing media and government discourses of migration as out of control and in need of greater restriction. As in Lynn's comments, the minoritised pupils and their families are constituted as part of the inner city problem, particularly in their failure to assimilate by adopting 'British' practices.

The issue of 'race' or ethnic group was not a common feature of talk among the adults in these Reception classrooms, but the few occasions where it was discussed revealed that ethnic groups were largely seen as based on nationalities. There was, however, still an acute awareness of skin colour and other aspects of appearance, among both the adults and the children. The teachers were also conscious of the religion of the children and adapted their practices to suit their perception of Muslim sensibilities, as I discuss further below. Implicit within all of these discussions was a celebration of the exotic, for example in an emphasis on the 'mixedness' of the children, and in the sometimes clumsy attempts to be sympathetic to an 'unusual' cohort of children. I continue the discussion of these contradictions – where children are simultaneously constituted as the deficient Other and as exotic – in the section on the inner city below.

EAL and bilingualism

The concern over high proportions of EAL children noted above reflects a general positioning of EAL pupils as another 'problem group' alongside Special Educational Needs (SEN) pupils in educational documentation, including the EYFS Profile handbook (QCA, 2008). However, the discourses related to language that were cited at Gatehouse were not entirely based on this negative EAL connection; Jim also attempted to use a more positive discourse of bilingualism:

> "They're all learning ... I know they're not achieving, like, above the national average, or even the national average, but, most, the majority come in with English as a second language, so. They just do incredibly, I'm just, you know; they finish the school day and [clicks fingers] they're straight into another language. So I already think that this whole national average – levels and that kind of thing – I don't really think that's that relevant here because these children who achieve really highly according to the government statistics, I don't know if they could speak another language as fluently as these children, and I think that's a major skill in itself". (Jim, Gatehouse)

Here, Jim appears to rally against common attitudes towards bilingualism which are 'wrought with contradiction' in that they glamorise bilingualism when it involves European languages and higher education, but reject immigrant languages (Leonardo and Hunter, 2009: 157). His comment describes the children's home languages as worthy, and not as evidence of resistance to assimilation, as they are frequently described in popular press discourses (Chapman, 2009; Radnofsky, 2007). However, despite this positive stance, Jim also slips into the 'EAL as a problem' discourse: national averages are "not relevant here" and it seems there is no ambition for these pupils to reach the expected levels because they do not speak English at home. Thus, even when he appears to be sympathetic to his pupils' different situations, Jim actually rejects the possibility that they could do as well as White middle-class pupils. His later comments reveal further the limits of this attempt to reposition EAL status as positive rather than a problem:

> "I always wonder with these children – are they achieving as highly as I say they are, or is it that I just completely don't understand? I've never taught in a school where children speak English as a first language. Am I just really positive towards them because they know it in two languages, and isn't that amazing, or is their achievement actually lower than, you know, an English-speaking, White middle-class primary school in the middle of England? I don't know". (Jim, Gatehouse)

Jim uses the White middle-class referent already discussed to explain his doubts about his positive stance. In physically locating the norm of White middle-classness in "the middle of England" (probably a reference to popular conceptions of leafy and affluent 'Middle England'), Jim sets up a clear contrast with the urban location of Gatehouse. The Otherness of the Gatehouse children is emphasised by their EAL status, which positions them further from the White middle-class high-achieving ideal.

There were several practices in the classrooms which were based upon the large number of children learning English as an additional language, such as signs in many languages, opportunities to use home languages in songs and games, and writing in different scripts on posters and displays. Some of these practices, at times, served to mark certain children out as different, because they spoke English at home, or because their home languages seemed more valued than others. The use of foreign languages in the class seemed to be both a sympathetic accommodation to the particular needs of the children, and a celebration of the "mix" of ethnic groups which marked the teachers out as having a particularly unusual (difficult) intake of pupils. At Gatehouse, children who spoke English at home were few in number and seen as particularly helpful. Jim explained how useful it was to have some models of English among the children, and how much these children contributed because they could be relied upon to answer questions. On some occasions, two White British girls in the class were asked specifically to answer questions even though there were several pupils who spoke English at home or who spoke English at home sufficiently that they were all but fluent. These instances revolved around ideas or words which were seen as culturally English (for instance, identifying geese in a book), and these two White British girls, as discussed further in the following chapter, were seen as the White British pupils with 'positive' home backgrounds, who could be expected to have a wider vocabulary. Thus simplistic assumptions about the richness of children's home lives were at times hidden beneath practices which appeared initially to be based on language. These practices also had a dividing effect: in directing these questions specifically at the White British girls, the teacher constituted them as a class and racial Norm to the rest of the children's Other. Whiteness and middle-classness were again made central and desirable.

Parenting, class and 'needy' children

As we have already seen in Lynn's and Paul's comments, at both schools, local parents were regarded as lacking in parenting skills or the right educational values. This was particularly important given the links made in policy discourses regarding good parenting (Ball, 2008), and its impact on the community. This link between bad parents and difficult children was frequently made; for example:

> "I mean, there's a lot of them come from very, very difficult backgrounds, you know, and parents that have been through a lot and the children are kind of mirrors of what they see – they absorb it, they reflect it, and you see it coming out in different ways". *(Paul, St Mary's)*

In Paul's comments, the link between parents' experiences, home life and behaviour in school is rendered inevitable ("they absorb it") and obvious ("you can see it"). This certainty was reinforced by Paul's discussions of educational research on the subject: he described the findings of the Effective Provision of Pre-School Education (EPPE) project (a longitudinal study of provision for 3-to-7-year-olds), thus: "Actually says it is more about their bloody home life than the teaching. Ha ha! Surprise, surprise! [sarcastic]". Paul saw this finding as simply common sense – the research had just found what all teachers know anyway.[2]

Following on from these comments, I asked Paul if he saw a similar pattern in his class, where background was related to progress at school. He responded with conviction, making reference to Paige, a White working-class girl in his class:

> "I definitely, definitely think that's true. Definitely think that if you have a family – if you've got two children of equal developmentally, you know, ab- they're both at the same point in development and they both could probably move in a parallel way, and you put one in a home that's full of support and security, and one in a home with nothing; the one who's all secure and full of really good learning in their home life will shoot up whereas the other will just not, even though they've got the same potential. There's no question who will do, who will move forward faster, definitely. It's obvious. [...] There is no question who is going to do better, and it's the same thing with all, you know, one's sent to the TV, whereas the other one's taken to the ballet lessons, and mathematics and gymnastics [...] I mean Paige's mum has now got three, got one on the way. She started producing children when she was 16, she's had no life. She's not been modelled good living if you like". (Paul, St Mary's)

Paul's comments conceive of the problems he sees in the classroom as originating entirely from, and entirely because of, the parents of the children. He explicitly links certain homes and styles of parenting with quicker development. He juxta- poses stereotypically middle-class activities such as being taken to ballet lessons with the pupils in his class, using Paige, a White working-class girl, as an example of the effects of poor parenting. Here he is using a constructed notion of the supported middle-class child (Vincent and Ball, 2007) to emphasise what he sees as the deficiencies of the parents at St Mary's. His comments also reflect, as Ball (2010) has argued, a division between the kinds of children produced by extra- curricular 'edutainment' services available to middle-class families and those who do not experience these. All of this is cloaked in terms of sympathy with these families and support for 'interventions': Paul went on to talk about family literacy projects and said, "Why are we even bothering to target the children? You must target the adults". Nonetheless, despite this sympathy for parents, Paul comments that Paige's mother has "not been modelled good living", which suggests that she is unable to improve her life and is trapped. This is similar to Lynn's comments on parents at Gatehouse. These teachers engage with the idea that there is a correct way of parenting and that this is something that they can recognise, even when they acknowledge the difficulties faced by some parents. In Paul's comments, there are also overtones of a discourse of the 'deserving' and 'undeserving' poor in his discussion of a White working-class family: Paul seems to suggest Paige's mother has not helped herself by having several children.

At St Mary's, much of this discourse of poor parenting and low-income families was tied up with the idea of 'needy' children. For Paul, the term 'special educational needs' included issues of emotional maturity and sociability, as well as formally recognised educational needs. This 'neediness' was linked to the children's backgrounds, to what Paul called the "social things" which he listed alongside EAL as being linked to 'needy children'. He appeared at times to conflate emotional and social issues with SEN and EAL, as if being socially disadvantaged were another 'special need'. This is a complex deficit discourse, where the socially disadvantaged are seen as lacking in terms of emotional and social skills as well as economic capital; it is discursively reinforced by the government's targeting of low-income families with projects such as SureStart which focus on parenting and social skills. The vagueness of Paul's comments about 'needy' children do not lessen the force of this discourse; it worked powerfully to constitute these children at St Mary's as challenging.

The inner city

The urban inner city location of the two schools was critical to the discourses used in relation to the pupils who attend them. As the data has shown, the inner city was linked to poverty, minority communities and deprivation in social as well as economic terms. These discourses are reinforced, I would argue, by policy which is focused on urban regeneration, such as Education Action Zones, which construct inner city populations as inevitably problematic (Gulson, 2006; Lupton and Tunstall, 2008). As in Connolly's (1998) study of infant classrooms in the inner city, the teachers engaged in a discourse which links the school's physical location with particular expectations of the cohort as a whole.

Leonardo and Hunter's (2009) discussion of the 'urban' and education, although based on US cities, is useful here in considering the significance of discourses about urban spaces for schools. They argue that the urban can be 'imagined' in three ways: as a sophisticated space, as an authentic place of identity, or as a disorganised 'jungle'. I would argue that the teachers in my study predominantly imagine the urban mainly as a disorganised jungle. The teachers' descriptions of a lack of activities at home, the doubt cast upon parents' educational values, and their contrasts with the 'White middle class' engage with a discourse of disorganisation and a lack of civilisation, similar to that described by Leonardo and Hunter in their comments on the 'internal colony': in this imagining, 'the urban resembles the colonies frequented by the colonists who never feel out of place, never not in charge' (2009: 148). Here, the inhabitants of an 'internal colony' need to be improved through education:

> These spaces are complete with colonial-like education systems that treat the urban 'natives' as something to be assimilated, civilised, and converted. Real

urban dwellers [...] may not be constructed as sophisticated, but through proper education, it is believed they can become modernised. *(Leonardo and Hunter, 2009: 149)*

The pupils at Gatehouse and St Mary's are seen as needing to be civilised, modernised and improved through education. This civilising process is constructed by Lynn as part of early years education, important because it is the first point of access. For Paul, the dubious "educational values" of the parents who come from "who knows where" need to be improved (though some White parents also need to be taught "good living" in his view). The discourses of the inner city at both schools suggest the teachers imagine their urban locations as 'internal colonies', where they are needed to begin the process of assimilating the children into civilised life.

However, this is a complex situation where children are simultaneously constituted as the deficient Other *and* as exotic. As Said describes in *Orientalism* (1978), these non-Western children are constituted as removed from Western culture and as inevitably deficient, but also as exciting and interesting. In Jim's discussion of the children's bilingual skills and his occasional positive comments about diversity, he attempts to engage with the first of Leonardo and Hunter's ways of imagining the urban: as a cosmopolitan place of interest. Here, they argue that 'urban' can be used to mean 'the right amount of diversity' or the 'urban without the burden' (2009: 146). In this imagining, people of colour are 'recast' in a positive light, for example through 'appropriating diversity or urbanism [which] is a way of marketing a school or program as "cutting edge"'. Jim used this view of the city when he engaged superficially with the idea that the minoritised groups in his class are exotic and interesting (though not sophis-ticated, as Leonardo and Hunter describe). At Gatehouse, the heterogeneity of the pupils seemed to be seen as an important feature of the class: these children were symbols of an exciting, 'international' city. When we were discussing the new January children, Jim said to me, "We've got such a range. We've got kids from Korea, Cambodia, Ecuador. We're going to have to make new flags. Flags we've never made before". Here, Jim is engaging with discourses of the exotic Other (Donald and Rattansi, 1992; Said, 1978). The growing number of different flags that indicate the children's families' origins is cited as evidence of the international nature of the class; Jim appears to be citing a 'melting pot' discourse, where diversity is valued. Similarly, in a discussion of the children's attainment, Jim focused on the variety of different ethnic groups, listing them in turn to show the number. This variety of different ethnic identities seemed to obfuscate any concern for which groups do particularly well or poorly in the assessment; there is just "a real mix". Yet at other times, children were rendered homogenous in their Otherness: during a game, another teacher commented on the fact that most children had the same colour hair, which also reinforced the difference between this and an imagined White class (where, it seemed to be assumed, hair colours would vary more widely).

This view of the inner city as exotic resonates with all of the teachers' attempts to position themselves as having particularly difficult jobs, as having taking on the greatest challenge. Leonardo and Hunter argue that in this construction, 'educators who deal with the urban are constructed as positive, but the urban students and families themselves are not' (2009: 146). We see this in Lynn's comments when she argues it is easy for schools with White middle-class parents to do well. The teachers at Gatehouse and St Mary's manage to combine these two imaginings to cast themselves in a positive light: they work in difficult areas (the 'urban jungle') and so have more problems to deal with, but this also means that their work is 'cutting edge', important, and somehow more exotic or interesting because they deal with 'diverse' populations, unlike the teachers in White middle-class areas who have it easy. This complex construction of the 'urban' is a fundamental part of the 'difficult intake' discourse: the inner city is both exotic and a problem.

Religion

Issues of religion took very different forms at the two schools because of St Mary's status as a faith school, but nonetheless, at both schools there was an awareness of the religions of the children which again served to render them Other to an external White/Christian Norm. At Gatehouse, this took the form of being very conscious of the (assumed) Islamic faith of most of the pupils. This faith was seen in simple terms, and as a homogenous entity. There were several incidents in the classroom which appeared to be attempted accommodations to the Muslim pupils, and incidents that showed the teachers' ideas about Islam. A large display involving pictures of life-size children included a girl wearing hijab, for example, while other comments concentrated on known features of Islam, such as not eating ham, missing school for Eid, and not drinking alcohol. A page of a reading book involving beer was glued shut, because it was thought "it wouldn't be appropriate for Muslim children". These practices seemed to be tinged with a perception of Muslim parents and children as inflexible and easily alarmed: the parents were described as unhappy about calling it a 'Christmas' play, for instance. At St Mary's, there were similar accommodations to the Muslim religion of some of the pupils in the class (fewer than at Gatehouse), including a lesson about Eid. However, as it was a Church of England school, most of the RE lessons were based on Bible stories and Christian festivals. This led to some confusion at times between religions: Paul at one point described praying as something directed at "God, Jesus, Allah, Diwali" and later explained he used the term "Diwali" even though it is a Hindu festival so that the children connected up the comment with some previous work on the subject.

The different religions of the children formed an important part of their constitution as Other, particularly for the Muslim children. There was very little discussion of the religion of the White or Black pupils: it seemed to be assumed at both schools that these children would be Christian, if they were religious at all. On one occasion, a White British child in the class was asked to identify a picture of a church, even though there was a church near the school which most children would have seen. Religion seemed to be an important issue in both schools and a significant part of what made the classes unusual and interesting. The teachers appeared to be torn between a desire to make concessions to the Muslim pupils and parents, and an underlying scepticism about and stereotypical view of the Islamic faith. As several researchers have argued, young Muslim men have become stereotyped as problematic in recent years, due to fears about Islamic extremism following the terrorist attacks of September 2001 and July 2005 and the 'race riots' of 2001 (Alexander, 2004; Archer, 2003; Shain, 2010). While the children in these classes were perhaps too young to be tinged with much of these damaging discourses, I suspect that the interest which the Gatehouse teachers showed in their majority Muslim class was partly due to an increased focus on Islamic communities in the press and popular debate in recent years. The presence of children from Iraq and Afghanistan, countries where British troops were at the time deployed against Muslim groups, further emphasised international issues around Islam in the classroom. Although the different nationalities of the children were seen as exotic, it seemed that the Muslim religion of the children was not; instead, the 'backwardness' of Islam was cited in comments about how it restricted behaviour. This is perhaps due to popular discourses which have positioned Islam as a socially conservative and potentially dangerous faith. However, the idea of Islam as 'backward' and repressive is also consistent with Said's argument that in Orientalist discourses the exotic and the uncivilised cannot be separated (Said, 1978).

Prevailing discourses constitute acceptable Muslim subjectivities as passive and Westernised, and it was this particular element of the minoritised children's identities that seemed to be regulated more strictly than others. Youdell writes, in her research on a 'multicultural day' at a multi-ethnic school in Sydney where White teachers patrolled the grounds:

> In post 9/11 western contexts, perhaps this pluralism and policing are reconciled in the subjectivation of the good teacher and good citizen who celebrates diversity as long as it remains minoritized, marginalized and willing to be (impossibly) Westernized. *(Youdell, 2006c: 524)*

This balancing act is seen in the discussions at Gatehouse of the Christmas play and the beer page of the reading book. The Reception teachers were willing to make accommodations to 'minority issues', as long as they remain positioned as the minority and are subject to Western/White/majority regulation.

The significance of the 'difficult intake' discourse

As shown in the data discussed, a discourse of a 'difficult intake' operated in these classrooms in complex ways to position these children as distant from a White middle-class ideal learner. Issues of race, religion, language, parenting and class worked to constitute these children as a group as unusual and challenging. The 'difficult intake' discourse is implicitly and explicitly racialised: it draws upon ethnic groups, religion and language to define children as different and atypical. The external idealised image of White middle-class children reinforces the centrality of Whiteness in a Norm/Other dichotomy, where the Other is inevitably deficient. The Otherness of the children at St Mary's and Gatehouse positioned them as a group outside educational success. Individual pupils may have the status of good learners, but when talking about the children as a group, the teachers focused on their 'difficulty' and unusualness. The 'difficult intake' discourse frames much of the discussion of learner identities in the following chapter; it limits and enables how the pupils in the Reception classes can be talked about and how they can be assessed.

The teachers' use of this discourse should not, however, be seen in isolation from education policy discourses, which position certain groups of pupils (including those from minoritised backgrounds, those learning EAL, and those on low incomes) as needing extra help to succeed in school. As I have argued elsewhere, the implication that some groups will *inevitably* fare better or worse in the education system is apparent in policy (Bradbury, 2011a). The 2008 EYFS Profile document itself has a whole section on 'Inclusion', which deals with four groups: 'Children who are learning English as an additional language', 'Boys', 'Children with special educational needs' and 'Children from minority groups' (QCA, 2008). The teachers in this study had classes with large proportions of children who would fit into these groups; their descriptions of them could be seen as a genuine concern to deal with particularities of their cohort. In their use of these terms and descriptions, the teachers could be seen as merely suffering from the form of 'ventriloquism' described by Morley (cited in Ball, 2003b), where teachers use policy terms in everyday discussions; certainly, the idea of concern for EAL or minority pupils appears common sense in these teachers' comments. As with all analysis of their comments, the teachers' discussions have to be seen as constrained by the discourses which, for example, mark out what is involved in being a 'good teacher' who cares about their pupils. That said, the assumptions about deficient home backgrounds, poor parenting and the inevitability of low attainment shown in the teachers' quotes show that the 'difficult intake' discourse is not simply about a concern for underachieving groups; it has the potential to embed low expectations of pupils in their first year of schooling, and define who can be a good learner. Youdell argues that the use of categories such as EAL and 'special needs' can be associated with the exclusion of certain identities from positions of success:

> proliferations [of category] also have the potential to box us into tighter and tighter spaces, to open us up to closer scrutiny, to render some bodies and selves possible and others impossible. *(Youdell, 2006b: 28)*

With the 'difficult intake' discourse, the Reception teachers have boxed their pupils into a clearly defined space where poor parenting, religion, language and 'race' render the majority of their classes as 'impossible', incapable of high levels of attainment.

We see most clearly how this discourse constitutes these children as a whole outside educational success in the teachers' comments on assessment. Lynn commented, "If you measure against the country, we're just always going to look hopeless". Also at Gatehouse, Jim argued that the EYFS Profile was irrelevant due to the nature of the parents:

> Jim: There's no real way of explaining it to some of the parents because their English themselves is just so … so bad.
>
> AB: So it's not useful in that way?
>
> Jim: No, god no. Not at all, I don't think.
>
> AB: Do you think it might be in some schools?
>
> Jim: Yeah, I think it might be in, like, middle-class White England. Might be very good.
>
> AB: Because the parents will come in and get a lot of detail about–?
>
> Jim: Yeah. But then again, whether they are better able to assess White middle-class English kids, using that system, I don't know, I've never done it before. *(Interview with Jim, Gatehouse)*

Here, the 'difficult intake' means that the EYFS Profile information cannot be relayed to the parents. On another occasion, Jim told me that he found parents' evening difficult because the parents "don't have a clue". Thus the 'difficult intake' intersects with the assessment process to create discourses which constitute EAL parents as inappropriate users of the education system, unable to take an interest in their child. This means that, unlike in "middle-class White England", the EYFS Profile fails to fulfil its stated aim of informing parents about their children's progress. As I discuss further in Chapter 6, these ideas about the role and appropriateness of the EYFS Profile in an inner city play a part in the process of deciding the final results and the children's official levels of attainment.

Gender and the ideal learner

In this final section, I consider one further element of how children were constituted as learners in these Reception classes, before I explore children's individual learner identities in more detail in the next chapter. As is apparent in the individual stories that follow, gender intersected with the 'difficult intake' discourse in complex ways. However, they also operated alone in ways which deserve particular attention, given the contrast to much other research on gendered ideal learner identities.[3]

The teachers were keen to discuss gender, to use it to organise their classrooms, and to base assumptions about the children on their gender. This was reinforced by differences in uniform and which toilets the children went to, and official listings in the class register. Nayak and Kehily argue that '[a]t an ontological level, the processes of schooling assume the presence of sex categories as known and knowable'; gender is a 'comfort zone' in schools, 'a settled certainty of the educative experience' (2006: 470). These categories provide 'an unassailable presence, a constant', they argue, 'amidst the turmoil of the reform and new initiatives' (2006: 470). For these Reception teachers, gender had a similar comforting function: it was a difference that was acceptable to talk about, due to its official status and the long history of scientific study into the different ways in which boys and girls learn (part of the development discourse). It also helped to explain processes in the classroom which the teachers felt uncomfortable about, such as the boys at St Mary's who played with the train set all day, every day. In Paul's explanation, gender differences provided further evidence of the distance between official advice and reality (advice which, he argued, along with current research, sought to deny that boys and girls learnt differently). Gender appeared to be a 'safe' difference to discuss, less likely to be seen as indicating prejudice or snobbishness, as was perhaps the risk when discussing 'race' or class with a researcher.

Given previous research on boys as ideal rational subjects (Walkerdine, 1990), the characteristics associated with a 'good' learner might seem more associated with boys than girls in Reception. Furthermore, the idea that girls are simply 'plodding' hard-workers while boys are inherently more inspired (Francis and Skelton, 2005) might suggest that boys are more likely to be constituted as authentic learners with innate skills. However, I would argue that these discourses do not operate in such simple ways in these classrooms, not least because gender discourses intersect with 'race' and class in complex ways. The discourse of rationality does have an impact in that boys are still constituted as better at subjects such as maths and science. This renders the constitution of some boys as 'intelligent' recognisable, and allows authentic good learner status to be viable for some boys. However, I would argue that boys are *not generally* more likely to be constituted through classroom discourses and practices as 'good' learners, because this subjectivity requires not only rationality, but also flexibility, passivity, and conscientiousness, all of which were discourses used in relation to girls.

Essentialist notions of how boys and girls learn informed this distinction between girls as good learners and boys as 'flawed consumers' (Bauman, 2005), unable to choose well. Paul in particular made explicit comments on the differences in how boys and girls learn: "This sex difference is interesting. They do want to do different things, and their interest comes from ease. They just learn differently. It's so clear, I don't know why there's even any question about it. It's just obvious". When asked about differences between boys and girls in his class, Paul commented:

> "I've got very capable boys, and I've got very capable girls, and I've got very developmentally behind sort of boys; not behind, but at the level of

development they're at, you know. Similarly with the girls, you know, in here, it's irrelevant. And I think it's because partly it's play-based and the boys get a chance – I try to put the literacy and the numeracy into what they like […] It's very, very clear that boys are different from girls in their play … it's really clear […] boys like big movements *[does big movements with arms]*, they like cars going round, they like trains going round, they like anything going around, so if you introduce big movements into their play, and introduce numbers, introduce the words, introduce anything, but they can do all the bouncing around, while you're working with them, they take it on. You try to do what you would do, more girl-type stuff, they won't, they don't want to be there". *(Paul, St Mary's)*

Paul's describes himself as 'genderblind', as it were, and yet describes how he provides different activities for boys and girls based on simplistic ideas about how they learn. His description of how he manages to fit in the literacy and numeracy around what the boys like suggests that boys are inherently less likely to independently choose these high-status forms of learning, and need further encouragement in order for them to move away from "anything going around". Thus boys are rendered less likely to be authentic good learners who display the entrepreneurial spirit of seeking out and joining in with a range of learning activities. Like other 'problem groups' like EAL and SEN children, they need to be provided for separately. This is a discourse which is increasingly apparent in policy, and indeed 'boys' are listed as one of the groups requiring additional support in the EYFS Profile handbook (QCA, 2008).

Boys were also distanced from 'good' learner identities by discussions of their behaviour, which was often seen as not submissive enough (or not at the right times); Paul commented that "their behaviour is hellish". This is in keeping with long-standing ideas about boys as 'naughty' in school, which have traditionally run alongside the idea that boys are more intelligent. I would argue that these traditional discourses which, in the past may have worked to position boys as good academic learners but not good students, work in this situation, where 'learning' has a wider remit, to distance boys from being 'good' learners. The specific notion of the learner that operated within these classrooms appeared to value the 'reliable work' linked to girls – who produce and display a range of learning – over moments of brilliance: consistent good work is more useful in the EYFS Profile than infrequent achievements in a few areas.

At Gatehouse, Jim talked explicitly about what the EYFS Profile valued and how this related to boys' and girls' characteristics:

"Generally speaking, girls seem to be higher […] But I think that's because girls are more interested in literacy and reading than boys. Boys are more interested in riding [bikes], playing football, fighting, building stuff. Girls are more interested in sitting down and making, and talking, and reading,

and if you're more interested in reading and talking, then you're going to do
well in literacy and that's where you score the most points". *(Jim, Gatehouse)*

Jim's explanation of the gendered nature of high- and low-status and acceptable
and unacceptable activities has wider implications than simply getting the most
points. It shows how boys are constituted as not only failing to engage in the kind
of activities that are important in being a learner (including both passive "sitting
down" and more active "reading and talking"), but also as doing things which are
anathema to the socially adept learner, such as fighting. Furthermore, the boys'
activities he lists are all physical rather than mental pursuits, further distancing
them from ideas of 'high ability' learners. This is linked to a number of discourses,
such as developmental explanations about boys talking later than girls, boys being
less interested in books (Moss, 2007), and to wider ideas about men as generally
more physically competent (with comments such as 'you throw like a girl'). In
Reception, where physical activity is included only within parts of one learning
area of the EYFS Profile[4], being physical is only valued at particular times and
particular ways, not in general. The idea that boys are only interested in these
lower-status activities means that they are understood as having chosen badly.

In arguing that boys are no longer associated with being 'good' learners, I am
not suggesting that the discourses surrounding what boys are like has changed
dramatically (although policy discourses about 'failing boys' have probably eased
this transition by making it intelligible to talk about boys as 'bad' learners); instead
I am arguing that what it means to be a 'good' learner is different in Reception. In
particular, the need to be a good 'all-rounder', an idea associated with girls more
than boys, has worked to place girls as the vehicles of educational success. The
idea that boys may be 'gifted' remains, particularly in maths and science, but this is
irrelevant if boys score badly in other areas. At St Mary's, where Paul talked about
the difficulties he faced with boys, one boy (Ryan) was constituted as high-ability
in maths, and scored the only 9 (the maximum) that was awarded in the class for
the Shape, Space and Measure scale. This was completely intelligible within the
discourse of boys as good at maths and, more specifically, as better able to cope
with spatiality (Francis and Skelton, 2005: 81). However, his scores for the other
areas varied, and his lowest score was 6 for the writing scale. In contrast, all of the
five top scoring girls in the class scored either 7 or 8 on every scale, but scored no
nines at all. The high-attaining girls were constituted as good all-round learners:
they were able to score highly on the 'boy' areas such as maths and physical development as well as on the emotional and physical scales.

This leads me to the other impact of this specific notion of what it means to
be a learner: that in Reception girls are *completely intelligible* as 'good' learners.
They are the rational choosers who select the high-status reading and talking, and
they do not need extra provision in order to become engaged with learning. This
also makes them more authentic, because being a learner is understood as coming
naturally to girls, and the sort of innate brilliance traditionally associated with
boys is not required. General educational discourses about (White middle-class)

girls' high attainment in recent years also make the girls' success more intelligible. Although much of this discourse has focused on 'failing boys' and feminist work has critiqued the construction of this issue as a problem (Epstein et al., 1998), the idea that girls can and will do well at school is now well established in school discourses. This is particularly apparent in early years: every year the EYFS Profile data have been collected, girls have outperformed boys overall (DCSF, 2008a; DCSF, 2010a). I would argue that the idea of girls as 'good' learners is also connected to the broadening out of discourses of women's places in the workforce, especially for middle-class women, which provide for different femininities:

> [M]iddle class girls and women today are involved in a repositioning and the construction of slightly different variants of femininity which allow the possibility of academic excellence within schooling and leadership within the labour market. They have been more adept than their male peers at assuming the 'gender multiculturalism' which Connell (1995) argues opens up and broadens the possibilities of gender. *(Reay, 2001: 163)*

It is intelligible that the ideal learner can be female because the learner must be self-reliant, adaptable, and hard-working, all of which have come to be associated with modern femininity.

Although I am arguing that these overarching gender discourses play a part in the constitution of individual children as learners, I do not wish to overstate the importance of this idea given my commitment to using concepts of intersectionality. As commented on in the quote above, this connection between women and academic excellence has largely involved middle-class women, and popular discourses continue to pathologise working-class women as lazy and uncivilised (Gillborn, 2010). Moreover, the constitution of these children as 'difficult' through 'race', religion and class applies to girls as well as boys. As with all identities, these children are constituted within competing and overlapping discourses regarding all aspects of their identities. Indeed, the minoritised boys in these classrooms are also subject to a complex matrix of discourses regarding their 'race', urban location and class positions:

> frequently portrayed in 'folk devil' terms, being associated with inner city social problems such as crime, deviance and unemployment, the causes of which have been linked to the boys' problematic subcultures and/or class/ ethnic cultures and their 'anti-education' masculinities. *(Archer and Yamashita, 2003: 115)*

While, as Alexander (2004) has argued, these discourses distance minoritised boys from the ideal learner, it is important to note that this works in more complex ways than the idea of 'multiple disadvantage'. I am wary of suggesting a simple binary of girls as good/boys as bad: as we shall see in the individual examples in the next chapter, the constitution of children as different types of learner is rarely simple. It is also worth noting that negative ideas of femininity were still present: Jim made a comment about "a lot of silly girls who like to mess around and chat" in Liz's class and explained, "that's why her class seem to be a bit lower". Nonetheless, despite this concern, I think it is important to consider these specific gender discourses because they have an impact on the recognisability of some children as good learners.[5]

In this chapter, I have explored how discourses of a 'difficult intake' (involving 'race', class, the inner city, religion and language) worked to exclude the children at St Mary's and Gatehouse from positions of educational success. In the following chapter, I consider who was recognisable as a good learner on an individual basis, and the possibilities for minoritised pupils to have positive learner identities.

5

'GOOD' AND 'BAD' LEARNERS IN THE CLASSROOM

Introduction

In this chapter, I examine how, despite their constitution overall as a 'difficult intake', some individual children were constituted as 'good' learners in the Reception classrooms at Gatehouse and St Mary's, and that this was made possible by the discursive provision of some 'intelligible space' where they could be recognisable as 'good'. I also consider the children who were constituted as 'bad' learners, the children's agency in their constitution as learners, and the importance of performing their learner identities in ways which allowed them to remain recognisable as learners. I begin with a discussion of the 'good' learner identities of a group of Muslim girls at Gatehouse, before I use one of the girls as an example of how minority success can be discursively dismissed as inauthentic. I then use another example of a Black girl at St Mary's to consider the limitations of intelligible space for some pupils, before I consider the learner identities of the White pupils at Gatehouse. The second part of the chapter focuses on negative learner identities, particularly those of the Black boys at St Mary's. I end the chapter with a discussion of the implications of these findings for children in schools.

Throughout the discussion of individual learner identities in this chapter, Judith Butler's use of the concepts of intelligibility and recognisability are key (Butler, 1990; 2004a). Being a learner is a performative identity, which must be coherent within established discourses in order to be intelligible. Butler has argued that to be non-recognisable as a subject is to fail to be constituted as human at all (2004a). She writes:

> What counts as a person? What counts as a coherent gender? ... By what
> norms am I constrained when I ask what I may become? And what happens

when I begin to become that for which there is no place within the given regime of truth? *(Butler, 2004b: 58)*

It is this final question which is of most importance here: what happens when a child becomes something for which there is no place within the regimes of truth relating to their intersectional position? How does this limit who can be recognised as a 'good' learner? As Davies writes: 'Subjects, and this includes school students, who are constituted as lying outside intelligibility are faced with the constitutive force of a language that grants them no intelligible space' (Davies, 2006: 434).

Discourses operate to limit the 'intelligible space' open to children in terms of how they perform their identities and the idea of the 'good' learner. In these Reception classrooms, minoritised children in particular were more limited in how they could perform their identities while remaining intelligible, as they were bound by complex overlapping discourses specific to the historical, political and geographical location of the classroom, which rendered all but a few subject positions unrecognisable. I am concerned here with which children's identities, and their performance of these identities, enabled them to inhabit positions as 'good' learners, and which found this position foreclosed to them. This work builds on Youdell's (2006c) research in an Australian high school, which considers the unintelligible nature of positive learner identities for Lebanese and Turkish students:

> [A] series of political, educational, popular and (sub)cultural discourses
> that circulate in this school setting and beyond [...] provide the discursive
> terrain on and through which these students are subjectivated. [...]
> Lebanese and Turkish students (collectively called 'Arabic' in this setting)
> are subjectivated in ways that render apparently incommensurable consti-
> tutions of the good-Arabic-student-subject and the bad-Arabic-subject
> through the citation and inscription of an Orientalism (Said, 1978)
> reinvigorated by post-9/11 anti-Islamic discourse (Lipman, 2004).
> *(Youdell, 2006c: 512)*

Although my analysis draws on Youdell's work on the intelligibility of the good-student-subject, I would argue that the incommensurability of the 'good' 'Arabic' student, to use her terms, is more complex in the case of the Reception classrooms in my study. In these classrooms the discursive terrain of Orientalism and anti-Islamism was layered over with gendered discourses about Muslim families and discourses of displacement and refugee status regarding children from countries in conflict. The political and international context nearly a decade after 9/11 included competing concepts of recovery, withdrawal, and 'good' and 'bad' Muslim states, which have an impact on the possible subject positions of 'Arabic' pupils. The 'reinvigoration' of Orientalism in the immediate post-9/11 years has been replaced with longer-term fears about global radicalisation, the stability of

Muslim states such as Iran, and the danger of so-called 'home-grown' terrorists (Winnett, 2008). To begin to unpick the impact of these ideas on the classroom, the first section of this chapter discusses how some Muslim girls at Gatehouse were constituted as 'good' learners.

Muslim girls as 'good' learners

During the year of observation at Gatehouse, it became clear that a group of girls – Farah, Khadija, Maira and Anna – were constituted as 'good' learners in this classroom. These girls came, respectively, first, fourth, fifth and sixth of the girls in the class on the EYFS Profile (the pupils who came second and third are discussed later in this chapter). These four girls are all Muslim; Farah, Khadija and Maira were Afghan; Anna is Kosovan. All had reasonable fluency in English, and it is likely that, as Jim had mentioned, this was helpful in the classroom. Within this classroom setting, the 'conditions of possibility' for these girls were demarcated by a complex web of discourses of Muslim femininity; fortunately for them, the possibility of academic success was not foreclosed. The following examples show how these girls' 'good' learner status was manifested in the classroom. Several extracts, from notes made between September and June, are presented in order to emphasise the small, everyday ways in which these children's subject positions were maintained:

> Anna is chosen by another teacher as the line leader. Jim says, "It's a good choice, she'll be making sure we all do the right thing".

> Jim writes 10 wrong as 01 on the board, but the children say it is right. He asks Maira, she chooses 10. Jim says, "Maira is right". He uses her to prove to others that he was wrong.

> In free play time, Farah appears quiet, studious, and is often alone. Later, when Jim is reading a book, Farah calls out, "It always rhymes". Jim says, "Yes, that's right Farah. It always rhymes". He is impressed.

> Khadija is picked as an "extra special helper" – Jim says this person has "got to be *so* good". Khadija laughs when she realises she has forgotten to put her name card on the board. Jim laughs too; they seem to have a special bond.

> The class are playing a game. Susan asks the class about the song for the game. Anna explains it all and then gets to be first "because you've explained it so well".

> The class have been on a trip, and Jim is grumpy because they didn't say thank you for the trip and going to the park. Maira is worried about Jim being grumpy. He says to her, "I'm not worried about *you* saying thank you, don't worry Maira". It seems she isn't at fault.

> Jim is reading a story about some naughty rabbits. When he reaches a line which says one 'piddled' on the carpet, he pauses and looks mock shocked.

Farah reads out 'piddled'. He says, "Say that again" and she repeats. He says to everyone, "It's just frustrating when you've got someone who's Level 20 and you're trying not to read something but someone can read it". He says this jokingly and fondly. When Jim picks up the next story, he says, "And who wrote this story?" as a rhetorical question (it is the same as another book); Farah immediately reads "Eric Carle" as if it were a genuine question. The children don't want any of the books Jim chooses, so he gets Khalid and Farah to choose one. Khalid picks the 'Bottoms up' book which makes them all giggle. Jim reads it, replacing words that are too rude, but Farah continues to correct him, reading out the rude words, but not loudly. *(Field notes, Gatehouse)*

These examples show how Anna, Maira, Khadija and Farah gained access to and re-inscribed their positions as 'good' learners. Jim treated these girls differently from other children: he made jokes with them, had quiet chats, and praised them more in whole class groups. They were given positions of responsibility more often, and were asked to answer questions more than other children. Their 'high ability' was made obvious within the classroom through Jim's displays of mock shock at their achievements. These girls were not *ideal* learners – the ideal is never achievable, much like gender performatives are never complete but remain 'illusions of substance' (Butler, 1990: 146) – but they were as close as Jim had, and were constituted repeatedly as 'good' learners. These girls' identities within the class were also maintained by the teachers' 'knowledge' of the children, which affected how their behaviour was perceived. For example, these girls were seen as good when they called out and were not reprimanded, because what they said was usually helpful or correct. When Farah (in the last quote above) reads out the rude words in the book, she is not seen as questioning Jim's authority, but as providing evidence of how well she can read. Thus, once the learner identity is established and the child is 'known', the child's behaviour is usually seen in this light, as further evidence of their 'good' learner status. There were however some exceptions, as I discuss later on in the chapter.

These girls' 'good' learner identities were made possible and recognisable, I would argue, because they fitted into a small intelligible space created by discourses linked with Asian and Muslim girls. Shain's research has suggested that female Asian pupils are perceived by teachers as passive, timid and shy and are positioned as victims, caught between two worlds (Shain, 2003: 123). In this study, I would suggest that these girls were similarly subjectivated through discourses of Islamic gender relations which position Muslim women as compliant and oppressed; this is linked to popular debates about the wearing of the hijab and the veil in recent years (Gereluk, 2008). Simultaneously, however, they were constituted positively as female pupils who were enthusiastic about learning and articulate, in line with popular discourses relating to girls' success in school; thus they combined gendered qualities of being conscientious, obedient and subservient with many of the other valued aspects of being a learner. They held intelligible subject positions within dominant discourses of Asian femininity as passive, sensible and hard-working.

Furthermore, for the Afghan girls, these positive learner identities were made intelligible by specific discourses relating to 'good migrants'. Maira, Khadija and Farah were constituted in a very specific intelligible space as 'good' Afghan girl learners. It is only through a quite detailed consideration of their particular 'diaspora space' (Brah, 1996) that the discourses which allow for their intelligibility are revealed. First, these girls' families were described positively in terms of having the right educational values and their fathers as having good jobs. In moments such as when their mothers helped out on school trips, their parents displayed some of the practices associated with middle-class parenting (Ball, 2003a), unlike the parents discussed in the previous chapter. But the positive perceptions of these parents were also linked to discourses of immigration which constitute them as 'good migrants' – aspiring, hard-working and keen to assimilate. This is particularly potent given a policy context of 'contemporary assimilationism', where 'integration' means learning English and contributing to the community (Gillborn, 2008). In addition, their particular status as Afghan Muslims has to be seen within the political context of the time. The years 2008 to 2009 saw an increased number of British forces deaths in Afghanistan and a growing unease about the purpose and effectiveness of military action there (BBC News, 2009a; Loyd, 2009; Reuters, 2009); so, the issue of Afghanistan was prominent in popular discourse at the time. In the run up to the Afghan elections in August 2009, much of the press coverage focused on an Afghan population that was reluctant to adopt 'Western' values of democracy and anti-corruption (Boone and Nasaw, 2009). In contrast, these families had implicitly rejected Islamic extremism and accepted Western values by living in London: therefore they were constituted sympathetically as 'good migrants', models of Westernised, submissive, moderate Islam. The migration of these girls' families from Afghanistan also suggested that they were relatively affluent families with aspirations, and thus close to the more middle-class backgrounds associated in popular discourse with the 'model minorities' – Indian and Chinese communities. This classed position was reinforced for Khadija in particular by her father's job at a broadcasting company.

Although the teachers at Gatehouse never talked about these identities specifically, at St Mary's, Paul did make some comments which illustrate this 'good migrant' discourse:

> "In my last school, it was a lot of Kurdish children, who'd come from villages, whose parents didn't know what … They really weren't that interested in education, to be honest, and so they did no work with them at home [...] Those children seriously didn't move the way that some of our Arab-speaking children from Baghdad do, whose parents have fled the country but are very highly educated, who can't speak much English, but they've got high education ethic". *(Paul, St Mary's)*

Here, we see the complexity of discourses of class, 'race' and the urban in relation to migration. Paul sees greater potential for the children from "Arab" countries; I would argue that the Afghan girls at Gatehouse are constituted through similar discourses as coming from families with the "education ethic". Paul's comments also suggest a rural/urban division that could also be applied to migrants from rural Bangladesh and from modern and comparatively 'Western' Afghan cities.

Although these girls were still subject to Orientalist/racist discourses as the Other compared with the White middle-class ideal, their status also as Muslim girls allowed them to be seen as engaging with learning and well behaved. Not subject to discourses of Muslim boys as the 'new folk devils' and as potential terrorists (Shain, 2010), these girls could provide a model of the kind of submissive, assimilating, liberal and Westernised Islam which is valued in the current policy context. Like the emphasis for working-class children on 'upward mobility' in the past (Walkerdine, 2003), these children are constituted as migrants who should be aspiring to higher social status through education; thus their educational success is welcomed by the teachers. These discourses also allow greater proximity to the neoliberal subjects of schooling, who take responsibility for their own learning in a discourse of individuality.

These complex webs of discourse opened up conditions of possibility whereby these girls could be recognisable as 'good' learners. In this quote, Jim's descriptions of Khadija, one of the Afghan girls, reveal the complexity of this position. Here, we are discussing whether the new January children had been as he expected:

Jim: Khadija's exactly how I knew she was going to be.

AB: Which is what?

Jim: Which is exactly what Claire [nursery teacher] said. Which is just amazing, kind of, just funny and "How do you know that?" kind of girl. Like knowing who Barack Obama is, and Gordon Brown [fondly]. And all these other things which are – and it's because her dad works at [broadcasting organisation] so he's kind of, not political, but he obviously talks about stuff at home. So she picks up on it and knows about it, which I think's just amazing that a four year old … She's really with it. She's one of those, the ones I was talking about earlier, who just, it's, English-speaking girl, where it's not all about hair braids and playing with the skipping rope and that kind of thing, and making up new games. It's about almost like political and, I don't know, just totally different. *(Interview with Jim, Gatehouse)*

Here, Khadija is constituted through discourses of globalisation as the bilingual international child: she is politically aware and a moderate Muslim (she did not wear hijab) whose family have chosen to live in a Western state rather than an Islamic state. Khadija is a thus a 'good' Muslim, unthreatening and submissive to the demands of living in the UK (as shown by parents teaching her English before she went to school). However, she is still constituted through Orientalist discourses as exotic and interesting, as shown when Jim was very impressed with her writing her name in Pashtu.

Youdell argued in her work on Lebanese and Turkish pupils in Australia that, 'the "Savage Arab" once in need of taming and Christianizing comes, in contemporary Western discourse, to be in need of westernizing, "democratizing"' (2006c: 521–2). I would argue that in the late 2000s, Afghan children such as Khadija, Farah and Maira come to represent the triumph of this 'westernizing and democratizing' process: successful, international, moderate Muslims fully assimilated into life in Britain. This is a precarious position which requires constant maintenance, however; there is always the risk of being subsumed back into general minority subjecthood through discourses of low attainment, disruptive behaviour and lack of 'ability', and the possibility of 'good' learner 'high ability' status being withdrawn.

The fragility of minority success

Bronwyn Davies writes: 'Teachers, in shaping the conditions of possibility of their students, do not wholly determine who their students are' (2006: 430). All of these girls also made use of their discursive agency in performing idealised feminine studenthood, in terms of actions and speech. For example, Maira would take work to show Jim, knowing he would be impressed, and Farah frequently took control of the large whiteboard in the classroom during free play time, which offered a very public opportunity to show off her writing skills. However, the changing learner identity of one pupil – Khadija – revealed the fragility of minority success. This analysis is informed by ideas of discursive agency and identity performance drawn from poststructural theory and from CRT. In particular, I make use of Carbado and Gulati's examination on the 'identity work' required by minoritised individuals in order to be successful in the workplace (Carbado and Gulati, 2000); this identity work involves making oneself acceptable within a White-dominated space, through behaviour, appearance and choice of associations. They argue that to be acceptable and succeed, minoritised workers are forced to engage in particular identity performances. I apply some of their arguments here to the very different context of Reception classrooms.

Khadija's deployment of her discursive agency towards the end of the year, which involved some unconscious resistance of her subjectivation as a passive Muslim girl, moved her beyond recognisability as a 'good' learner. First, Khadija began to question Jim's authority within the classroom, and was disobedient:

> Everyone is coming to the carpet for the end-of-the-day story. Khadija doesn't come to the carpet. Jim calls her over. She refuses, "Because there are beans everywhere" (these have been used for an activity). He says, "I'll pick them up later". Khadija replies, "No, I'll pick them up" and carries on. Jim says, "We've finished now so come and sit down". He starts to read the

story. Five minutes later, Khadija is still tidying – she has ignored Jim. He sees her and calls her over, "It does make me a little bit cross that you're not listening. You've done a fantastic job, but you do need to listen". Khadija sits down, and doesn't seem upset by this.

Just before lunch: the children are sitting waiting to be chosen to go and wash their hands. Khadija and Jena are running around the carpet while they wait; they don't seem to care that they will be last. Their behaviour seems very silly – they are giggling and running in circles while everyone else sits still. Lynn says, "Khadija and Jena, that's a little bit silly for in here". She doesn't seem too cross. They carry on, ignoring Lynn. She then says again, more crossly, "Girls, little bit silly". They are the last ones in.

On the carpet, some children are at the front showing their work. Khadija is reprimanded for talking when the speakers have not finished – Lynn says, "Khadija, they're still talking!"

In free play time, Jim is sitting with a group, absorbed in an activity. I am the only other adult in the room. Khadija, Bilqis and Jena have been playing together. Khadija and Bilqis go out into the corridor, which is forbidden without permission. Jena stays. The two girls giggle outside, and look back in to see if anyone has noticed they have broken the rule. They come back in and look at me guiltily, but they run off giggling. *(Field notes, Gatehouse)*

Here we see how Khadija's actions and words start to push at the boundaries of acceptable learner subjectivities: she is both verbally and physically rejecting the norms of being a 'good' learner, and, particularly, the norms of being a good female Muslim learner. This different 'identity performance', is not simply a failure to engage in the kind of identity work required for a minoritised child to maintain their positive subject position, but it is proactive step outside of and beyond acceptability.

In the following weeks, Khadija's behaviour seemed to become more challenging of authority, and the teachers began to speak to her more like they did to the other children, who were not usually understood as 'good' learners. At this point, discourses surrounding girls as better-behaved pupils began to be questioned: as Connolly (1998) found in his study of infant classrooms, girls' behaviour transgressions tend to be seen more negatively than boys'. Also relevant is Reay's finding that older girls who appropriated 'girl power' were labelled as 'real bitches' and 'a bad influence' (2001: 152). Khadija was similarly subject to discourses which view assertive, challenging girls as inherently problematic. Furthermore, her increasing tendency to play with Jena and Bilqis, two girls who were seen as "middling" and "silly", also began to position her in contrast to the other 'good' learner girls. This move towards a certain 'silly' femininity was compounded by Khadija's changing choice of clothes and footwear:

Khadija falls over and I mention it to Lynn. We talk about her shoes, which are not designed for running in the playground. Lynn says, "They're not the worst that we've had. We do try to tell them". Lynn says maybe she should ring home to get them changed, and asks Khadija if she should, but this doesn't happen.

Khadija seems to be a totally different position – much naughtier and more feminine. She is wearing high-heeled black sandals, with bows on the front (which she can't walk in properly), tracksuit bottoms, and a polo shirt, and sparkly bracelets. The other girls are mainly wearing summer dresses. *(Field notes, Gatehouse)*

The embodied identities of the children matter because they are a significant part of the performative: 'The way we style our bodies is neither a matter of sex (nature) nor simply an adjunct of the prevailing gender order (culture), rather it is one of the techniques through which we perform, enact and "do" gender' (Nayak and Kehily, 2006: 467). Here, the way Khadija 'does' her gender is unaligned with discourses surrounding Muslim women: she wears shoes that are overtly feminine and impractical (in contrast to the less pretty and more practical trainers that the other girls wear). These shoes physically restrict her from joining in with activities and being a 'normal' pupil. This is in stark contrast to Jim's comments earlier in the year about how Khadija was not interested in hair braids and skipping, when her lack of overt femininity was seen positively.

Lynn's comments on Khadija's parents' failure to provide appropriate footwear are linked to 'difficult intake' discourses about the deficiencies of immigrant parents, and by wearing these shoes, Khadija is suddenly moved away from the idea that she has 'good migrant' parents who want her to succeed as a pupil. Her jewellery and shoes are evidence of an unacceptable femininity in Reception classrooms, where all children are supposed to be practically dressed so that they can engage in all sorts of play. There is an acceptable femininity, which involves wearing the school summer dress and having nice hairbands, but Khadija rejects this in favour of her sandals and jewellery, which represent a more adult, impractical femininity that is unacceptable in this context. In wearing high-heeled shoes and jewellery, Khadija is constituted though discourses of 'silly' superficial femininity, but her non-feminine clothes (tracksuit bottoms and polo shirt) are completely incongruous with these displays of adult femininity. I would suggest that her appropriation of the outward displays of adult femininity contributed to the shift in how the adults understand her subject position, because they drew her away from the intelligible space she held as a conscientious hard-working Muslim girl.

Khadija performed her identity in ways that negated a viable, recognisable subject position; it was beyond the bounds of the discursively prescribed norms of 'good' learner Muslim femininity to be disobedient, silly and overtly feminine in this way, and thus she became unintelligible as an able Muslim female pupil. I was only just becoming aware of this process when Jim showed me how he had organised the ability groups. I was surprised to see Khadija in the second-to-top group, given Jim's earlier comments about her being "amazing". He explained (as mentioned in Chapter 3): "She's very vocal, but she's there for consolidation. I'm not sure it's all there". Thus Khadija was suddenly rendered inauthentic as a learner; being articulate and answering questions became merely evidence of her being "vocal", not of some underlying intelligence. Jim almost seemed to suggest that Khadija had tricked the adults into thinking she was 'clever' when really she was just chatty. The authenticity discourse is deployed here, when she becomes unrecognisable. There is no intelligible space for Khadija as a disobedient and overtly feminine authentic learner subject, so she is relegated within the hierarchy of the class. Khadija becomes another of the Muslim girls in the class who is a bit "silly", and has parents who are disapproved of; her articulate language skills become just a smokescreen for what she 'really' is, no longer evidence of her 'high ability'. She is discursively constituted in another viable subject position of silly, disobedient Muslim girl; this shift means she remains intelligible as a learner, but with a different learner identity. Although she is in some ways still a 'good' learner, as she will do well on the EYFS Profile, she is no longer inhabiting this position with any authenticity.

How can we understand Khadija's fall from grace in terms of how this sort of process might disadvantage minority pupils more widely? Carbado and Gulati argue in their paper 'The Fifth Black Woman' (2001), that discrimination based on identity performance is still discrimination. They give the example of a law firm which promotes four Black women but fails to promote a fifth, and cites this as evidence that no discrimination took place. Carbado and Gulati argue that, if the rejection of the fifth woman is based on her identity performance – as evidenced through her choice of dress and hairstyle, her association with 'controversial committees', where she lives, her attendance at social events, and her professional associations – then this is still discrimination. In this situation, they argue, the concept of intersectionality alone is not enough: 'Intersectionality does not capture this form of preferential treatment' (2001: 718); some discussion of identity performance is necessary. Similarly, Farah, Maira and Khadija cannot be understood only in terms of their intersectional identities as Afghan Muslim girls: *how they perform this identity, albeit unknowingly, and how this relates to dominant discourses in the setting, affects how they are understood in the classroom.*

A further example of this emerged from the data collected in the Reception class at St Mary's relating to another girl pupil, Abeje. In this case, however, Abeje was not only dismissed as inauthentic due to her identity performance, but removed from the possibility of 'good' learner status entirely. Abeje engaged in many practices that were associated with good learning in the classroom, such as helping the teacher, answering questions and engaging in a range of activities, and she was described as "very clever" by the teaching assistant. As a bilingual African-Caribbean girl, there was perhaps some intelligible space open to her to be constituted as successful within circulating discourses which associate speaking two European languages (English and French) with middle-classness and also an international, even exotic status. Mirza has argued that Black girls' educational success is little recognised because they fall between two discourses of race (which focuses on Black masculinity) and gender (which focuses on White femininity): 'this dichotomy explains the blind spot; the invisible location that leaves the complex, messy and untidy issue of Black women's success unaddressed' (Mirza, 1998: 121). Perhaps this ambiguity could have allowed Abeje to be constituted as a 'good' learner if she had engaged in the right sort of 'identity work'. However, her identity performance, like that of the 'Fifth Black Woman' in Carbado and Gulati's work, was incompatible with this intelligible space, and she was constituted through an alternative sets of discourses which position Black girls as 'difficult'.

Abeje was very confident in the classroom, and often tried to be helpful to the teacher. This behaviour was, at times, construed as challenging. On one occasion, Abeje played a significant role in a lesson which involved using several different types of toy animal. She recognised and found each of the animals in the classroom, and brought them to her teacher, Paul, and single-handedly kept this complex lesson going. However, this helpfulness was complicated by Abeje's commitment to getting the right animals for the story, as shown in this field note:

> Afternoon maths lesson on the carpet. Abeje is handing Paul animals on request.
>
> Paul: Now we need a goat.
>
> Abeje: This is a goat.
>
> Paul: No, that's a sheep.
>
> Abeje: That's a goat.
>
> Paul: It's a sheep.
>
> Abeje: *[quite irritated]* No, look *[points to horns]*.
>
> Paul: It's a sheep.
>
> Abeje: *[patronising]* No, goats have these [horns].
>
> Paul: OK *[takes the animal]*. *(Field notes, St Mary's)*

Shortly after this exchange, despite Abeje organising all the resources required, she was sent away from the carpet for talking. This was a common sanction, but talking would not always warrant this punishment. Abeje's reasonable argument about why the toy is a goat and not a sheep was not seen by Paul as capable, but as annoying, even though she was displaying the kind of attention to detail that at other times was valued in this Reception classroom. Her confidence was regarded as problematic: as in Archer, Halsall and Hollingworth's (2007) study of inner city working-class girls, Abeje's exercise of agency positioned her in conflict with the school because this assertiveness was understood as deviant and aggressive, particularly for minoritised girls. Abeje's lack of deference here allowed Paul to constitute her as challenging and difficult, and deploy discourses of a 'feisty', loud

Black woman. This 'challenging' learner identity was compounded by perceptions of Abeje's mother, who regularly wanted to speak to Paul, as interfering and 'difficult'; she complained on two occasions about what was happening in the classroom, and Paul made it very clear to me that he found her to be irritating. Her interest in Abeje's learning was regarded as inappropriate and uninformed, rather than as evidence of positive educational values. Research has indicated that many Black mothers are keen to be involved in their children's education (Crozier, 2000, 2005; Reay and Mirza, 2005); however, 'these approaches may still be read by schools as exemplifying "the wrong cultural currency"' (Archer and Francis, 2007: 168), as in Abeje's case.

Abeje's identity performance in terms of appearance was also a factor, I would argue, in her learner identity in the classroom. She styled her hair in a large afro, and wore a 'Rasta hat' woollen cap in green, red and yellow stripes. These physical manifestations of her Black identity are the opposite of the identity work that Carbado and Gulati argue is needed to fit in as a minoritised individual, whereby minoritised individuals engage in 'racial comfort' for White people by de-emphasising their racial status (2000, 2001). On other occasions, Abeje was reprimanded for dancing and singing when she should not have been, and so failed to display the kind of bodily control required to be a 'good' learner. These performative practices also resonated with discourses of Black musicality and physicality (Sewell, 1997). In combination with her assertiveness, these elements of her identity performance prevented her from accessing 'good' learner status; proud Black femininity appeared to be incommensurate with being a 'good' learner, as this involved passivity and obedience to authority. Abeje was in the process of learning, like the Caribbean women in Phoenix's study (2009), that she can be constituted as an inadequate learner even when she shows signs of success. Her gendered and raced position affects the way that her assertiveness is interpreted, and counters normative ideas about idealised middle-class femininity (Archer, Halsall and Hollingworth, 2007). Abeje was also being taught that there are limited ways in which her femininity can be performed that are commensurate with becoming a 'good' learner, and that her performance, so far, was not one of them.

It is important to note that I am not suggesting that Abeje (or the other children) were in some way responsible for their learner identities, even though they had some agency in the classroom. Abeje's behaviour could have been understood as helpful or enthusiastic, and as Carbado and Gulati (2001) emphasise, discriminatory views based on identity performance are still discriminatory, even if they are less obvious. Like Khadija, Abeje is understood through her intersectional identity, the discourses surrounding her which limit the ways in which she can succeed at school. She has perhaps an even smaller intelligible space as a high-ability pupil open to her, and fails entirely to occupy it. I would argue that, without the possibility of westernised (perhaps 'reformed') Muslim subjecthood, the possibility of Abeje as a Black girl attaining 'good' learner status is extremely limited: after all, Black pupils never approximate 'model minority' status in popular discourse. That is not to say it is impossible, but that, for Abeje, it would be quite difficult to ever reach 'good' learner status; it would require a very specific identity performance. I return to this issue of the reduced intelligible space for minoritised pupils to be constituted as 'good' learners later in this chapter.

Considerations of the conditions of possibility for pupils, or the intelligible space that is open to them in terms of being a successful learner, are an important part of understanding how some pupils come to be disadvantaged. These conditions include the different levels of acceptability of performative practices in relation to different identities. For Khadija, her identity performance moved her outside recognisability as a successful 'able' Muslim girl, but another pupil behaving in the same way might not have had the same effect on her learner identity. Discriminatory processes in classrooms are not as simple as a teacher engaging in unconscious racism: for some children, doing well is simply not possible given the constraints prescribed by the discursive construction of their intersectional identities, particularly if they engage in certain performative practices. These performative practices can have significant effects on how children are constituted as learners.

My argument in relation to these two girls is in many ways more pessimistic than Youdell's work on the possibilities of using 'discursive agency' to think about 'how the self might be made again differently' (2006c: 512). She argues for a performative politics which 'insists nobody is necessarily anything, and what it means to be a teacher, a student, a learner might be opened up to radical rethinking' (2006b: 519). In my data, discourse and its effects do indeed 'exceed the intent or free will of an agent' (2006b: 519), so that, for minoritised children especially, moving beyond a narrow realm of particular subject positions renders them unintelligible and removes the option for them to be 'made again differently'. In these classrooms, the balance of power heavily favours the restraints of discourse, to the extent that alternative subject positions which are not recognisable within circulating discourses must be quickly rectified. I am not arguing that there is no room for interruption, merely that we need to be aware of the extreme constraints of who can be constituted as a 'good' learner. I discuss the potential for resistance in more detail in the concluding chapter.

White pupils as intelligible learners

As discussed in previous chapters, in general White middle-class identities operated as the idealised Norm within these Reception classrooms, rendering almost all of the pupils at Gatehouse and St Mary's as Other. However, the relationship of the individual White pupils in these classes to this ideal was mediated by complex discourses relating to their class positions. In their discussions of identity performance in the workplace, Carbado and Gulati argue that in a law firm, White employees do not have the burden of 'identity work'. People of colour are divided into those that do 'identity work' in order to 'fit in' to a majority White workplace, and those that do not, and that the 'interracial problem is that White people are not subject to this subcategorization' (2001: 720). Although I think their theory of identity performance is very useful in its application to this school context, I would question this argument regarding identity performance among White individuals. I argue that the identity work required to be deemed a 'good' learner in these Reception classrooms *was* necessary for these White pupils too, but took on different forms more related to class positions. Moreover, identity performance is different in a context where minoritised groups are in the majority, as was the case in these classrooms. It is worth remembering that, as a small minority of the pupils, the White children were very noticeable, and were at times rendered explicitly distinct from the other children (for example, on sports day when the TAs only put sun cream on the White pupils).

An intersectional analysis is just as necessary in relation to the White children: their gender and class affect what 'kind' of White child they can be, and the relative access they have to the privileges of Whiteness (Leonardo, 2009). Within CRT literature, there is much discussion about the benefits of being White for poor or working-class White people within the context of White privilege (Leonardo, 2004b; Roediger, 1991). I agree with Allen's contention that people whom he terms 'poor Whites', 'are invested in Whiteness and receive the benefits of White privilege, even if their returns on their investments are not as great as the returns for nonpoor Whites' (Allen, 2009: 216). Nonetheless, they are also 'in a *relational* sense oppressed people who do face institutional and everyday forms of dehumanization' (2009: 214, *emphasis in original*). It is important to note here that a CRT framework considers Whiteness as a constructed concept, which is flexible given the historical and political context (Ignatiev, 1995), and that wider literature has noted a long history of poorer White people's 'precarious and contingent relationship to Whiteness' (Nayak, 2009: 29). Different forms of Whiteness, and the importance of identity performance within these, were apparent even within the group of White working-class girls at Gatehouse, the only White children in the class.

White working-class girls have, to some extent, been absent from discourses of educational success and failure in recent years, due to the specific focus on White working-class boys (Archer, Halsall and Hollingworth, 2007; Francis and Skelton, 2005). Where there is discussion, discourses of White working class femininity have largely been concerned with negative subjectivities such as the 'ladette' and 'chav'. These discourses, which follow from ideas about 'laddishness' as a working class male culture, position White working class girls as 'shameless and brash', and 'unrespectable' (Jackson, 2006: 346). Research on working-class girls has argued that they engage in heterosexual hyperfeminine performances, despite the masculine associations of some of their attitudes and behaviours, and that these girls are constituted within school discourses as 'problem' girls – disruptive, rude, and anti-academic (Archer, Halsall and Hollingworth, 2007; Jackson, 2006). More recent discourses about the 'underclass' and 'broken Britain', which hark back to ideas of the 'deserving' and 'undeserving' poor, often represent White working-class women as 'degenerate' (Gillborn, 2010). White working-class girls have been affected by the 'poor White boys' discourse, because they are still constituted as the contrasting group in the boy/girl (failing/succeeding) binary[2]; thus, I would argue that they are expected to succeed at school, to some extent, because they do not have the 'disadvantage' of being White working-class boys.

Ideas about the importance of aspiration (which, as we have seen above, when combined with discourses of migration can play out in complex ways) have been reinvigorated by government policy on raising aspirations such as the Aim Higher project, which implicitly apportions the blame for working-class 'under-achievement' (and therefore gaps in wealth) to the working class, who are accused of lacking ambition. This deficit discourse, present in policy from early years to higher education (Burke, 2002), divides working-class children into either hard-working and aspiring to 'better' themselves (and close to middle-class ideals), or as having negative educational values. For these girls at Gatehouse, their identity performances constitute them through these deficit discourses as either 'good' (hard-working, aspirational) or 'bad' (failing to take up learning opportunities) White working-class girls.

There were four White British pupils across the two Reception classes at Gatehouse, all girls – Chloe, Bethany and twins Ashlee and April. While Chloe and Bethany were constituted as 'bad' learners, Ashlee and April had positive learner identities. For example, when discussing the results of the White children in his class (which included only Bethany and Ashlee of these four), Jim commented, "Bethany's way down and Ashlee's way high". I would suggest that the differences in the White girls' learner identities were based on subtle differences in how their family backgrounds were constructed by the teachers, including their perceived proximity to middle-classness (and therefore positive learner attributes), and their performance of White femininity in the classroom.

All the girls were constituted through the inner city and 'difficult intake' discourses as distinctly working class, but there were subtle differences in how their families were constituted in terms of educational values. For instance, Ashlee and April brought in pictures they had drawn at home, talked about their sister and about family events, and used a wide range of vocabulary (which was particu-larly obvious given the smaller vocabularies of the EAL children). Although they were never seen as middle class, in the absence of middle-class White children, they came closest to the ideal of English speaking, White middle-class pupils that operated at Gatehouse. In contrast, Chloe and Bethany's families were talked of disapprovingly and they were constructed as problematic, not because they were badly behaved, but because they were "needy", and had the wrong attitude towards school. Here are some examples of these children's experiences in the classroom:

> Jim talks about homework. Ashlee asks about a bit she can't do (and shows Jim). Jim says, "Ask your mum or your sister. How about [sister]? She'll know".

> On a day where it is colder than expected, Ashlee and April's mum turns up with their jumpers for them.

As soon as she arrives in the morning, Bethany has her face cleaned by Lynn. It is not clear why. No other children have their faces cleaned.

Jim asks Bethany where she was yesterday (a school day), she says, "At the park". Anne (TA) and Jim look disapproving.

Chloe has a runny nose and adults constantly give her tissues, all day long. It seems to take up a lot of time. The adults recoil when discussing it.

Sports day: Laura (TA) puts sun cream on Bethany as she is very pale. She is disapproving about the fact that her mum didn't do it before.

Bethany and Chloe's new short haircuts come up in conversation with Jim. He says it's due to "N.I.T.S. – a last resort". *(Field notes, Gatehouse)*

We see from these examples how Bethany and Chloe's families are seen as unhelpful, while Ashlee and April's family is seen as educationally orientated and caring. These episodes resonate with ideas about the 'deserving' and the 'undeserving' poor which are present in popular discourses about working-class White families (Gillborn, 2010): April and Ashlee's family have the right values, while Bethany and Chloe's are not trying hard enough. There was also something corporeal about Bethany and Chloe's negative status, which resonates with Allen's argument relating to marginalised White groups in the US:

> 'The 'White but not quite' positionality of poor Whites is perpetuated not just by attitudes toward their economic status or alleged cultural dysfunction but also by beliefs about their biological inferiority'. *(Allen, 2009: 214)*

Allen is referring here to discourses about 'inbreeding' in White Appalachian populations. Although I am not suggesting there were explicit or implicit references to a 'biological inferiority' at Gatehouse, the suggestion that Bethany and Chloe had continual head lice infections and that Bethany was not clean did suggest a certain physical dimension to their negative learner identities. Paul's comment in Chapter 4 regarding a working-class White girl's mother "producing children" from a young age similarly resonates with this perception of some families as being outside the boundaries of 'respectable' Whiteness.

More importantly, Bethany's failure to care about being at school matters because it positions her outside the working-class aspiration discourse, as part of the 'undeserving poor' or even the 'underclass'. She did not do her homework and her attendance was described by Jim as "shocking". Discourses of individual responsibility position a disadvantaged child who does not come to school as failing to help themselves to 'escape' their situation; as Bauman argues in relation to poverty in neoliberal discourse:

'Not doing what is needed, in a country of free choosers, is easily, without a second thought, interpreted as choosing something else instead'. *(Bauman, 2005: 75)*

At Gatehouse, Bethany and Chloe are constituted as 'bad' learners because they 'choose something else' and therefore fail to demonstrate the enthusiasm for learning, commitment and hard work prescribed by the EYFS Profile. Therefore, the position of 'good' learner which is intelligible in relation to their raced, classed and gendered identities (an aspiring White working-class identity) is foreclosed.

In contrast, when Jim talked about Ashlee, he described her positively as enthusiastic about learning; he commented that she "asks some amazing questions" and would go away to think about a problem and then come back with an answer. Thus Ashlee performed a 'good' learner identity and was recognisable as such as a White working-class girl – she asked probing questions and took time to think, both of which are practices compatible with the intelligible space open to her. These behaviours, which might be seen as evidence of 'slowness' and as challenging or disruptive with another child, provided evidence that Ashlee is "with it", keen to learn and thoughtful. Her intersectional position meant that this was an intelligible learner identity for her, and her authenticity was never questioned, unlike other children.

The gender of these pupils was also important in constituting them as quite different learners: their adherence to a model of hard-working femininity (which, as we have seen, is easily elided with a 'good' learner identity) differed greatly. Bethany's lack of enthusiasm contrasted with Ashlee asking for help with her homework in the field notes above. As I discussed in the previous chapter, girls have more access to 'good' learner positions because the attributes of the learner as prescribed by the EYFS Profile are more associated with discourses about girls. Thus the distance from this identity created by Bethany's and Chloe's lack of enthusiasm is more stark *because* they are girls. Exempt from the 'failing White working-class boys' discourse, these girls are expected to be 'good' learners, albeit within discourses about the hard-working, aspirational working classes. Furthermore, their different performances of femininity brought up quite different discourses: like many of the girls in Reception, Ashlee engaged in displays of femininity such as caring about her hair, but crucially not to the extent of being seen as 'ditzy'. She would get annoyed with anyone playing with her hair on the carpet, for example, showing a commitment to learning. In contrast, Chloe and Bethany were marked out as unattractive and not engaging in appropriate displays of femininity by their constant head lice infections, runny noses and faces that need to be publicly cleaned.

Bethany and Chloe's resulting identity performances were incompatible with the intelligible space open to them as white working-class girls. While they reaped some reward from their Whiteness (for instance in relation to language), they were still seen as 'bad' learners because they did not display the kinds of educational values (hard work, commitment) associated with aspiring, 'deserving' working-class pupils. Therefore, in contrast to Carbado and Gulati's comments on adults in the workplace, I would argue that the White children *do* have to engage in some identity work in order to be constituted as 'good' learner subjects. The competing discourses of Whiteness, working-classness and femininity open up an intelligible space for pupils like Ashlee and April, in contexts like the Gatehouse classroom, to be 'good' learners; however, they also create the possibility of negative White working-class femininity, as discussed by Gillborn (2010) and Allen (2009), for pupils like Bethany and Chloe.

Negative learner identities

Thus far, I have discussed the complex ways in which some pupils are intelligible as 'good' learners and some, through a combination of their intersectional identities and their identity performances, are *un*intelligible as 'good' learners. I turn now to pupils who not only fail to occupy a 'good' learner position, but are actively constituted as 'bad' learners. For these children, who are mainly boys from minoritised groups, I argue that there is more intelligible space as a 'bad' learner created by their intersectional identities; in other words, it is far easier for them to make sense as 'bad' subjects of schooling than as 'good'. This is in keeping with a long history of research on minoritised boys (Archer, 2003; Gillborn, 1990, 1995; Sewell, 1997). I discuss in detail here how the specific conception of the learner in Reception operates to distance 'good' learner identities from discourses connected to boys and minoritised communities. However, as I suggest at the end of this section, there are possibilities for shifts in what is intelligible when a child's class identity is constructed differently.

Black boys at St Mary's

At St Mary's, the Black boys (Reece, Ryan, Mike and Dylan) were constituted as 'bad' learners through discourses of poor parenting and single-motherhood, violence and neediness. Given the prevailing discourses regarding Black boys and men as problematic and the long history of research into racist attitudes toward young Black men (Gillborn, 1995; Mac and Ghaill, 1988; Rollock, 2007; Sewell, 1997), this is not a surprising finding. However, I was surprised to find how quickly and how powerfully these discourses worked to distance the boys from positive learner identities, and how 'impossible' they were soon seen as being.

In their classroom, the boys' negative learner identities were quickly established and became common sense. In the first few weeks of term, Reece and Ryan appeared to be singled out as disruptive and in need of extra help with "settling" into Reception. Reece and Ryan were initially frequently confused and their identities seemed to merge: Ryan had been "diagnosed" as hyperactive, and Reece had also gained this label within a few days, despite no official diagnosis. The two boys were a constant focus of attention and seen as problematic from the very start of term. These field notes are from the first week of school:

During a lesson on the carpet, everyone is sitting in a circle. Reece is moved to sit on a chair for picking up a bag twice. Then Reece won't put his hands in his lap while the others sing and he gets taken away. Paul says to the rest of the children, "Reece isn't doing the right thing". Reece has to sit apart with the egg timer.

The children are moving off the carpet for free play when they are told to. Ryan is last but one to go. He starts to move, but is told off. *(Field notes, St Mary's)*

From the very first week of their educational careers, Reece and Ryan were seen as 'bad' learners, unable to display the sort of behaviours associated with 'good' learning, such as learning to sit without fiddling and waiting for instructions. At times, these negative identities were given validity through pseudo-scientific discourses; Paul said about Ryan, alongside his "hyperactive" label:

"He's like a boy, but an extreme; you know, if there's a normal distribution of the boy behaviour *[draws bell curve in air]*, he's quite at the end of it sort of thing, you know; he's not average in concentration".

Thus the discourse of boys as 'bad' learners worked with the idea of Ryan as "hyperactive" to position him as an "extreme", far removed from educational acceptability. Similarly, Reece's negative learner identity was maintained through the first term, as we saw in Chapter 3 when Paul and Kelly swapped the names on the supply teacher's observations. Soon, the idea of Reece as being anything other than difficult became entirely impossible for Paul to imagine, as shown in this incident:

It is fruit time, mid-morning. The children sit in a circle and the bowl of fruit is passed around, while two children (Amy and Naima) give out the water bottles. When they go to sit down, their own water bottles aren't in their places. Everyone looks around for them. This goes on for several minutes until Paul is quite agitated (there are several other things he is dealing with at the same time). Paul tells Reece, who is sitting against the main teacher's chair, "Stand up!". Reece looks confused. Paul assumes he has hidden the water bottles and looks under the chair. There is no sign of the bottles anywhere. Naima and Amy are told, "Never mind" and don't get any water. Later that day, at lunch time, Paul brings up the loss of the water bottles. He looks again under the chair and they are there, further to the side. Paul says he knew Reece hid them; it is "One of his things he does. I knew he had a twinkle in his eye". He then tells the other children that Reece had hidden them. *(Field notes, St Mary's)*

The certainty with which Paul accuses Reece of hiding the water bottles shows how strongly Reece is constituted as a 'bad' learner who breaks the rules in this classroom. Paul's contention that this is "one of his things he does" shows how 'teacher knowledge' can work to constrain how a child can be understood. Paul believes he can predict Reece's behaviour (as seen when he predicted Reece would start a fight in the swapped observation in Chapter 3), and decides he has taken the bottles even though he has no proof.

The 'bad' learner identities of these boys were made clear to the whole class both explicitly (as in the episode above) and also implicitly through the use of sticker charts. These were colourful pieces of card mounted on the wall, on which the boys were instructed to put any stickers given to them (all children were given stickers as a reward for good behaviour or learning), while other children simply stuck them on their jumpers. Reece was given a chart in the first week, and in the second week, Paul told Ryan, "I hear constant interruption. We're going to make you a sticker chart. That is going to help". Behaviour management practices such as this played an important role in constituting children as different types of learner, and maintaining these learner identities on a day-to-day basis.

For Reece, his negative learner identity had an impact on how he behaved in the classroom and how his behaviour was understood. One of the effects of his position as a 'difficult' boy was that he became increasingly withdrawn through the first term of school, and often appeared confused about what he should be doing and what he was doing wrong. This only further reinforced his negative identity as a learner because he did not display the required enthusiasm and motivation of a 'good' learner. Reece became reluctant to do any activities other than play with the train set, and had to be strongly encouraged to join in with adult-led activities; thus he appeared to reject the model of learning presented to him by only doing one activity in free time, and failed to be a 'rational chooser'. His negative learner identity was maintained through repeated reprimands and the constant perception that his behaviour was challenging of authority, as in this incident:

> It is tidy-up time before break. Paul does his usual routine for getting the children's attention, involving dinging a triangle and the children showing three fingers, then two, then one, after each ding. Reece is tidying up and is holding eight or nine bits of toy train. He is confused about what to do because he has no hands free to do the fingers action. He gets told off for not holding up a finger when the triangle dings. Paul says crossly, "Reece, I need a finger!" *(Field notes, St Mary's)*

Here Reece is reprimanded and his negative learner identity is reinforced, even though he is trying to help tidy the classroom. There appears to be very little space for him to be positioned positively. I would argue that the strength of Reece's negative learner identity was based on the recognisability of the Black boy as a 'bad' learner; the intelligibility of this position in relation to circulating discourses may have led to Paul's certainty about him.

This recognisability of the Black boy as a 'bad' learner is based on popular and educational discourses which have for decades positioned Black boys as a problem in education. Furthermore, at the time that this research was conducted there was a growing concern with 'knife crime' and 'gang violence' in London that was linked to Black young men (BBC News, 2009b, 2009c, 2009d). This popular discourse tapped into longer-standing concerns about Black male crimi-nality, social breakdown in Black communities and Black single mothers that have historically limited how Black boys can be understood within classrooms (Alexander, 2000; Archer and Yamashita, 2003). It is within these frames of reference, I would argue, that the Black boys at St Mary's were understood. These boys all came from single-parent families and Paul was quite critical of their mothers in conversations. He experienced several problems with parents arguing with each other in the classroom and using threatening behaviour, and described "really, really aggressive angry parents", one of whom "threatened to kick people's effing heads in". As well as the complex racialised discourses of bad parenting and Black aggression and violence, these boys were constituted through discourses of poor educational values and the 'undeserving' working class. On another occasion, Paul openly criticised Reece's mother for her attitude towards her son:

> Lunchtime. Reece isn't well, so he has been given an extra jumper and is curled up on a soft chair. The adults look at him and discuss sending him home. One of the TAs says, "But take that jumper off him first; it's ours". Paul says he will call Reece's mum, but to me he is quietly doubtful if she will come; he says, "She's got to do her swimming *[cynically]*. She's all, 'That effing boy, he's such an effing pain'". *[Then to Reece]* "But we know he's such a special person in our class". *(Field notes, St Mary's)*

This boy's Black single mother was thus constructed as violent, neglectful, poor and potentially criminal (as shown by the implication that she will keep a school jumper). This link between parent and child was particularly important in Paul's classroom, as he had strong views on how parents have a "huge impact" on their children. Paul's views of the parents played a key role in constituting these Black boys as inevitably bad learners, as shown in this incident relating to another boy, Dylan:

> In free play time, there is a fuss in the home corner – Dylan doesn't want to be Liam's friend. Paul argues with Dylan about whether his mum would want him to be kind. Dylan says, "My mum isn't kind, not if people aren't nice to her". Paul later talks to me about an incident that week when Dylan's and Ryan's mums were swearing and shouting at each other and threatening to stab each other in the head. Paul says it is all coming out in Dylan's behaviour – "He sees it, you see". *(Field notes, St Mary's)*

Within generally poor perceptions of the home lives of the children at St Mary's, these Black boys' backgrounds were seen as particularly damaging to them.

Another Black boy, Mike, was also described in terms of his "major home problems". These boys were thus constituted simultaneously as victims of their circumstances and as problematic as individuals. There was a strong sense of inevitability about these boys being 'bad' learners, which further suggests that being a 'bad' learner was the only intelligible position for them in school. This inevitability was extended to their adult lives: the teaching assistant, Kelly, commented when discussing Mike, "It's just scary to think [what are] these children going to be like as adults? What are they going to be like then?". Thus these boys' learner identities seemed likely to continue to position them negatively throughout their school careers.

However, the need for subjectivities to be maintained and repeated constantly and the scope for discursive agency which I have discussed throughout this chapter, also applied to these negative identities. This was particularly the case for one Black boy – Ryan. Paul's discovery of more information about his home background made his bad identity unintelligible, and opened up the possibility of a more positive learner identity. The discussion of Ryan at the EYFS Profile meeting in November where his and Reece's observations were switched was the first indication I saw of these changing ideas:

> EYFS Profile meeting. Paul and Kelly are present. They have already switched Reece's and Ryan's names on the two supply teacher observations. They now look at an observation for Ryan. It is about Ryan playing with the fire station, then the play-dough, then going to the writing desk. Paul defends Ryan moving around: "It was early days". Then Paul says, "And Ryan's really clever; he's really developed. Clever's not the right word".
>
> A while later: Paul says he is not going to write about Ryan moving about as "He's not doing that now". They discuss how some observations can be no use for the profile as "it all moves on, but it's useful for teaching and that's the point" (Paul). *(Field notes, St Mary's)*

Here we see how the first observation about Ryan describes behaviour that is not commensurate with being a 'good' learner: he is moving around too quickly without being focused on one activity, not exercising choice effectively. However, this information can be dismissed through the development discourse – he is now "really developed" because he does not move around as much. Paul uses his 'teacher knowledge' to constitute Ryan more positively.

This change in Ryan's learner identity appeared to coincide with Paul finding out more about Ryan's home life and the distancing of Ryan's mother from other Black single mothers:

> Paul talks about Ryan's mum from parents evening; he says, "She's actually very nice. She's a nursery nurse, you know". Kelly is surprised. Paul continues, "I was honest with her, and I told her that when he first came in

I thought, 'What support are we going to need?' [...] She was really nice. I told her how he's changed". *(Field notes, St Mary's)*

With these comments, Ryan's class and 'race' position is shifted to being more 'respectable': his mother is a nursery nurse (a profession requiring qualifications) and "actually very nice", which is implicitly connected to this occupation. Later in the discussion, it was mentioned that Ryan's mum was a single mother because his father died from an illness. Thus Ryan's home life was constructed as unfortunate, but importantly not a result of the hypersexuality and promiscuity attributed to Black communities in enduring discourses of raced sexuality. This information appeared to disrupt Paul's perception of Ryan's particular 'constellation of identity markers' (Youdell, 2006b), and renders his initial assessment of him as a 'bad' learner unintelligible. Ryan cannot be understood through simplistic discourses of Black boys with single mothers; instead, he is constituted as the 'deserving poor', the victim of unfortunate circumstance, with a mother in a caring, respectable occupation. This opened up another recognisable identity for him in the classroom: as a Black working-class 'success story'. In explaining this shift at the end of the year, Paul drew on developmental discourse: he said, "He just developed emotionally, he's a thousand, thousand times better". Ryan's "hyperactivity", initially seen as an official diagnosis, was now 'solved' and he was removed from the special needs register.

Ryan's changed identity allowed him to be seen as authentic and "clever", but only within a particular discourse of masculine intelligence. Ryan scored the only 9 on the EYFS Profile for a maths scale, and this was entirely intelligible given discourses of boys as good at maths, and the idea of a gifted working-class boy. But, despite these positive shifts, he was never seen as a 'good' all-round learner. This position was not recognisable for a Black boy, and furthermore, Ryan's identity performance (as with Abeje) allowed links to be made with negative discourses of Black aggression. Ryan's height (the tallest in the class) compounded this as he was often seen as too 'physical'. Also, when Ryan was keen to answer questions on the carpet, he tried to answer *every* question and thus while displaying the right kind of enthusiasm, did not display the self-regulating social skills described in the EYFS Profile. This led to him being reprimanded, even though Paul had a great deal of patience with him, as seen in this field note:

The class is on the carpet for an RE lesson about Noah's ark. Ryan answers a lot of questions – he knows about the dove in the story – and the lesson seems to be a conversation between Ryan and Paul. Paul is sympathetic to Ryan's enthusiasm for ages, and then says, "Everybody else has to have a turn; you're shouting out constantly". Some other children answer questions, but then Ryan asks more questions. He also picks up and reads a second Noah's ark book that is lying near him, and asks about that. Paul tolerates this for a while then says, "You're brilliant, but I'm tired!" He sends them off for free play. He asks Ryan what he wants to do, then says, "Everyone else, do what you like". *(Field notes, St Mary's)*

Here we see how, although Ryan was constituted differently from the other Black boys (from whom this behaviour would not be tolerated), it remained entirely recognisable for Ryan to be seen as difficult; there was a constant risk that he might be shifted again to being a 'bad' learner. Unfortunately for Ryan, this more negative perception of him prevailed in the rest of the school, so the durability of this more positive identity was doubtful.

Even though Ryan's home background had opened up some space for him to be seen positively as a learner in Reception, this space could also quickly be closed down. As with Khadija's shift from good to inauthentic learner, Ryan's position as "clever" could be temporary and was certainly more precarious than his original 'bad' learner identity. I would argue that when minoritised children are able to be intelligible as 'good' (or at least not 'bad') learners, these positions are very unstable and fragile; there is a constant threat that they will be returned to more easily recognisable 'bad' learner positions at any time.

Other ways to be a 'bad' learner

Although I have focused here on the Black boys at St Mary's, I am not suggesting that it was only Black children who were recognisable as 'bad' learners, nor only boys. Other minoritised children in these classrooms were constituted as failing to be a 'good' learner through quite different discourses, and they too had some discursive agency. I provide here two brief examples of these alternative negative learner identities.

At St Mary's, Dinesh, a Bangladeshi boy, was constituted as an inadequate learner through discourses of Asian boys as weak, effeminate and lacking in independence. Dinesh was very shy and quiet, probably at least partly due to his limited English, but was described as lacking in confidence because of his overly concerned parents:

> EYFS Profile meeting: Kelly, Paul and Asif (a student teacher) are looking through the observation labels. Asif mentions there isn't much for Dinesh. Kelly reacts by saying, "Oh, bless him!" and they say there isn't much as he hasn't done much. Kelly tells them about seeing Dinesh walking very slowly with his dad, "like precious porcelain". They discuss if this is because he is the only boy in the family, or the first child. Paul tells the others about how Dinesh is scared of PE, and got hit by a bean bag when he was sitting out. Paul explains that he didn't say anything as he was waiting for Dinesh to "express his feelings" (an EYFS Profile point). They laugh because Dinesh didn't say anything. *(Field notes, St Mary's)*

Dinesh is constituted here as failing to demonstrate the social skills described in the EYFS Profile, and this is connected to discourses which position some

Asian boys as overly 'mothered', like the boys in Connolly's (1998) study of infant classrooms; Kelly commented that "they do everything for him". Further evidence of this was provided in the same meeting when Kelly told a story about Dinesh's pencil falling on the floor and him expecting her to pick it up. Thus Dinesh was constituted as failing to become the independent, flexible learner required of the EYFS Profile, which was intelligible within discourses related to Asian boys; at the same time, the effect of the language barriers he faced were ignored. Dinesh's constitution as a 'bad' learner was compounded by the lack of evidence he provided for the Profile by being quiet; Paul decided that Dinesh was unable to do most of the Profile points and he was awarded the lowest score in the class.

At Gatehouse, another boy, Tahir, was constituted negatively as a learner through another set of discourses related to 'race' and class. Tahir came from a Lebanese family, but was constituted through similar discourses as Bethany and Chloe (the two 'undeserving' working-class White girls discussed earlier) as indicated by these field notes from the classroom:

> During the morning register, Tahir sits and does his homework with Susan, the support teacher. He ends up being the first one to hand it in. It is not clear why he is getting special treatment – they seem to assume he won't do it at home. Later that day, Tahir is doing an activity which involves porridge oats. He gets told off for eating the oats. I ask later why he ate them, and Susan tells me that he's probably hungry.

> Before the dance class, Tahir doesn't have any socks on – he is only wearing plimsolls despite the cold. They give Tahir some school socks. One of the teaching assistants says, "We won't get them back!"

> Jim is sorting out some of the children's belongings. He says, "lovely hat" to someone, but then to Tahir he says, "You need new shoes, don't you? You've worn a hole in your shoes".

> At the end of day, the children go to the cloakroom outside to get their bags. Jim says to Tahir, "Tahir, you don't have a bag, you shouldn't be going outside". He is the only one without a bag. *(Field notes, Gatehouse)*

Tahir's lack of possessions, his inadequate footwear and his hunger positioned him as 'needy' and, as with Reece at St Mary's, this led to the teachers predicting the family would steal school clothes. These perceptions of a poor home life were associated by the adults with unacceptable behaviour in the class, such as eating the oats which were supposed to be used for an activity. In Tahir's case, his learner identity was not only affected by perceptions of parents with the wrong 'education ethic', but also by discourses of 'bad migrants' who fail to assimilate into British ways. In failing to provide Tahir with the right shoes, his parents were also positioned as failing to understand the needs of school, as in Lynn's quotes about parental failures in Chapter 4.

Tahir's behaviour was a constant issue in Jim's classroom, with regular reprimands for not sitting still, calling out and fiddling with things. The way in which he was reprimanded often sought to isolate him from the other children, by emphasising how differently they behaved; the teachers made comments such as "no one else is calling out" and "we're all waiting for Tahir". Like the sticker charts at St Mary's, these dividing practices worked to solidify Tahir's identity as a 'bad' learner. This identity was entirely intelligible, I would argue, given Tahir's intersectional identity and the way in which his home life was understood.

Discussion: Who is recognisable as a 'good learner'?

In this and the previous chapter I have argued that in these Reception classrooms, the idea of what a 'good' learner looks like and the association of these attributes with White middle-class (and to some extent, female) identities works to distance almost all of the children from positions of educational success; but, at the same time, some children are still recognisable as 'good' learners within the web of discourses associated with their intersectional identities. In this concluding section of the chapter, I want to emphasise how I see these findings as adding to our understanding of classroom practices that discriminate.

This exploration of who is recognisable as a 'good' learner has attempted to examine the complex ways in which it is possible for some children to be constituted as successful in the classroom, while for others this is almost impossible. I have attempted to map the ways in which the extent of the intelligible space open to different children varies, and how moving outside recognisability can lead to shifts in a child's learner identity or them being remade as inauthentic. These findings show that there cannot be set rules for how children are understood in terms of their learner identities, as there is always room for discursive agency. However, we can identify some key themes which have arisen from this data. These points build on my argument in Chapter 4 that girls are more intelligible as 'good' learners in Reception, because discourses of girls as hard-working and compliant and as all-rounders are valued in the EYFS Profile.

A first point is that all learner identities are precarious, and this is particularly the case for minoritised pupils who are seen as successful. There is the constant risk that minoritised children's successes may be dismissed as inauthentic, or rendered completely unintelligible. Second, there is quite different intelligible space open for minoritised girls from that boys: for the Muslim Afghan girls discussed in this chapter, their gender was key to them being recognisable as successful. Similarly, the Black boys at St Mary's were understood through specifically gendered discourses of Black behaviour and single parenthood. Thus I would argue that the intersection of gender and 'race' is particularly powerful in constituting these children as successful or not. Third, for White children, class was a key issue, but operated in complex ways: there was a generally positive association of Whiteness and middle-classness and there were recognisable White working-class female 'good' learners, but White children too could be constituted as lacking the appropriate 'education ethic' if they were seen as the 'wrong type' of working class. Finally, the data from these schools suggest that some children, such as Black boys and Bangladeshi boys, are most recognisable as 'bad' learners, and any move beyond this identity is only possible with a significant shift in how their identity is understood.

The implications of this argument are, in many ways, pessimistic in terms of inequalities in early years education. I argue that only a small number of children from minoritised groups and working-class families can approximate 'good' learner identities, and it is important to remember that this may only be possible in these classrooms where there are no White middle-class pupils. Even when success is recognised, it is fragile and can easily be dismissed as inauthentic. But, the case of Ryan also provides an example of how disruptions in how a child is understood can open up small spaces for him to be recognisable as succeeding, at least in some parts of learning. As Youdell argues, with a performative politics there is the possibility of *re*signification or *re*inscription – this is 'not simply a doing again, but a reversal or a doing again *differently*' (Youdell, 2006b: 49–50, *emphasis in original*). There is the potential for interruptive work that seeks to introduce different discourses into the web, and perhaps widen the intelligible space open to these children. I return to these questions in the concluding chapter.

6

PLAYING WITH NUMBERS

Learner identities and assessment

Introduction

This chapter considers how the EYFS Profile results are produced in ways which are intelligible within the contexts of the study schools and the policy requirements.[1] The EYFS Profile functions in these classrooms in particular ways, and this has an impact on how the final results are decided by the teachers. Following this, a second stage of 'moderation' may occur, during which the Local Authority (LA) has an influence. There is also pressure from the school management, particularly in relation to the need for EYFS Profile results to provide a baseline figure for children's attainment as they progress through the school. These twin pressures can result, as I discuss in relation to the data collected at Gatehouse, in Reception teachers 'playing with numbers'; that is, changing their results to make them both acceptable, in terms of other patterns of attainment, and intelligible, in terms of discourses of inner city 'underachievement'.

How EYFS Profile results are produced: fabrications and performativity

The final results reported to the Local Authority were produced through a process which was influenced at many levels and constrained by a number of forces, at classroom, local and national level. The EYFS Profile results can be conceptualised as 'fabrications', in that they are performances created for the purpose of accountability:

> Fabrications conceal as much as they reveal. They are ways of measuring oneself within particular registers of meaning, within a particular economy of meaning in which only certain possibilities of being have value. However,

such fabrications are deeply paradoxical [...] Fabrications are both resistance *and* capitulation. They are a betrayal even, a giving up of claims to authenticity and commitment, an investment in plasticity. *(Ball, 2003b: 225, emphasis in original)*

In these schools, both the final results (the 'fabrication') and the performative practices which produce them (the 'cynical compliance' discussed below) are regulated by discourses of attainment gaps, deprived communities and 'underachievement', which render some results intelligible and some not. Just as identity performances need to be intelligible in order for recognition to be conferred, these results must comply with circulating discourses in order to be accepted as 'accurate'. The final results are not a neutral, scientific process of assessment, but a fabrication, a produced set of numbers which sets particular children on trajectories of educational success, and all but forecloses this possibility for others. Thus the process of producing final results and adapting them works to reproduce inequalities in early years education.

Classroom practices of 'cynical compliance'

Any discussion of how the final EYFS Profile results are decided must be framed by some examination of how the Profile functions in the classroom throughout the year, and concomitant pressures on the teachers involved. The Profile includes 117 points across the 13 different scales, which are awarded or not awarded at the end of the academic year. Teachers are advised to base these decisions on what they have observed through the year and the evidence they have collected in EYFS Profile folders. As discussed previously, the teachers described the Profile as inappropriate because it was too lengthy and the points were vague, and were frustrated by the time-consuming nature of the assessment. They engaged in a discourse of 'teacher knowledge' as neutral and factual, and yet saw the Profile as an inaccurate vehicle for this 'knowledge' to be recorded. These tensions and contradictions are indicative of the complex processes of renegotiation that occur when policy is translated into reality in the classroom; what Apple terms, the 'recontextualisation' of policy 'at every stage of the process' (Apple, 2006: 71; see also Ball, Maguire and Braun, 2012). This disenchantment with the EYFS Profile led to a range of practices in the classroom which, I would argue, are examples of what Ball called 'cynical compliance' when discussing the performance required by school inspections:

What is produced is a spectacle, game-playing, or cynical compliance, or what one might see as "enacted fantasy" (Butler, 1990), which is there simply to be seen and judged. *(Ball, 2003b: 223)*

These practices were in keeping with the rules of the EYFS Profile requirements, but also showed the teachers' ambivalence towards it. At both schools, there was an approach of resignation towards the requirements, a 'we've got to do it' attitude: at Gatehouse, Jim commented that he needed to get observations in the folders because "we need to show that we're doing work". The frustration felt at this specific practice of collecting observations, and the resulting impact on the comparative time spent teaching and collecting observations of the impact of this teaching, reflects Lyotard's 'law of contradiction' (1983 in Ball, 2003b): Ball explains:

> This contradiction arises between intensification – as an increase in the volume of first order activities (direct engagement with students, research, curriculum development) required by the demands of performativity – and the 'costs' in terms of time and energy of second order activities that is the work of performance monitoring and management. *(Ball, 2003b: 221)*

Providing activities meant producing observations, which then had to be filed, thus reducing the amount of time available for planning and preparing new activities. This contradiction led to one example of cynical compliance – the tactical selection of which observations to file. At St Mary's, Paul was aware that some of the folders might be checked by the Local Authority at the end of the year as part of the 'moderation' of results, so he decided to focus on only six children, based on the idea that the LA would request "two high, two middle, two low". This practice was justified by the fact that, as he explained to a teaching assistant in their meeting, "We know where the other children are at, 'cause we're observing them all the time". Thus the idea of 'teacher knowledge' could be deployed to justify practices of cynical compliance. Later in the year, when Paul found out he was not being moderated by the LA, he continued to observe, but explained, "We're not being moderated, so we don't need to worry about sticking everything in". The Profile folders became 'there simply to be seen and judged' (Ball, 2003b: 221), not used by the teacher for any other purpose.

This is not to say, however, that the EYFS Profile had a limited effect on these classrooms: it was a constant presence, in the form of observations being written, photographs being taken, and tick sheets for activities. It also affected planning, which was often based on Profile points; as Jim commented, "How can we teach it if it's not a target?". Hundreds of observations were written and stuck into folders over the course of the year and all of the adults in both classrooms were involved in the process. For some teachers, the performative need to comply with regulations became their entire role; the 'enacted fantasy' (Butler, 1990) had become real. Susan (the support teacher at Gatehouse), who was still collecting observations after the final results had been submitted to the LA, explained, "If I didn't do it I wouldn't feel like I was doing my job". The process of recording learning had become the focus, for this teacher. As I have argued elsewhere (Bradbury, 2012), the pressures of the EYFS Profile led to teachers constructing their roles as enablers and recorders rather than teachers, providers of learning 'opportunities' which the children could take up if they chose. This was evident in Lynn's comment that, if the children get low Profile scores, "you're failing them in that you're not providing an appropriate situation for them". These ideas were tied in with the construction of the child as having individual responsibility for their own learning, but were also legitimised by development discourse, which suggests that the 'natural' process of development will happen inevitably and all the teacher can do is provide the space for it to happen.

The impact of the EYFS Profile on classroom practices can be understood as two processes running in parallel: first, a process of producing evidence which exists only to be checked, and second, a process of gathering 'knowledge' which will eventually be used to score the children. Within these, 'teacher knowledge' always had precedence over observations in terms of perceived legitimacy. Both of these processes are necessary for the teacher to appear and feel professional, but they do not necessarily need to interact, unless the LA moderator relates the folder to the EYFS Profile scores. It is only at this point (and for only six children in the class), that these two parallel processes need to converge. Nonetheless, these processes did, of course, feed into each other through the year (for example, the 'knowledge' collecting process feeds into the folder production by determining what is included). But they were not regarded as one and the same; the performance required involved two different processes, running along in parallel in order to be checked at key points.

Producing final results: 'teacher knowledge'

The production of results that are intelligible within the discursive terrain of these schools began with the teacher's 'knowledge' of the child, which (as we have seen in Chapters 3 and 5) is far from neutral. This understanding of the child as a learner, which is informed by discourses relating to their intersectional identity and their identity performance, was used by the teachers to make decisions about which EYFS Profile points to award to which children. At times, teachers described this knowledge as entirely adequate for this task: Jim commented, "Sometimes you don't need to look at the folder – you know or you don't know if the child has achieved that, just from your own brain". During one meeting at St Mary's, Paul realised the data had gone missing for one child on one scale, and he and a teaching assistant simply filled it in without reference to the child's folder or other evidence. This process was made simpler by their view that, as the TA commented before they began, "It won't be much", meaning the child would not be awarded many points. Even when folders of evidence were used (bearing in mind only what correlates to the teacher's 'knowledge' was included anyway), this was only in conjunction with what was already 'known'.

At other times, however, the teachers attempted to resist the idea of the EYFS Profile as accurate, and rendered the entire system dubious; this revealed the extent to which the teachers regarded the process as a performance and fabrication. When asked how confident he felt about his assessments, Jim commented:

"I don't feel confident about that, and I never have done. And I've always thought that when I was filling out their Foundation Stage Profiles at the end, that it's always just a best fit, it always has been. It's just there's no way you can quantify everything that they've said and done throughout the whole year and give them a tick for it. It's impossible. It's a way to make people do their job and do it properly". *(Jim, Gatehouse)*

This acknowledgement that teacher knowledge is inadequate and the results are "just a best fit", ties in with Jim's other criticisms of the assessment. The teachers' belief in the system as objective was only ever partial – Jim also commented that grades "depend on your mood when I'm marking", for instance. Nonetheless, this idea of teacher knowledge as objective remained powerful within these classrooms, as a means of providing status perhaps, and to justify the huge amount of effort involved in producing EYFS Profile results.

Further contradictions were evident in the teachers' descriptions of how they ranked and checked the children's EYFS Profile results. The teachers drew upon their 'knowledge' to determine whether their individual assessments were 'right' when children were compared against each other. This process of confir-mation worked as a second check of intelligibility, following the first check if the individual scores were recognisable in relation to the child's learner identity. At Gatehouse, Jim put the children into rank order by score, to see if there were any "glaring inaccuracies" in his own assessments. This practice was based on the idea that Jim has an accurate overall picture of the children in his class as compared to each other; he is able to find the "glaring inaccuracies" because he knows how high or low each child should score, and this overrides the decisions made through the painstaking process of going through each point in turn and ticking yes or no. Thus he is able to deem his own decisions as inaccuracies if they do not fit his overall model of the class. This model is perhaps informed by ideas of tripartite 'ability' groups and also a normal distribution (a bell curve): Jim commented on another occasion, "They want us to fit into a bell curve, that's all it is. You know – a few low, a few middle and a few high". At St Mary's, Paul used other methods to check that results were recognisable, including colour-coding high, middle and low scores. He commented that these aided his checking because "These [low scoring children] jump out at you". However, he also explained that 'reviewing' results sometimes only proved his 'teacher knowledge':

"There might be a number and I think, 'Shit!' [surprised voice] and I look at the point, the profile point, and I have to rethink. Oh yeah, I mean I've reviewed it definitely before the final data. I'll scan; I'll go through it and think, 'Shit, why is that 6? That kid, why is that 6?' And then I'll look at it again and think, 'Oh yeah, they can't do that.' […] I've never been asked a question that I didn't have that for". *(Paul, St Mary's)*

Thus, as with many of their practices, the teachers engaged in an alternative discourse where they dismissed the idea of changing any figures: as Jim put it, "They get what they get". When Jim was asked if he thought any children were in the wrong place, he commented, "No, there weren't and that's actually – it's really nice", seeing this as a confirmation of his 'knowledge'. Therefore, despite their doubts about accuracy and these checking processes, the results were eventually constructed as neutral and objective. Paul went further in criticising teachers who try to grade children based on simple categories:

> "I mean, to me, there's absolutely no point in saying, 'This is a child who we clearly know is nursery level in most things, make sure he's only got 3, 4. Whereas this child is, like, an average child, he should be getting 6, 7. Whereas this is a sort of exceptional child, he should be getting ...'. You know the sort of high/low/medium group, and then expect them accordingly to be getting 6 ... My feeling is that a statement is a statement; the Profile points, although vague, there's exemplification, now available, which we've now got". *(Paul, St Mary's)*

Paul's contradictory position dismisses his role as a subjective assessor; he argues that exemplification means that there is no need for simple allocations of points based on top, middle or bottom assessments. Both teachers appear to deny their roles as arbiters of accuracy (at least at this point) in favour of a construction of the EYFS Profile as accurate. This is critical in the operation of the Profile as an assessment: even when there are doubts, discourses of accuracy can be deployed which constitute these results as definite. This matters hugely if those grades deem a child to be definitively below a 'good level of development'.

Producing final results: the need for intelligible and acceptable scores

Although there was a need for the final EYFS Profile results to be recognisable in terms of individual learner identities, the need to produce intelligible results operated at another level over and above the teachers' decisions about which points to award to which children. The influence of the school management and LA superseded the 'knowledge' of the teachers, as they operated as the final arbiters of what was accurate. At this moment, 'teacher knowledge' was delegitimised in favour of the LA advisors and school management, who fulfilled this regulatory function both informally and formally. The formal process was conducted through 'moderation' across schools, but results could also be influenced through informal chats with teachers. Throughout these processes, the LA's role in deciding what was accurate was not questioned. This flexibility over the idea of correct results, whereby 'accurate' means that which is intelligible in that particular context, derives at least in part from national policy documents regarding the EYFS Profile particularly in the years immediately after its introduction as the Foundation Stage Profile. In these years, when the FSP data was published by the Department for Education and Skills (DES), the statistics would come with this caveat:

> *The results should be treated with caution as this is the first year that such data have been collected.* The data result from a new statutory assessment for which teachers have received limited and variable training and the moderation of results within and between local education authorities (LEAs) has been patchy. Therefore, there is less confidence in the quality of the assessments and the consistency between teachers, schools/settings, and LEAs. In addition, we know *some* of the data to be of poor quality and completeness, although we are satisfied that these do not affect the results significantly at a national level. *(DES, 2004: 1, emphasis in original)*

Implicit in this statement is the idea that teachers need to learn to assess properly, and that the local authorities or national government can ultimately define what accurate assessment is (and what is 'poor quality') and recognise it when the teachers produce it. This idea turns the idea of accuracy on its head, by defining it as something which can only be recognised after the results have been produced, not something which can be ensured through the careful application of fair practices (as in scientific discourse, for example). This flexible definition of 'accuracy' allows the government department to decide when the teachers have got it right, and therefore which sets of results should be taken as indicative of children's progress. In the evidence below, we see how this idea is transferred to the Local Authority, which defines what the accurate set of results for the Reception class at Gatehouse should look like. This definition is based on powerful discourses in education which prescribe what constitutes intelligible results in an inner city school and, in the process, exclude many children from educational success.

An additional pressure operated alongside the need to make results intelligible for an inner city school: the need to produce results which were advantageous in terms of 'value added' scores. These are a measure whereby a school is judged on the progress made between two tests several years apart; it aims to judge the 'value' added by the school during the children's time there. Although there are no official measurements of value added scores based on the difference between the EYFS Profile and the Key Stage 1 Sats tests (two years later), the data suggests that this has not prevented schools (and possibly LAs) from beginning to apply value added principles and calculations to EYFS Profile results, and indeed to relate the Profile scores to Key Stage 2 results. This practice is also indicated by the adoption in many schools of assessment software which tracks children's progress in several tests as they move through primary school. At both schools here, and particularly at Gatehouse, the dual pressures of producing intelligible results for a 'difficult intake' and value added measures had major effects on the final EYFS Profile scores.

The moderation process

All of the teachers commented regularly on the pressure they felt from the LA, and within these comments, it was clear that the teachers did not hold the LA advisors in high regard and often found their advice to be confusing or inappropriate. Nonetheless, they felt they needed to comply with the LA's demands, particularly with regard to 'moderation'. This practice is explained by the EYFS Profile handbook:

> Moderation activities within the context of the EYFS profile involve professional dialogue to ensure practitioner judgements are based on assessments of children consistent with nationally agreed exemplification and that attainment of individual scale points is a reliable, accurate and secure process. The moderation process is a supportive one, designed to develop practitioners' confidence in their approaches to assessment and their understanding of the EYFS profile. *(QCA, 2008)*

Moderation in these schools took the form, as mentioned, of giving a number of folders to the LA advisors, who would assess them against the final scores and perhaps come in and assess the children as well. Thus moderation was seen by the teachers as an assessment of their ability to score children accurately. However, the advice given was described as being conflicting; for example, Jim commented, "We were told that, like, a score of 4 was an average score. The following year … we were told 6 is a good score". He also commented:

> "I was moderated, which was a total farce. They told me [each year] that I'd been marking too high, then too low and then too high, and that basically I need to make sure I mark the children a certain way. And I was, like, well, you know, I can't mark them a certain way; they come out with what they get". *(Jim, Gatehouse)*

Significantly, the advice appeared to be based on the school's intake; the moderation process seemed to be informed by discourses of inner city schools similar to those expressed by the teachers. Jim explained why his marks had been "too high" in the past in this section of interview:

> Jim: [Our scores] were "too high", they were way above the national average. And because the school is in an EEZ, or education action …
>
> AB: An EAZ? [Education Action Zone]
>
> Jim: Yes, we shouldn't be that high, because we're achieving really high, so, by the time they've got to Year 6 they've gone down, and what are we doing wrong? *(Interview with Jim, Gatehouse)*

Jim's comments suggest that, in the past, he has been told directly to keep his results low because of the intake of the school. Here we see how the idea of teacher knowledge and the careful observation of children to assess each point is superseded by pressure to keep overall results lower. Education Action Zones were areas designated as needing additional funding due to poor educational results through a New Labour policy. Jim's comments suggest that it is easy for labels such as 'EAZ' and their class and 'race' associations to be collapsed into 'low attaining'. The LA's definition of what is accurate is informed by raced and classed discourses of the inner city which view 'challenging' areas as incommensurate with educational success. Jim was critical of this association, despite the operation of a very similar discourse within his classroom: he was clear that this advice was not a one-off, and fully expected it to be the case in the future:

"I'm sure it'll be exactly the same. It's all because, you know, we're in, shouldn't really, we're in an EAZ, underprivileged children – [cynically] there should be no chance of them getting 9s".

Although Jim is critical here (and in other comments where he made clear that he felt the low expectations of his class were unfair), the similarity of the discourses allegedly used by the LA to those used by Gatehouse teachers suggest that the link between the 'difficult intake' and low results works powerfully to remove the possibility of educational success for these children. Although the LA may talk in terms of EAZs and "too high" marks, there are clear commonalities with the comments relating to parents who do not look after their children or take them to the park, or when the school was compared to a "White middle-class primary school in the middle of England". Nevertheless, these comments do remind us of the power of policy decisions to define who is likely to fail and who to succeed. As mentioned, the EYFS Profile booklet lists ethnic minorities as a group with particular needs, alongside boys and SEN pupils. At a wider level, policies such as Educational Action Zones and, more recently, London Challenge schools might aim to weaken the link between deprivation and educational underattainment through 'intervention', but simultaneously have the effect of solidifying this association in that area or that school. This raises serious questions about the long-term effects of social policies, which I return to in the concluding chapter.

The policy-legitimised idea that teachers can get assessment 'wrong' has an impact on the teachers' ambivalence about the EYFS Profile and their ability to decide accurately on Profile points. This quote from Lynn reveals the frustration felt following the LA moderation process; I had asked her if she felt under pressure to produce particular scores:

"I mean, look, you're human – obviously if someone keeps saying to you, 'Oh that's not right, no, that's not right, that's not right. I don't want you to mark them into a curve, I don't want you to fit them into a pigeon hole, I want you to mark them how you think you mark them' and then you get told off for that, then you think – and you do get to the point where you think I'm just going to fill this out – 'What do you think I should write, so that you will stop bothering me please?'" *(Lynn, Gatehouse)*

Here Lynn describes the LA's advice as contradictory and critical; asking the teachers not to mark into a curve and then telling them they are wrong when they do not. Her frustration with the EYFS Profile system and the LA is evident, and this frustration leads, she suggests, to teachers completing the Profile in ways that will discourage the LA from criticising them. This shows the regulatory function of the LA, who define what is accurate, but also blur the requirements of accurate assessment (while emphasising its importance) to such an extent that Lynn feels she just wants them to stop "bothering" her. Paul made similar comments about how other teachers complete the EYFS Profile:

"[With] the Profiles, you can make up any number and they're not going to bloody know. They do come and moderate every two or three years, whatever it is, and you show them three samples ... and they check that you're making the correct assumptions. Well, my experience is that most people just go and say, 'Right, what do we have to write to make them that level?' They know the child is at a different level, but then they just go ahead and make up the points. [LA] say the average child would be expected to get up to 6, the lower child would be expected to get no more than 3, and the sort of super-duper child who should be in Year 1 by now will get, you know, 7, 8 and at absolute most 9. They tell you *[agitated]*, so all you have to do is decide which child, where it fits in, through your year's experience, and give them a number! That's what people clearly do *[quieter]*, sometimes. And it's just crap". *(Paul, Gatehouse)*

Here, Paul suggests first that the limited sampling involved in moderation encourages teachers to write whatever is necessary to ensure the child really is the level they say they are; and secondly, that the LA advice on what low, middle and "super-duper" children will get also encourages teachers to decide on which category and "give them a number".

In these quotes, we see how the ambiguity of the policy can be used to justify the fabrication; if the system provided is impossible and the teachers are always wrong, there is no reason to try to provide accurate results. Issues of professionalism, pride and pressure contribute to this fabrication and the teachers' obfuscation of the issue of accuracy. Before I consider further how discourses of low attainment affect results, I consider the role of national policy in the form of value added results in more detail.

The impact of national policy

National policy relating to value added scores provided a second pressure and constraint during the production of the final EYFS Profile results. At St Mary's, Paul made comments which suggested that other teachers produced results in ways which were affected by value added scores. He commented in relation to teachers who produce results which are not based on evidence:

> "With value added, if you've got a bunch of children who are really developmentally very behind, and you're telling everybody that they're normal – [correcting self] that their kind of expectation would be a normal expectation, you're really setting up for massive failure, for the kids. So personally, I think it's stupid". (Paul, St Mary's)

These comments demonstrate how value added systems serve to further regulate what results are deemed acceptable, and how the school is encouraged by these performative technologies to engage in tactical assessment practices (Stobart, 2008). Value added scores are included in league tables for primary and secondary schools and this principle of measuring 'progress' over several years appears to be spreading in education. As I have argued elsewhere (Bradbury, 2011a), the inclusion of 'contextual' data in these scores sanctions low expectations for particular ethnic groups, pupils receiving Free School Meals, and boys. At both schools, the teachers mentioned the need to keep results lower in order not to make life difficult in later years. These comments often ignored the fact that value added scores have little meaning (and are never published) at an individual level – they only have significance in terms of judging a school. Thus Paul's comment that it will be "a massive failure, for the kids" perhaps obscures the real impact, which is on the school. Both class teachers were also critical of practices associated with value added scores. Paul commented that using these scores was "completely wrong, 'cause what they're assessing there is not national-curriculum-level-type predictable". At Gatehouse, Jim also thought it inappropriate to use the results of the EYFS Profile and Key Stage 1 Sats together, saying:

> "It's not the same, so I don't know why they're using the figures and [hand action of comparing two points]. It's just ridiculous ... I mean there are similarities – it's in a school, it's a document, but you know, it would totally skew it". (Jim, Gatehouse)

The issue of value added scores was important in both schools as a factor which determined what results were acceptable and even desirable. (Jim's comments below reveal the role of these scores in the production of the results at Gatehouse.) One of the functions of value added scores, and particularly contextual value added (CVA) is to recognise the achievements of schools with lower overall attainment through a focus on 'progress'. With contextual scores, this progress is calculated within a statistical framework which expects slower progress for children from some minorities, those on FSM and from more deprived areas (Bradbury 2011a), and boys; as such, CVA has often been presented as a mechanism which is 'fairer' to schools in deprived areas with high proportions of pupils receiving FSM and minoritised pupils. These schools' positions in local league tables, importantly, are likely to be far higher when ranked by CVA than by raw scores. Therefore, value added measures are particularly important to schools like Gatehouse and St Mary's; they provide a chance to demonstrate the quality of the school in the light of 'contextual' issues.

It would seem from the comments made about value added that the importance of these scores means that they function as a powerful but complex regulatory mechanism. The school management and LA find desirable results that are low enough to show that children make progress as they move through the school; there is an incentive to mark low. Combined with the pressure to deflate results that are deemed "too high" for a deprived area, value added scores work powerfully to ensure that EYFS Profile results at these schools remain below national averages. However, these scores remain one of several different ways of judging a school; just one disciplinary technology in the accountability system. There is always a danger for low-attaining schools that they will not be judged on value added, and so lowering scores may be self-defeating. The ambiguity of the relative importance of different measures was shown in 2008 when the government used raw GCSE percentage scores to define 638 schools as 'failing', whatever their CVA scores (BBC News, 2008), an apparent reversal of previous policy which had prioritised progress and improvement over percentage figures. The introduction of additional measures of success such as the 'English Baccalaureate' since the election of the coalition government in 2010 have furthered this trend of unpredictability. CVA itself has also been removed from league tables. In this policy context, the 'fairer' measure, presented as a positive step to low-attaining schools, can also be taken away without warning. As Ball explains, in a performative system, 'constant doubts about which judgements may be in play at any one point mean that any and all comparisons and requirements to perform have to be attended to' (2003b: 220). At Gatehouse and St Mary's, the concern over value added in the Early Years Foundation Stage, where it is not even officially used, suggests the power of this disciplinary technology to regulate results in all areas; confusion allows the regulation to spread beyond its original remit.

Playing with numbers, changing the results

As we have seen, the production of final EYFS Profile results was subject to competing demands in order to be intelligible and acceptable: the need to fit to some extent with 'teacher knowledge', the need to be low enough not to skew value added scores, and the need to be recognisable within circulating discourses about inner city pupils and educational attainment. As discussed, at Gatehouse, Jim had felt under pressure in previous years to produce the 'correct' results, as defined by the LA. He was concerned to avoid being told he had marked "too high" again. He commented in September that:

"What blatantly came out from the thing [moderation] last year, you know, was that the children can't, they really should not be scoring that high, according to the government figures".

This suggested that he felt limited in what scores he could possibly give the children by the LA's insistence that they "can't" and "should not" be getting these scores – a clear definition by the LA of what they deemed intelligible, which is backed up by "government figures". During the year I spent at the school, Jim speculated with some pessimism about what would happen when he calculated that year's results. I observed the production of the results and all seemed to be going smoothly; however, in my final interview with Jim, he explained the more complex process of producing the final results and the influence of the school management. The complexity of this issue requires quoting this interview extract at length:

Jim: So, basically [bit awkward], Liz had a couple of days off with a bit of illness, and hadn't got her reports sorted. So [the head] gave me a day and got some cover in and I went off and looked through her reports [...] Printed them off, got rid of spelling mistakes [laughing] and had to change some of her results. And we had the early years specialist in 'cause when I – I put them all into my own table as they were. Divided it by 56 and came out with a 78.5 which made the class half a per cent, made the *school*, sorry, half a per cent above the kind of required mark, of 78. And [guiltily], although I was not told to change any of the figures, the question arose as to how a school with a very difficult intake could achieve half a per cent like average, how could it be average? And it also would then skew the [...] Key Stage 1 Sats results which had come out just below average. Which would show, if you were to chart it on a graph [cynically], would show that the children haven't achieved, well, have gone backwards from the end of Foundation to the end of Year 2. So therefore [laughing], stuff was changed.

AB: Because it was thought they were too generous, it was just too –?

Jim: Yeah, so anyhow, I prioritised Liz's – I looked at Liz's results 'cause I had to.

AB: And also, she hasn't done it before, so, it's –

Jim: Yep. So, basically, I had all of the children, I put them all in a list, from top to bottom, and I picked out the ones that looked in the wrong place. And then had a closer look. I noticed that Liz had marked quite a lot of children as achieving I think point 7 in the third section of maths, which is about shape, space and measure 7, which is something to do with uses of mathematical language such as 'larger', 'greater', 'smaller', and she ticked quite a lot of children as achieving that. But the children who had achieved that hadn't achieved point 6 and 5 and 4, and so. Now, this has been a big push for her this year, mathematical vocabulary.

AB: Yes, it was a whole school thing.

Jim: Yes, and she's really pushed it in her maths lessons. But I think, and I'm quite confident in the fact that I took it away from the majority of her class – I don't think I gave it to very many children in my class. They're perfectly capable of being able to copy the words in lessons and being able to use the words in lessons, but they don't use it independently, and because they don't use it independently … Well, it's a bit cheeky, 'cause I'd be upset if another teacher came and crossed off loads of my results, but … I would have left it, personally, but, because of the conversation I'd had about the average marks, I had to kind of revisit …

AB: And that was one that's more kind of –

Jim: That was one that is actually very difficult to get – I don't know many children who use 'greater', specifically 'greater', 'larger', 'smaller', so I knocked those off. And at the end of it, because I knocked it off for most of the lower-ability children, that took the average up, because the lower went further down but the higher didn't move. So the overall average went up by another half per cent after I spent two hours on it. I gave up; I wasn't going to change it any more.

AB: So you just decided?

Jim: I think it's actually – what I think, I didn't take away stuff that wasn't fair to take away.

AB: Right. You took away the stuff that was …

Jim: That I thought was a bit overly generous. Things like Yuhannis *[with incredulity]* being able to use 'greater' and 'smaller' – in a lesson fair enough with a bit of prompting, but I don't think independently.

AB: So you could say it's inexperience, or ambiguity?

Jim: I actually think Liz's done incredibly well this year. And I think, actually, I don't think we do a bad job. I don't know what other schools are like, and this is the issue. We don't know what kind of other scores, other schools are like. We have about – we have a fair few 9s, across the board. *(Interview with Jim, Gatehouse)*

Jim explains here how he was either told, or felt under a great deal of pressure, to lower some of the children's marks because the overall percentage of the class was too close to the government's benchmark of 78 (one of the criteria for a 'good level of development'). As he had described about previous years, his marks were "too high" for the kind of school that Gatehouse is; they are unintelligible within the discourses of 'race', class and deprivation present in the inner city. A further consideration was that the school's low Key Stage 1 results (though obviously for a different group of children) would look even worse if the EYFS Profile results were good, or even just average – this is the power of value added to function as a performative technology, often in illogical ways. Jim's concern is not to boost his results to make the school look better, but to lower them in order to fit the LA's perception of the school as "challenging", and to make sure the school's 'value added' scores do not look like the children are going "backwards". The non-sensical nature of this value added theory is perhaps obscured by a view of the local population as homogenous.

We see here how these two elements – value added scores and the 'difficult intake' discourse – work together to ensure that the school has a vested interest in keeping marks low *and* has a ready-made justification. It is acceptable for the Reception children to do badly because they are still so influenced by their homes and backgrounds, so it can be argued that the school has not had a chance to 'add value' yet. This playing with numbers, a deflation of the EYFS Profile scores, will only make the school look better in the long run, *and* it makes sense as the only intelligible set of results given the dominant discourses around poverty, 'race' and the local area. Despite the school-wide focus on a particular area of maths, Jim removes the marks from this very area; success is regulated away, even in the subject area that has been specifically targeted.

The removal of marks, which appears logical and even sensible in Jim's explanation, plays out in complex ways, as shown by the removal of marks from the "lower-ability" children. This reveals the relative difference in value of the children in the class: these children, already assessed as "low", are expendable within the system – it does not seem to matter so much if they lose a few marks. Jim does not take a point away from *everyone*, thereby keeping the same pattern of attainment but lowering overall scores; instead his tactic increases the spread of results in the class, distancing the 'low ability' even further from the 'high ability'. This is, perhaps, informed by the need to produce a normal distribution of scores: removing these marks will just produce a longer tail end to the bell curve without flattening it out. But the effects are not just statistical; these children, already given low scores, are further disadvantaged by a system in which they are unimportant as individuals. They will arrive in Year 1 with an EYFS Profile assessment which states that they cannot use this mathematical language, despite their teacher observing that they can; they are victims of the external definition of what can be 'correct'. Furthermore, this will not seem incongruous, given the strength of the 'difficult intake' discourse. This process of lowering 'low-ability' children's scores can be seen as the beginning of a process which maintains a spread of results: research in secondary schools has suggested that processes of setting and tiered exam entry repeatedly disadvantage certain groups of pupils (Gillborn and Youdell, 2000; Tikly et al., 2006).

In the interview extract above, we see how Jim relates the production of his marks to other schools' systems. His comment, "I don't know what other schools are like, and this is the issue" shows the wider pressure to produce intelligible results, not just for the LA, but in terms of comparisons with other schools. Jim knows that his school cannot intelligibly score higher than schools in more affluent areas and so is worried that they have too many 9s. The implication of this is not that he might have accurately assessed the children (whom he himself described as "very intelligent") and they did very well, but that he might have done it 'wrong'. Here, the teachers' complex positions as professionals contribute to the production of results: they feel simultaneously trusted to get the right results by the 'teacher knowledge' discourse, but this can be taken away in a moment by the LA. The fear for Jim is that the other schools will make his results look unintelligible, but without access to this information, he is left guessing what will be seen as realistic. This mirrors Ball's description of the uncertainty inherent in many accountability systems, which leave us 'ontologically insecure', 'unsure about whether we are doing enough, doing the right thing, doing as much as others' (Ball, 2003b: 220).

The situation at Gatehouse reveals the intricate balancing acts involved in transforming early years into an 'auditable commodity' (Shore and Wright, 1999 in Ball, 2003b), and the necessity of engaging in 'fabrications' (Ball, 2003b). In submitting to the school management's concerns to change the results, Jim is engaging in 'both resistance *and* capitulation' (Ball, 2003b: 225, emphasis in original). On the one hand, the deliberate changing of results is a resistance to the detailed, year-long build-up of 'knowledge' prescribed by the EYFS Profile; it shows he can assess without collecting information into folders, and that he is prepared to cynically produce results which he understands to be inaccurate (though he attempts to deflect this) and therefore undermine the principles of teacher assessment. However, changing the results is also capitulation; there is no doubt that he will produce the results, and that they will be as acceptable as he can manage given the ambiguity of what is 'accurate'. He does give up what Ball calls 'claims to authenticity and commitment' (2003b: 225) by changing the results, although the perception of the EYFS Profile in general as inaccurate and impossible underpins this as it renders the authenticity of the Profile doubtful from the start.

Jim's decision to remove marks from some pupils reveals his investment in a fabrication, but by arguing this I do not mean to apportion individual blame. It is clear, given the data in this and previous chapters, that Jim was severely limited in his capacity to resist the pressure to produce a fabrication. Having been told in previous years that his assessments were 'wrong' because they were too high or low, Jim is familiar with the ways in which his assessments can be deemed incorrect on the basis of the "difficult intake". His comments throughout have suggested that he is resigned to the need to "produce a figure", and although he might at times mobilise other discourses to challenge the EYFS Profile processes, in his words, "I still have to do it". Later in the interview, he commented that despite the changes, "They'll probably say something like they're too high", suggesting he feels that, whatever results he produces, he will be criticised. Within his professional context, Jim is unable to resist the need for a fabrication due to the pressures of the LA and school management; he is constrained by local and national discourses which define how well pupils can do so that the results remain intelligible. However, he is not willing to admit to this capitulation: his claim that "I didn't take away stuff that wasn't fair to take away" can be seen as an attempt to justify a process which he knows to be controversial. It is also, perhaps, an attempt to deny the extent to which he is constrained by local and national pressures when producing the Profile results. His willingness to tell me about changing the results at the beginning of our final interview, when he could have simply avoided the issue, suggests he has serious misgivings about the practice, however he presents it later; as such, this very act of telling a researcher how results are changed can be seen as a form of resistance against the dominant discourses in education.

We see in the example of Gatehouse how the need to produce acceptable and intelligible results is a powerful determinant of the scores that are allocated; however, it also shows how performative technologies require constant work and maintenance. The 'enacted fantasy' (Butler, 1990) does not happen in one moment, but must be built up and performed throughout the year, in the production of folders of evidence and through continual observation. The fictive accuracy of the EYFS Profile must be resignified though the regular collection of data and the allocation of points, up until the final scores. Even then, success (in the form of getting intelligible results) is only ever fleeting – it will need to be reproduced, refabricated again next year, and the next; there can be no respite. The need for coherence between fabrications is determined by long-term analysis of results, as well as by value added measures.

Any discussion of these assessment practices must be informed by an awareness of the effects of the EYFS Profile on the teachers. Practices at St Mary's and Gatehouse reflected the deep ambivalence felt towards the Profile and the conflicting pressures associated with it. The Profile reinforced the Reception teachers' understandings of their roles as based on particular early years developmental knowledge, which made them accountable, expert professionals. The 'teacher knowledge' discourse legitimised this position further, and worked powerfully to create great flexibility in the production of results. However, the EYFS Profile simultaneously also devalued the teachers' status, by requiring them to produce evidence (which they do only cynically) and designating them through moderation as 'right' or 'wrong' in their assessments. The Profile seemed to give the teachers greater status, but then also constantly threatened to take this away. This ambiguous position is inextricably linked to the assessment practices discussed in this chapter: the teachers engage in cynical compliance with the requirements for folders of evidence because they need to show they are 'good teachers' who can build up a view of a child. They need to engage in the performance of assessment, because that is an important part of defining them as 'good teachers'. There is little room for resistance, but they know that the performance will rarely be checked and that it is hugely time consuming, so they only do what is necessary. They rely on the 'teacher knowledge' discourse to produce the scores initially, and then undermine the legitimacy of this 'knowledge' by admitting that they cannot know all of the required information about every child. This 'knowledge' is then undermined by the LA's judgements about their accuracy. The performative technology appears paradoxical: it gives teachers status but also pressure in producing results, and also burdens them with the danger of being told they are assessing inaccurately. The ambiguity of this situation gives rise to competing discourses about accuracy through which the teachers understand their role as deliverers of intelligible results.

These teachers' investment in the fabrication is immense: it is a judgement on a year's work, their professionalism and their pedagogy. While they have some power to determine who will be designated as successful in the EYFS Profile, they are also limited by circulating discourses associated with inner city schools and minoritised learners. In the final chapter, I discuss how fabrications such as the EYFS Profile results might work at a systematic level to reproduce educational inequalities.

7
POLICY, EQUALITY AND 'LEARNING'

Introduction

As I explained in the opening chapter, this book tells a story of who gets to succeed at school and who does not. In many ways, this is a story that is very familiar in the sociology of education, but what I have aimed to elaborate on is how, within this simple story, there lies great complexity: a multitude of different discourses and practices operate in classrooms to regulate who succeeds at any one time. In this concluding chapter, I summarise my arguments in relation to the making of intelligible learners and intelligible results, and discuss the implications of these arguments and the possibilities for interruption of the practices. I begin with the notions of learning implicit in the EYFS Profile and its related practices, before moving on to discuss the lessons that can be learnt from this policy in early childhood education in the UK and internationally, and (in my view most importantly) the role of assessment in the reproduction of educational inequalities.

Notions of 'learning'

This book has aimed to contribute a detailed analysis of exactly what is involved in being constituted as a 'good' learner in Reception classrooms in an era of accountability and early years reform. The EYFS Profile affects who is recognisable as a 'good' learner: it prioritises independence, enthusiasm and responsibility for your own learning, and at other times values submission and obedience. It is organised so that those children who take up the position of 'learner' effectively are marked out, and those who are constituted as having failed to become learners are labelled and excluded. The terminology involved, particularly the division of children into those reaching or failing to reach a 'good level of development', organises children at the age of four or five into those who have adequately become learners, and those that have failed to take up this opportunity. The children have some agency in how they are constituted learners, with some engaging in performatives that position themselves positively as entrepreneurial learners engaging fully with the opportunities on offer. However, the teacher remains powerful in constituting the children on a spectrum of learners, with assessment of their learner identities taking in a wide range of factors both academic and relating to behaviour and attitudes. Some children's learning is deemed authentic, while other children are seen as merely appropriating the attitudes and behaviours of a 'good' learner; in particular, successful children from minoritised backgrounds are at risk of being rejected as inauthentic.

The notion of learning that the EYFS Profile proposes is, I would argue, inherently neoliberal: learning is something to be engaged in on demand, by a flexible, enthusiastic and self-regulating child. The situation is created by adults, but the learning must be driven by the child's initiative and commitment. Links can be made with the contention that young children are positioned as 'consumers-in-waiting, with their care and education increasingly located as a private and individual concern' (Woodrow and Press, 2008: 96). At the same time, the EYFS Profile legitimises particular ideas about learning that are long-standing in early years: the idea of 'discovering' a child, which is linked to development discourses, and the idea that a child has inherent characteristics that can be identified over time, described as 'talents' or, more commonly, 'ability'. The workings of these combinations provide further evidence of what Dahlberg and Moss have called 'a new normality of the child', whereby a system produces children who are 'developmentally ready for the uncertainties and opportunities of the twenty-first century' (Dahlberg and Moss, 2005: 7). The effect is that the EYFS Profile limits the models of good learning that operate within classrooms, and closes down opportunities to think more freely about how we can envisage learning in this context.

Assessment in the early years

As well as affecting notions of learning, the EYFS Profile turns the Reception classroom into a site for the specific types of learning that form the Profile points to be produced and recorded. There is a process of surveillance, through the moderation activities of the Local Authority and the senior management of the school. Statutory assessment positions the teachers in new ways as enablers and recorders, and encourages them to collect 'knowledge' of children which is constructed as neutral and objective (though not always accurate). The EYFS Profile can be seen as part of an international trend involving the standardisation of curricula and the spread of accountability measures into early childhood education. Assessment plays an important role within this trend, as it is seen as providing evidence of improvement and progress through objective data, part of a belief in scientific approaches and quantifiable measurement, described as 'an orchestrated return to modernity' (Hatch, 2007: 2). There is evidence, in the teachers' constructions of their knowledge as objective, and in the construction of the EYFS

Profile results within government, of 'a particular form of modernity ... [which is] highly regulatory, foregrounding order, control and certitude' (Moss, 2008: 8). Further evidence of this trend has been apparent in the time since my fieldwork was conducted: the UK coalition government has made some changes to the EYFS Profile, but the underlying principles of assessment by teachers of identifiable and measurable targets remain. These statistics will continue to be reported to parents, inspectors and, on a national scale, to the public, in ways which construct this data as accurate, definite and scientific, despite evidence from studies such as this which question such assumptions.

One of the most significant findings of this study relates to the production of the EYFS scores: these results are a 'fabrication' (Ball, 2003b), cloaked in a façade of accuracy, produced to satisfy the requirements of accountability and performance. They cannot be taken as accurate indicators of children's progress or of differences between groups of pupils' levels of attainment. This does not reduce their power, however, in repeatedly constituting whole groups of pupils as 'underachieving' when the results are published each year, and setting children on educational paths with widely differing expectations.

Systematic disadvantage

The data presented here has demonstrated that the EYFS Profile's model of what a 'good' learner looks like and who can be recognisable as one works *systematically* to disadvantage minoritised and working-class children and, to some extent, boys. Although each individual is constituted in different ways, there is far less intelligible space for a minoritised, working-class child to be constituted as a 'good' learner. There is *some* space for minoritised children to be 'good' learners, but this is very precarious, and the wrong identity performance can result in a learner being seen as inauthentic; success can always be explained away by this idea of authenticity. White pupils are more recognisable as 'good' learners, even if they are working-class. Furthermore, all of these processes can operate in the absence of any idealised White middle-class children.

This book has examined the layers of discourse and practice which work to systematically disadvantage some pupils, right from their first days in school. I have explained how discourses of low expectation are reinforced by national policy which aims to alleviate the effects of poverty, but can work to reduce the possibility of inner city schools ever having high results that are seen as accurate. Meanwhile, policy technologies such as value added scores also work in unexpected ways to provide an incentive to keep scores low, even when the scores themselves are not used in official value added measures. If, in line with a framework informed by Critical Race Theory, one assumes that racism is endemic in education, then the systematic ways in which these classes of mostly minoritised children are constituted as failing represent merely a small section of an educational trajectory that is determined by 'race' (and other social factors). Yet the very certainty with which these children are assumed to be 'difficult' as learners is still shocking; low expectations determine and limit the possibilities for these children at the age of five. There are individual stories within this overall picture, of children who are apparently successful, but are deemed 'inauthentic' learners, and children who are constituted as failing before they even arrive in the classroom. But the complexity of the discourses which position these children negatively can at times obscure the systematic disadvantage that occurs. I deliberately use the term 'systematic disadvantage' in order to avoid excluding the aspects of children's identities other than 'race' that constitute them as 'bad' learners from this analysis, in line with the intersectional approach taken throughout this book. I understand systematic disadvantage, like institutional racism, to mean processes which produce unequal outcomes, whatever the intentions.[1] At this point I think it is important to make my arguments about intentions and outcomes clear; to do this I employ a CRT technique of storytelling.

Using CRT to understand intentionality and outcomes

In 2006, David Gillborn published an article which examined the first sets of the (then) Foundation Stage Profile (FSP) results. In this paper and in his 2008 book *Racism and Education*, he argued that the poor attainment of Black pupils on the FSP compared with their previous levels of attainment at age five and the lack of public outcry over this reversal revealed a deeply ingrained racist system in education. He used a CRT-style story to explain this phenomenon, based on an imaginary 'deeply racist society', where 'racism leaves its imprint on virtually every aspect of life, from birth to death' (Gillborn, 2006c: 324):

> In my story, the despised group is excelling at a test that every pupil must take. You see, in the place I'm asking you to imagine, the state has decreed that all children must be tested throughout their school careers. They are each stamped with a unique code number, and a log of their successes – and failures – follows them throughout the system.
>
> And so everyone must take the test. But if the dominant group cannot restrict entry to the test, it seems that only one course of action remains; change the test.
>
> The test must be redesigned so that the despised group no longer succeed. Simple.
>
> But, of course, such a crass and obviously racist set of events could never occur in the real world. There would be an outcry. Wouldn't there?
> *(Gillborn, 2006c: 326)*

In this story, Gillborn does not suggest that the EYFS Profile was deliberately introduced in order to make children from minoritised groups do badly; instead, he offers this analogy to show that the *results* of this policy are the same as if they *had* been intentionally racist. This is an important distinction which I wish to emphasise; my concern here is with the *results* of these processes, not the conscious intentions. In the same manner as Gillborn's story, I offer here a story which focuses on the processes I have observed at St Mary's and Gatehouse. This tale takes as its premise the same racist society outlined above:

A new test is introduced; the despised group do badly, and the status quo is preserved. But, the new test is for very young children, and so has to be based entirely on teachers' judgements and observations. There is a risk that the despised group might start to get better scores. How can the system be organised in ways which ensure the scores are kept down? Two processes make certain that the despised group continue to get low scores. First, the idea that this group will and should do badly must become common sense in the school system. This can be achieved by mentioning this group as a particular problem alongside other 'problem groups' who will be expected to fare badly, or by creating policies which single these groups out as problematic. Particular features of the despised group, such as their non-majority language, are emphasised to ensure that everyone has a reason for why this group are doing badly. Because the entire test is based on what the teachers 'know' about the children, any lower expectations of this group will not be too obvious; this can be legitimised by the idea that a good professional teacher can gather 'knowledge' accurately. Thus the teachers can give lower scores to the despised group, without it ever seeming unfair.

A second back-up process ensures that if the teachers do start to give children from the despised group high scores, this can be monitored and prevented. Each teacher's scores must be monitored by the local authority 'expert' advisors, and checked. These advisors have the power to deem teachers' scores right or wrong, and they are feared by the teachers, because the teachers know they are judged on these scores. The 'experts' give contradictory advice, so the teachers are always unsure quite what the advisors want. The teachers have become so confused with and pressured by the system that they just want to produce what the advisors want to see. When the advisors tell the teachers that their scores are too high, the teachers respond. So, when results from a school with a large number of children from the despised group are above the national average, the advisor can simply declare them 'too high' and the school will change them. In turn, this is helped by the official designation of schools like this into special zones which are identified as having low attainment levels; being in this zone provides further proof that the teacher simply must have got the scores wrong. Perhaps soon the advisors will not even have to say the scores are wrong because the headteachers will begin to understand the system, and make sure that their teachers give low scores to avoid the pressure from the advisors.

Through these two processes, the group gets low scores. The results are published each year, and this backs up the idea that it is only common sense that the despised group do badly, and no one is to blame. Everyone is quietly pleased with the wonderfully circular, self-perpetuating way in which the group stays lower than the other groups in this test, especially since it provides the benchmark for all of the children's further progress. As long as the advisors keep checking, the teachers keep feeling that they need to get it 'right', and the idea that the group will inevitably do badly keeps circulating, the despised group will get poor scores, and keep getting poor scores.

It is important to reiterate here that I am not suggesting that this hypothetical story is what actually happened with the EYFS Profile; I do not believe that this is a deliberate, planned strategy to ensure that minoritised or lower income pupils do badly in schools. However, as with Gillborn's story above, the *results* are the same: my data has shown that the teachers expect their schools to do badly because of their "difficult intake", and the EYFS Profile scores are changed if they are too high for a school in an area with low educational attainment. The children's final scores in these two classes were lower than the national average; *the results are the same as if it had been deliberate*, and this is deeply concerning. Gillborn writes, following his story:

> But there is no evidence of conscious intent: there is no conspiracy. It is more frightening than that. Rather than being generated by a deliberate strategy (one that is readily open to exposure and reversal), these changes appear to have resulted from the *normal* workings of the education system – a system that places race equality at the very margins of debate and takes no action when Black students are judged to be failing. *(Gillborn, 2006c: 334)*

The idea that the 'normal workings' of the system result in minority groups being disadvantaged is a familiar concept to CRT scholars who take racism as an endemic aspect of society, but it is a shocking idea to many educators. I am arguing here that the 'normal workings' of the EYFS Profile and Reception practices in general work to disadvantage some children from minoritised and economically disadvantaged backgrounds, without anyone ever consciously intending to do so. My intention is not to blame the teachers for their situation either; as I have argued throughout, they are entirely constrained by the discourses surrounding them and their professional context.

Policy and inequality

At the heart of the story I have told is the need to constitute children as intelligible learners, who correspond to both the dominant discourses linked to their intersectional identities and the particular conception in Reception of what being a 'learner' means. Simultaneously, there is a need to produce intelligible assessment results for these children, though the relationship between these two processes is itself complicated. The demands of performativity ensure that the final EYFS Profile results are a 'fabrication' produced to be acceptable and recognisable, not necessarily a reflection of how the children are constituted as learners. The production of intelligible learners and intelligible results are merely two parts of a vast assemblage of different processes that take effect in classrooms. My exploration of the effects of the EYFS Profile on Reception tells a familiar story about the negotiation of policy into practice and its unintended effects (Ball, 1993; Ball, Maguire and Braun, 2012; Gillborn and Youdell, 2000). However, other policies are implicated too in the analysis, particularly value added measures and the creation of Education Action Zones, with similar unintended effects; at times, these work with teacher assessment to produce the systematic disadvantage discussed above.

In these two schools, it is apparent that principles associated with value added measures have spread in their application from Key Stages 1 and 2. There are no published value added data on progress between the EYFS Profile and Key Stage 1, yet the schools are concerned about this phenomenon or at least its potential to be used. This may be linked to other pressures which encourage schools to track children's progress, from Ofsted inspectors or the Local Authority, and to identify those who are failing to fit within a standard attainment profile. The idea of needing to be aware of the long-term effects of scores, which may take effect when the particular teacher has left, appears to be applied to all assessments, including the EYFS Profile.

Although in 2010 the coalition government scrapped the use of contextual value added scores in league tables (DfE, 2010g), measures of 'expected progress' continue to be used in the tables and it seems unlikely that the principle of measuring progress will become less important in schools. Indeed the revised Ofsted framework used to judge schools from 2012 includes, as one of the criteria, how well pupils 'make progress relative to their starting points' (Ofsted, 2012). As I have argued in relation to the more complex contextual value added scores (Bradbury, 2011a), this policy of using measures of progress to judge schools has been framed in policy documents as being a 'fairer' method of judging schools that takes into account the children's attainment on entry. But, it only functions as an accurate measure of 'progress' (setting aside the overtones of scientific predictability for a moment) if the previous attainment scores are accurate. EYFS Profile results, as the first set of scores to be recorded for each child, are therefore the best possible opportunity to make a school appear to be adding value; they are often used as a 'starting point' or 'baseline' figure, even though they are assessed after children have spent a year in school. There is therefore a real incentive to keep these scores low. Moreover, after only one year in the school, low results can easily be attributed to factors outside the school context, and thus low EYFS Profile results do not do too much damage to a school's reputation. What is particularly important in the case of these schools is that the incentive to give low scores is even greater for schools that predict they are unlikely to do well on raw results; valued added is their chance to show their success. Thus, unintentionally, this policy works to lower the EYFS Profile results of schools that are already seen as low-attaining; it plays a role in the perpetuation of educational 'failure' for some schools and some children.

Another policy which unintentionally reproduces inequality is the labelling of certain areas as in need of additional help. Policies such as Education Action Zones (EAZs) and its successors Excellence in Cities and London Challenge, aimed to reduce educational inequality through the allocation of additional funds. But, as the data show, the effect of this designation may be to constitute schools or an area as incommensurate with high results. There is a clear link in the teachers' explanations between this specific label and the intelligibility of low results. EAZs ended in 2005, and yet, in 2009, Jim at Gatehouse was still talking about the area as an EAZ; we see how the negative effects of the label linger after the policy and the money have disappeared. The idea that policy which is notionally redistributive and should contribute to social justice could also have the effect of ensuring that results remain low should be of real concern to those involved in education policy-making.

If, as I have argued in relation to Reception, teacher assessments are informed by the need for them to be recognisable within the context of the school, this has implications for many schools which are designated as Challenge schools or are involved in other policies which aim to reduce inequality. This includes schools with a high proportion of pupils on the Pupil Premium, a government policy introduced in 2011 which gives additional funding for children in receipt of Free School Meals. The increase in teacher assessments as replacements for 'high stakes' tests in all schools (already in place for Key Stages 1 and 3, and possibly in Key Stage 2 in the future), makes this issue one which has the potential to affect all schools. It is important that schools are aware that the use of teacher assessment does not necessarily mean freedom and autonomy over how pupils are graded.

This study has demonstrated how teacher assessment can *create* inequalities in education, as well as record them (see also Bradbury, 2011b). What if teacher assessments are only recognised as accurate if they mirror the patterns of previous test results? Gaps in attainment and inequalities will be the only intelligible results and will be reproduced while the possibility for change is shut down. This is an issue which deserves more research and attention, particularly given the prominence of issues of poverty and attainment in recent political debates. This study has shown how policies can combine in complex ways to provide incentives for schools to keep some children's results low; these consequences may well be unforeseen, but they have a real impact on children's lives and educational trajectories.

Implications

The most common question I am asked about this research, having explained my findings, is 'What should we do instead?', and, although I strongly believe there is a purpose in critique without necessarily finding an accompanying solution, in this section I discuss how these findings offer possibilities for interruption and change. Before I do so, I want to acknowledge the limitations of the study. I am not arguing that exactly the same processes occur in the same ways in all Reception classrooms or all other schools. I accept that the teachers involved, in being willing to have a researcher in their classrooms, are likely to have more to say on assessment, or be more confident, or be more interested in research in general. Although, whenever I have presented this work, the reaction from other Reception teachers has been that these practices are not unusual, I do not present this data as anything other than a representation of what happened in these two classrooms in the year I spent in them. A further limitation is that the data used in this study represent only the voices of the teachers and support staff, not the Reception children themselves. As shown by Connolly's (1998) use of interviews with children, young participants can provide an alternative perspective. Despite these limitations, I would argue that this study has important implications.

In many ways, my arguments are pessimistic: the complexity of forces working within these schools makes it difficult to see how and where systematic disadvantage could be challenged. The current political situation in the UK is such that any reduction in assessment of children is unlikely; the change of government in 2010 has led to increased levels of assessment in primary schools, with the introduction in 2012 of a Phonics Screening Check at age six. Indeed, much of the current political discourse on 'early intervention' has the potential to strengthen the link between poorer families and educational failure, with comments from Conservative cabinet ministers suggesting that children living in poverty have been 'going to school with a brain the size of a child of one' so that they 'simply bump along at the back and at the bottom' (Iain Duncan Smith in Woolf, 2010). Furthermore, with the continued focus on White working-class pupils (BBC News, 2010; Paton, 2012; Vasagar, 2011) and on the Pupil Premium, racism remains an 'absent presence' (Apple, 1999) constantly working to maintain inequality.

However, I would argue that there *are* opportunities to disrupt systematic disadvantage, and that these can be found through understanding the detail of how classrooms work. The politics of the performative allow a questioning of what is intelligible and how alternatives can be opened up. Although the detail may be unique to each child, exploring the intelligible space where children can be recognisable as learners within prevailing discourses matters because we learn more about what the possibilities for change might be. Can the intelligible space where particular intersectional identities are recognisable as 'good' learners be expanded? Can different identities become commensurate with 'good' learners, if the discourses associated with them change? This analysis offers the potential for interruptive work: what would happen if a teacher was aware of the complex ways in which they constitute children as different types of learner? Could the associations between certain classed and raced identities and failure as a learner be interrupted, so that these children could be understood as successful at school?

These questions can only be answered by teachers and the school leaders who shape their priorities and practice. An awareness of the ease by which children become 'good' or 'bad' learners in their first few weeks of school, and how this can be based on perceptions of their home life and on their intersectional identity positions, would be helpful in interrupting these associations. I would argue that seeing the way in which tiny moments can change how a child is understood as a learner can help teachers think about how these moments might work in their classrooms without them ever being aware. This potential is inherent in seeing identity as performative: it means that no one is 'necessarily anything' (Youdell, 2006b). But this perception needs to happen within an understanding of how discourses frame what is intelligible more widely. In understanding how discourse shapes the intelligible space open to children as learners, and also the power of discursive agency in confirming or resisting these identities, we can see exactly where the potential for interruption lies. For example, could the recognisability of some Afghan and Kosovan Muslim girls as 'good' learners be extended to include boys, or other Muslim girls? Could these groups who have more recently become established in the UK come to be associated with 'model minorities' (taking into account the way in which these pupils are constituted as inauthentic) and become more recognisable as 'good' learners, even when their performance in the classroom is not submissive?

I appreciate that this suggestion – that we need to think about how discourses can be changed or stretched – can be criticised for not being ambitious enough, or for failing to deal with the structural issues at play. I would argue, however, that it is the endemic nature of racism and other prejudices which means interruption needs at times to be small in scale: suddenly trying to position a group strongly associated with educational under-attainment as model learners would be completely unrecognisable to teachers, and serve no purpose at all. This does not mean that we accept or ignore the wider inequalities, but that we 'choose our battles wisely' while also seeking to address broader issues. As the saying goes, we need to 'struggle where we are'; and where we are, I would argue, is entwined in a network of discourses which make low attainment by minority and working-class children common sense. This has not gone away despite decades of research with similar findings. Perhaps, alongside the important debates about institutional racism and structural disadvantage, we need to think about the small moves that can be made to disrupt the bigger pattern, particularly given the current policy terrain.

The future of the EYFS and possibilities for change

The review of the EYFS conducted in 2011 and 2012 was, overall, quite positive about the systems put in place by the previous Labour government.[2] Dame Clare Tickell, who led the review, commented on the popularity of the EYFS across the sector and its effect on 'improving outcomes' for children (Tickell, 2011). She identified key areas that needed to be reformed, including the EYFS Profile, which she described as 'burdensome'; this mirrors many of the comments made by the teachers discussed in this book. The majority of the review's recommendations were taken up by the government and the new system was introduced to schools in the autumn of 2012. In this final section, I speculate as to the impact of the changes to the EYFS on the issues discussed here.

The main changes of relevance relate to processes of collecting evidence and the reduction in the number of targets in the EYFS Profile. The Tickell review recommended that paperwork, including the recording of children's progress, 'should be kept to the absolute minimum required to promote children's successful learning and development' (2011: 31), and the new framework was described by the government as 'reducing bureaucracy for professionals' (DfE, 2012a). The early learning goals which form the basis for the 117 EYFS Profile points were reduced from 69 to 17, and, from 2012, teachers only need to make judgements on these 17 new early learning goals. Instead of either awarding or not awarding these points, teachers decide if children are 'meeting the expected levels, exceeding them or below them (emerging)' (DfE, 2012e).

At first glance, these changes appear to solve some of the problems associated with the Profile, including the overwhelming complexity of the assessment. However, in the light of the data discussed in this book, I would argue that there are real dangers involved in this 'slimmed down and more focused' EYFS (DfE, 2012d). The reduced emphasis on collecting evidence further promotes the 'teacher knowledge' discourse and continues to allow teachers' judgments to be taken as accurate assessments in the same way as test-based scores. This is significant because teachers' views of children as learners, as I have discussed throughout, are affected by children's intersectional identities and the dominant discourses surrounding these. Furthermore, the reduced number of goals and the three-level assessment of these goals have the potential to exacerbate the tendency to organise children into a tripartite top-middle-bottom schema, with only those recognisable as 'good' learners being awarded 'exceeding expected levels' in the new Profile. In this way, this assessment based on teachers' judgments, like the previous system, has the potential to *create* disparities in attainment. This matters particularly because, as the Tickell review comments, these scores provide a baseline for children's progress through school. For those who are deemed to be only 'emerging' in the early learning goals, a pattern of lower-than-expected attainment may well be deemed acceptable.

At a more fundamental level, the review and reform of the EYFS in 2011–12 embedded further the principle of statutory assessment in early years education. The ideas behind the new system are the same: discourses of development and ability remain, and the idea that learning can be effectively measured in a summative assessment prevails. Neoliberal ideas of accountability and performance continue to justify the expense, time and impact involved in the EYFS Profile, as shown by Dame Tickell's (2011) comment in the review: 'results should be published at national and local level so that the general public can hold government and local authorities to account for the quality of early years services'. However, Tickell also urges caution over the use of Profile results in judging schools: in the review she warns against using the figures for 'school-level accountability', due to 'the different rates at which young children develop and the subsequent risk of children being inappropriately pushed to do things they are not ready for' (2011: 33). But there is no comment on the use of the data for school-level accountability in the government's new EYFS framework, and in the light of the data presented in this book, it seems unlikely that the current trend of using EYFS data to judge a school's early years provision will be halted. Furthermore, the introduction in 2012 of an additional assessment in Year 1, in the form of a Phonics Screening Check – a reading test based on children's phonetic understanding – suggests that the direction of policy is in favour of more accountability in this phase of education.

Despite the continued existence of statutory assessment in early years and the pressures and contradictions this brings to classrooms in primary schools, I would argue there is still potential for disruption of these processes. There can be resistance, as seen in some of these teachers' comments, to the values and priorities of an accountability-based assessment system. There continue to be many questions that need to be asked – by teachers, headteachers, local authority advisers and policy-makers – about what the assessment is for, what it aims to measure, and what kind of learner the EYFS aims to produce. There also needs to be greater scrutiny of the role of teacher assessment in *creating* disparities in attainment by ethnic group, gender and class indicators, both in early years and more widely. In the future, I would hope that any further adjustments to the assessment system in early years take into account its role in perpetuating inequalities in education, and result from a wider debate into the need for statutory assessment of children at the age of five, and the alternatives.

Yet, even while the EYFS Profile remains a powerful force in classrooms, there is still potential for teachers to constitute children as learners differently, without recourse to the models of 'good' learning prescribed by the assessment. The constraints of an intelligible space relating to a particular intersectional identity can be altered, and the constitution of some children as failing when they first enter education is something that can be disrupted at an individual level, by teachers and other adults in early years thinking critically about the dominant discourses that operate in their classrooms. The current system appears to limit the possibilities of educational success for some children when they are just starting their school careers and sets them on paths of educational failure and success at a very young age; this is something that must be changed if every child is to have an equal chance in school.

APPENDIX 1

Early Years Foundation Stage Profile points

Personal, Social and Emotional Development 1: Disposition and Attitudes

1 Shows an interest in classroom activities through observation or participation.
2 Dresses, undresses and manages own personal hygiene with adult support.
3 Displays high levels of involvement in self-chosen activities.
4 Dresses and undresses independently and manages own personal hygiene.
5 Selects and uses activities and resources independently.
6 Continues to be interested, motivated and excited to learn.
7 Is confident to try new activities, initiate ideas and speak in a familiar group.
8 Maintains attention and concentrates.
9 Sustains involvement and perseveres, particularly when trying to solve a problem or reach a satisfactory conclusion.

Personal, Social and Emotional Development 2: Social Development

1 Plays alongside others.
2 Builds relationships through gesture and talk.
3 Takes turns and shares with adult support.
4 Works as part of a group or class, taking turns and sharing fairly.
5 Forms good relationships with adults and peers.
6 Understands that there needs to be agreed values and codes of behaviour for groups of people, including adults and children, to work together harmoniously.

7   Understands that people have different needs, views, cultures and beliefs that need to be treated with respect.
8   Understands that s/he can expect others to treat her/his needs, views, cultures and beliefs with respect.
9   Takes into account the ideas of others.

Personal, Social and Emotional Development 3: Emotional Development

1   Separates from main carer with support.
2   Communicates freely about home and community.
3   Expresses needs and feelings in appropriate ways.
4   Responds to significant experiences, showing a range of feelings when appropriate
5   Has a developing awareness of own needs, views and feelings and is sensitive to the needs, views and feelings of others.
6   Has a developing respect for own culture and beliefs and those of other people.
7   Considers the consequences of words and actions for self and others.
8   Understands what is right, what is wrong, and why.
9   Displays a strong and positive sense of self-identity and is able to express a range of emotions fluently and appropriately.

Communication, Language and Literacy 1: Language for Communication and Thinking

1   Listens and responds.
2   Initiates communication with others, displaying greater confidence in more informal contexts.
3   Talks activities through, reflecting on and modifying actions.
4   Listens with enjoyment to stories, songs, rhymes and poems, sustains attentive listening and responds with relevant comments, questions or actions.
5   Uses language to imagine and recreate roles and experiences.
6   Interacts with others in a variety of contexts, negotiating plans and activities and taking turns in conversation.
7   Uses talk to organise, sequence and clarify thinking, ideas, feelings and events, exploring the meanings and sounds of new words.
8   Speaks clearly with confidence and control, showing awareness of the listener.
9   Talks and listens confidently and with control, consistently showing awareness of the listener by including relevant detail. Uses language to work out and clarify ideas, showing control of a range of appropriate vocabulary.

Communication, Language and Literacy 2: Linking Sounds and Letters

1   Joins in with rhyming and rhythmic activities.
2   Shows awareness of rhyme and alliteration.
3   Links some sounds to letters.
4   Links sounds to letters, naming and sounding letters of the alphabet.
5   Hears and says sounds in words.
6   Blends sounds in words.
7   Uses phonic knowledge to read simple regular words.
8   Attempts to read more complex words, using phonic knowledge.
9   Uses knowledge of letters, sounds and words when reading and writing independently.

Communication, Language and Literacy 3: Reading

1   Is developing an interest in books.
2   Knows that print conveys meaning.
3   Recognises a few familiar words.
4   Knows that, in English, print is read from left to right and top to bottom.
5   Shows an understanding of the elements of stories, such as main character, sequence of events and openings.
6   Reads a range of familiar and common words and simple sentences independently.
7   Retells narratives in the correct sequence, drawing on language patterns of stories.
8   Shows an understanding of how information can be found in non-fiction texts to answer questions about where, who, why and how.
9   Reads books of own choice with some fluency and accuracy.

Communication, Language and Literacy 4: Writing

1   Experiments with mark-making, sometimes ascribing meaning to the marks.
2   Uses some clearly identifiable letters to communicate meaning.
3   Represents some sounds correctly in writing.
4   Writes own name and other words from memory.
5   Holds a pencil and uses it effectively to form recognisable letters, most of which are correctly formed.
6   Attempts writing for a variety of purposes, using features of different forms.
7   Uses phonic knowledge to write simple regular words and make phonetically plausible attempts at more complex words.
8   Begins to form captions and simple sentences, sometimes using punctuation.
9   Communicates meaning through phrases and simple sentences with some consistency in punctuating sentences.

Problem-solving, Reasoning and Numeracy 1: Numbers as Labels and for Counting

1   Says some number names in familiar contexts, such as nursery rhymes.
2   Counts reliably up to three everyday objects.
3   Counts reliably up to six everyday objects.
4   Says number names in order.
5   Recognises numerals 1 to 9.
6   Counts reliably up to 10 everyday objects.
7   Orders numbers up to 10.
8   Uses developing mathematical ideas and methods to solve practical problems.
9   Recognises, counts, orders, writes and uses numbers up to 20.

Problem-solving, Reasoning and Numeracy 2: Calculating

1   Responds to the vocabulary involved in addition and subtraction in rhymes and games.
2   Recognises differences in quantity when comparing sets of objects.
3   Finds one more or one less from a group of up to five objects.
4   Relates addition to combining two groups.
5   Relates subtraction to taking away.
6   In practical activities and discussion, begins to use the vocabulary involved in adding and subtracting.
7   Finds one more or one less than a number from 1 to 10.
8   Uses developing mathematical ideas and methods to solve practical problems.
9   Uses a range of strategies for addition and subtraction, including some mental recall of number bonds.

Problem-solving, Reasoning and Numeracy 3: Shape, Space and Measures

1   Experiments with a range of objects and materials, showing some mathematical awareness.
2   Sorts or matches objects and talks about sorting.
3   Describes shapes in simple models, pictures and patterns.
4   Talks about, recognises and recreates simple patterns.
5   Uses everyday words to describe position.
6   Uses language such as 'circle' or 'bigger' to describe the shape and size of solids and flat shapes.
7   Uses language such as 'greater', 'smaller', 'heavier' or 'lighter' to compare quantities.
8   Uses developing mathematical ideas and methods to solve practical problems.
9   Uses mathematical language to describe solid (3D) objects and flat (2D) shapes.

Knowledge and Understanding of the World

1   Shows curiosity and interest by exploring surroundings.
2   Observes, selects and manipulates objects and materials. Identifies simple features and significant personal events.
3   Identifies obvious similarities and differences when exploring and observing. Constructs in a purposeful way, using simple tools and techniques.
4   Investigates places, objects, materials and living things by using all the senses as appropriate. Identifies some features and talks about those features s/he likes and dislikes.
5   Asks questions about why things happen and how things work. Looks closely at similarities, differences, patterns and change.
6   Finds out about past and present events in own life, and in those of family members and other people s/he knows. Begins to know about own culture and beliefs and those of other people.
7   Finds out about and identifies the uses of everyday technology and uses information and communication technology and programmable toys to support her/his learning.
8   Builds and constructs with a wide range of objects, selecting appropriate resources, tools and techniques and adapting his/her work where necessary.
9   Communicates simple planning for investigations and constructions and makes simple records and evaluations of her/his work. Identifies and names key features and properties, sometimes linking different experiences, observations and events. Begins to explore what it means to belong to a variety of groups and communities.

Physical Development

1   Moves spontaneously, showing some control and coordination.
2   Moves with confidence in a variety of ways, showing some awareness of space.
3   Usually shows appropriate control in large- and small-scale movements.
4   Moves with confidence, imagination and in safety. Travels around, under, over and through balancing and climbing equipment. Shows awareness of space, of self and others.
5   Demonstrates fine motor control and coordination.
6   Uses small and large equipment, showing a range of basic skills.
7   Handles tools, objects and construction and malleable materials safely and with basic control.
8   Recognises the importance of keeping healthy and those things which contribute to this. Recognises the changes that happen to her/his body when s/he is active.
9   Repeats, links and adapts simple movements, sometimes commenting on her/his work. Demonstrates coordination and control in large and small movements, and in using a range of tools and equipment.

Creative Development

1 Explores different media and responds to a variety of sensory experiences. Engages in representational play.
2 Creates simple representations of events, people and objects and engages in music making.
3 Tries to capture experiences, using a variety of different media.
4 Sings simple songs from memory.
5 Explores colour, texture, shape, form and space in two or three dimensions.
6 Recognises and explores how sounds can be changed. Recognises repeated sounds and sound patterns and matches movements to music.
7 Uses imagination in art and design, music, dance, imaginative and role-play and stories. Responds in a variety of ways to what s/he sees, hears, smells, touches and feels.
8 Expresses and communicates ideas, thoughts and feelings using a range of materials, suitable tools, imaginative and role-play, movement, designing and making, and a variety of songs and musical instruments.
9 Expresses feelings and preferences in response to artwork, drama and music and makes some comparisons and links between different pieces. Responds to own work and that of others when exploring and communicating ideas, feelings and preferences through art, music, dance, role-play and imaginative play.

Source: QCA, 2008

APPENDIX 2

Additional EYFS Profile data

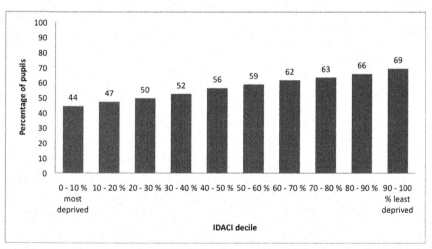

FIGURE A2.1   Percentage of pupils attaining a 'good level of development' by IDACI decile, 2010

Source: DfE, 2010b

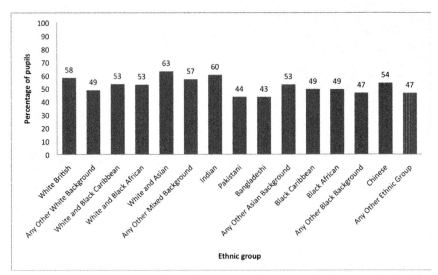

FIGURE A2.2 Percentage of pupils attaining a 'good level of development' by ethnic group, 2010

Source: DfE, 2010b

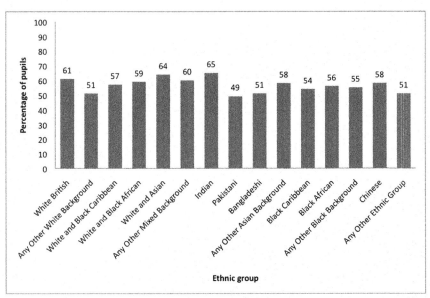

FIGURE A2.3 Percentage of pupils attaining a 'good level of development' by ethnic group, 2011

Source: DfE, 2012b

TABLE A2.1 Percentage of pupils attaining a 'good level of development' by ethnic group, 2009–2011 (full data as presented by the DCSF and DfE)

Ethnicity	2009	2010	2011
White	**53.3**	**57.3**	**60**
White British	53.9	57.9	61
Irish	58.2	64.1	66
Traveller of Irish Heritage	16.1	19.7	21
Gypsy/Roma	17.1	20.7	22
Any Other White Background	45.1	48.6	51
Mixed	**52.0**	**56.7**	**60**
White and Black Caribbean	47.7	53.2	57
White and Black African	51.2	52.8	59
White and Asian	57.6	62.8	64
Any Other Mixed Background	52.1	56.8	60
Asian	**45.3**	**49.7**	**55**
Indian	56.4	60.1	65
Pakistani	39.0	43.5	49
Bangladeshi	37.8	43.4	51
Any Other Asian Background	48.7	52.9	58
Black	**43.7**	**48.9**	**55**
Black Caribbean	43.0	49.4	54
Black African	44.3	49.3	56
Any Other Black Background	42.2	46.6	55
Chinese	**51.8**	**54.0**	**58**
Any Other Ethnic Group	40.4	46.5	51
Unclassified	50.7	53.9	56
All pupils	**51.6**	**55.6**	**59**

Source: DCSF, 2010a; DfE, 2010b; DfE, 2012b
Note: The data for 2011 are provided in whole percentages by the DfE.

APPENDIX 3

Key to transcripts

Key to transcripts	
italicised text	Emphasis
…	Pause
[…]	Material has been edited out
[square brackets]	Contextual information
[square brackets, italic]	Actions

NOTES

1 Policy and inequality in primary education

1   The department with responsibility for schools has been given a range of titles in the last two decades, including: the Department for Education and Employment (DfEE) 1995–2001; Department for Education and Skills (DfES) 2001–7; the Department for Children, School and Families (DCSF) 2007–10 and the Department for Education (DfE) from 2010. It is referred to here as the Department.

2   The law states that children must be in some form of educational provision from the term after their fifth birthday, but it is possible for parents to opt to educate their children at home.

3   Academic years start in September in England, and are divided into three equal 'terms' – autumn, spring and summer. Children with summer birthdays often attend from the January before they are five, spending only two terms in a Reception class.

4   The EYFS Profile results by pupil characteristics were published in November 2012, at a late stage in the publication of this book. The patterns of attainment are similar to those discussed in this chapter. Overall, the proportion of pupils reaching a 'good level of development' increased again to 64 per cent (DfE, 2012f).

5   All figures are rounded to the nearest whole percentage point, except in Table 1.3.

6   In 2012, the proportion of girls reaching a 'good level of development' was 73 per cent; for boys the figure was 55 per cent; this was consistent with previous years' results (DfE, 2012f).

7   The term 'ethnic group' is used by the government; there is further discussion of terms relating to 'race' in Chapter 2. In exploring these statistics, I use the descriptors for particular groups provided by the Department for Schools, Children and Families and Department for Education in the order they are presented.

8   In 2012, the data by ethnic group followed a similar pattern to that discussed here: the highest attaining groups were White (65 per cent), Mixed White and Asian (68 per cent) and Indian (70 per cent). The lowest attaining groups were Pakistani (53 per cent), Bangladeshi (56 per cent) and any other ethnic group (57 per cent) (DfE, 2012 f).

9   As discussed further in Chapter 2, I use the term 'minori*tised*' to emphasise that 'ethnic minorities' or 'people of colour' are only termed such in particular contexts, in this case England, where the majority of the population are White.

2 Understanding learner identities in the early years classroom

1 There is some debate over the labelling of Foucault's work as 'poststructuralist' (Dreyfus and Rabinow, 1983); however, for this study, I am considering Foucault's work to be part of poststructuralism.
2 Further biographical details of the adults in both schools have been omitted to preserve their anonymity.

3 Assessing learners in the first year of school

1 There is no way to find out if the two observations *were* the wrong way around: I am not making a judgement on this myself. However, whether or not the supply teacher made a mistake, the conversations are very revealing in that they show how strongly Reece is positioned as distant from a 'good' learner.
2 This is a game where wooden fishing rods with magnets on the end of the lines are used to pick up magnetic numbers from a large tray, intended to encourage numeral recognition and conversations about numbers.
3 Many of the children at St Mary's had been to some form of nursery before starting school, though not all of these provided information to Paul. At Gatehouse, most of the children had been to the school nursery, and so a report was passed up to the Reception teacher and there was also a 'handover' meeting.

4 Assessing a 'difficult intake': 'Race', religion, class and gender in reception

1 Families of Schools Data from the DCSF shows that approximately half of the schools in the LA had proportions of FSM as high or higher than Gatehouse and St Mary's. According to data based on 2008, White British pupils made up less than 20 per cent of the school population in over half of the schools in the LA. In London as a whole, over a third of schools have a White British minority of under 20 per cent of pupils.
2 This comment also engages with a common discourse among teachers which regards educational research as too academic and irrelevant to everyday practice.
3 I am conscious that I have not dealt with the issue of young children's sexualities, despite a growing body of literature on this interesting topic and on how sexuality is intermeshed with gender (Renold, 2005). I am taking as an assumption the presence of compulsory heterosexuality in these classrooms, and thus the need to perform masculinity as heterosexual masculinity, and femininity as heterosexual femininity. The denial of sexuality present in the classroom only emphasised heterosexuality as a taken-for-granted Norm. Moments where the issue of sexuality did arise involved the implicit Othering of homosexuality.
4 The Physical Development area of learning includes points about fine motor skills, such as holding a pencil correctly, as well as gross motor skills, such as running and jumping.
5 Although it is not the main focus, I think it is important to discuss briefly the significance of the gender of the main teachers in the study, particularly since much has been made of the importance of male teachers in primary schools in recent years. It is clearly unrealistic to suggest that male teachers will perform masculinity in the classroom in identical ways, any more than women teachers will perform femininity homogenously. At times, Paul used a particularly feminised construction of early years teachers to criticise them, but of course this cannot be extended to any discussion of male Reception teachers in general. Although I would not dismiss the teachers' maleness as irrelevant, I would argue that to come to any conclusions as to the effect of their gender specifically would be to essentialise both male characteristics and male teachers generally. Furthermore, this study is focused on these two classrooms as communities

of practitioners, and the female teachers and teaching assistants are prominent in these. The analysis is focused on systemic rather than individual responses to the EYFS Profile, involving the school management and Local Authority as well as the main class teachers. Responses to the Profile itself were reasonably consistent across the teachers and schools, and their practice is located in wider policy discourses about learning and assessment, and popular discourses about learners. Thus, although there may be some gendered aspects to their classroom practices, the data discussed does not represent a distinctively masculine response to the EYFS Profile.

5 'Good' and 'bad' learners in the classroom

1 This contrast is used less than the White boys/Black boys binary present in many press reports about 'poor White boys' (Gillborn, 2009), but remains potent given the wider educational discourses about boys' failure.

6 Playing with numbers: Learner identities and assessment

1 Some of the material in this and the following chapter appeared in my 2011 article 'Rethinking assessment and inequality: The production of disparities in attainment in early years education' (Bradbury, 2011b).

7 Policy, equality and 'learning'

1 I am aware of the power and necessity of naming racism where I see it, and do not wish to shy away from this aspect of the discussion. However, to focus purely on this aspect of the findings would be to dismiss important insights relating to class, gender and the urban.
2 Evidence from this research was submitted as part of the Tickell Review.

REFERENCES

Adnett, N. and Davies, P. (2002). *Markets for Schooling: An Economic Analysis*. London: Routledge.

Alexander, C. (2000). '(Dis)Entangling the "Asian gang": Ethnicity, identity, masculinity'. In B. Hesse (ed.), *Un/Settled Multiculturalisms: Diasporas, Entanglements, Transruptions*. London: Zed Books.

—(2004). 'Imagining the Asian gang: Ethnicity, masculinity and youth after "the riots"'. *Critical Social Policy*, 24 (4), 526–49.

Alexander, R. (2009). *Children, their World, their Education: Final report and recommendations of the Cambridge Primary Review*. London: Routledge.

Allan, J. (1999). *Actively Seeking Inclusion: Pupils with Special Needs in Mainstream Schools*. London: Falmer.

Allen, R. L. (2009). 'What about poor White people?'. In W. Ayers, T. Quinn and D. Stovall (eds), *Handbook of Social Justice in Education*. New York: Routledge.

Apple, M. W. (1998). 'Foreword'. In J. Kincheloe, S. Steinberg, N. Rodriguez and R. Chennault (eds), *White Reign*. New York: St Martin's Griffin.

—(1999). 'The absent presence of race in educational reform'. *Race, Ethnicity and Education*, 2 (1), 9–16.

—(2006). *Educating the 'Right' Way: Markets, Standards, God, and Inequality* (2nd edn). London: Routledge.

Archer, L. (2002). 'Its easier that you're a girl and that you're Asian: Interactions of race and gender between researchers and participants'. *Feminist Review*, 72, 108–32.

—(2003). *Race, Masculinity and Schooling: Muslim Boys and Education*. Maidenhead: Open University Press.

—(2008). 'The impossibility of minority ethnic educational 'success'? An examination of the discourses of teachers and pupils in British secondary schools'. *European Educational Research Journal*, 7 (1), 89-107.

Archer, L. and Francis, B. (2007). *Understanding Minority Ethnic Achievement: Race, Gender, Class and 'Success'*. London: Routledge.

Archer, L., Halsall, A. and Hollingworth, S. (2007). 'Inner-femininities and education: "Race", class, gender and schooling in young women's lives'. *Gender and Education*, 19 (5), 549–67.

Archer, L. and Yamashita, H. (2003). 'Theorising inner-city masculinities: "Race", class, gender and education'. *Gender and Education*, 15 (2), 115–32.

Ball, S. J. (1990). *Politics and Policymaking in Education*. London: Routledge.

—(1993). 'What is policy? Texts, trajectories and discourses'. *Discourse: Studies in the Cultural Politics of Education*, 13 (2), 10–17.

—(1994). *Education Reform: A Critical and Post-structural Approach*. Buckingham: Open University Press.

—(1997). 'Policy sociology and critical social research: A personal review of recent education policy and policy research'. *British Educational Research Journal*, 23 (2), 257–74.

—(2003a). *Class Strategies and the Education Market: The Middle Classes and Social Advantage*. London: RoutledgeFalmer.

—(2003b). 'The teacher's soul and the terrors of performativity'. *Journal of Education Policy*, 18 (2), 215–28.

—(2008). *The Education Debate*. Bristol: Policy Press.

—(2010). 'New class inequalities in education: Why education policy may be looking in the wrong place! Education policy, civil society and social class'. *International Journal of Sociology and Social Policy*, 30 (3/4), 155–66.

Ball, S. J., Maguire, M. and Braun, A. (2012). *How Schools Do Policy: Policy Enactments in Secondary Schools*. Abingdon: Routledge.

Bauman, Z. (2005). *Work, Consumerism and the New Poor* (2nd edn). Maidenhead: Open University Press.

BBC News (2006). *Fewer children able to write name*. Online at: news.bbc.co.uk/1/hi/education/6089412.stm [Last accessed 30 July 2010].

—(2008). *Raising the bar on school results*. [Online at: news.bbc.co.uk/1/hi/education/7444148.stm [Last accessed 18 October 2010].

—(2009a). *Afghanistan death toll surpasses Iraq*. Online at: news.bbc.co.uk/1/hi/uk/8145612.stm [Last accessed 24 Sepember 2010].

—(2009b). *Mapping UK's teen murder toll*. Online at: news.bbc.co.uk/1/hi/uk/7777635.stm [Last accessed 24 Sepember 2010].

—(2009c). *Raids target youth gang members*. Online at: news.bbc.co.uk/1/hi/england/london/8095312.stm [Last accessed 24 Sepember 2010].

—(2009d). *Two teenagers killed in stabbings*. Online at: news.bbc.co.uk/1/hi/england/london/7900687.stm [Last accessed 24 Sepember 2010].

—(2010). *White working class pupils left behind*. Online at: www.bbc.co.uk/news/education-10528359 [Last accessed 13 Sepember 2010].

Becker, H. S. (1952). 'Social-class variation in the teacher-pupil relationship'. *Journal of Educational Sociology*, 25 (8), 451–65.

Bell, D. (1992). *Faces at the Bottom of the Well: The Permanence of Racism*. New York: Basic Books.

BERA (2004). *Revised Ethical Guidelines for Educational Research*. London: BERA.

Bhattacharyya, G., Ison, L. and Blair, M. (2003). *Minority Ethnic Attainment and Participation in Education and Training: The Evidence*. Annesley: DfES.

Blaise, M. (2005). *Playing it Straight: Uncovering Gender Discourses in the Early Childhood Classroom*. London: Routledge.

Booher-Jennings, J. (2005). 'Below the Bubble: "Educational triage" and the Texas accountability system'. *American Educational Research Journal*, 42 (2), 231–68.

—(2008). 'Learning to label: Socialisation, gender, and the hidden curriculum of high stakes testing'. *British Journal of Sociology of Education*, 29 (2), 149–60.

Boone, J. and Nasaw, D. (2009). *Cloud hangs over legitimacy of Afghanistan election result*. *The*

Guardian. Online at: *guardian.co.uk/world/2009/aug/23/afghanistan-elections-hamid-karzai* [Last accessed 10 August 2012].

Bradbury, A. (2011a). 'Equity, ethnicity and the hidden dangers of "contextual" measures of school success'. *Race, Ethnicity and Education*, 14 (3), 277–91.

—(2011b). 'Rethinking assessment and inequality: The production of disparities in attainment in early years education'. *Journal of Education Policy*, 26 (5), 655–76.

—(2012). '"I feel absolutely incompetent": Professionalism, policy and early childhood teachers'. *Contemporary Issues in Early Childhood Education*, 13 (3), 175–86

—(2013). 'Education policy and the "ideal learner": Producing recognisable learner-subjects through assessment in the early years'. *British Journal of Sociology of Education*. 34 (1)

Bradford, S. and Hey, V. (2007). 'Successful subjectivities? The successification of class, ethnic and gender positions'. *Journal of Education Policy*, 22 (6), 595–614.

Brah, A. (1996). *Cartographies of Diaspora*. London: Routledge.

Brah, A. and Phoenix, A. (2004). 'Ain't I woman? Revisiting intersectionality'. *Journal of International Women's Studies*, 5 (3), 75–86.

Brown, C. P. (2007). 'Unpacking standards in early childhood education'. *Teachers College Record*, 109 (3), 635–68.

Burke, P. J. (2002). *Accessing Education: Effectively Widening Participation*. Stoke-on-Trent: Trentham.

Butler, J. P. (1990). *Gender Trouble: Feminism and the Subversion of Identity*. London: Routledge.

—(1993). *Bodies That Matter: On the Discursive Limits of "Sex"*. London: Routledge.

—(1994). 'Against proper objects'. *Differences: A Journal of Feminist Cultural Studies*, 6 (2 and 3), 1–26.

—(1997). *Excitable Speech: A Politics of the Performative*. New York: Routledge.

—(2004a). *Precarious Life: The Power of Mourning and Violence*. London: Verso.

—(2004b). *Undoing Gender*. New York: Routledge.

—(2006). 'Response'. *British Journal of Sociology of Education*, 27 (4), 529–34.

Cannella, G. S. and Viruru, R. (2004). *Childhood and Postcolonization: Power, Education, and Contemporary Practice*. London: RoutledgeFalmer.

Carbado, D. (2002). 'Afterword: (E)Racing Education'. *Equity and Excellence in Education*, 35 (2), 181–94.

Carbado, D. and Gulati, M. (2000). 'Working Identity'. *Cornell Law Review*, 85, 1259–308.

—(2001). 'The Fifth Black Woman'. *Journal of Contemporary Legal Issues*, 11, 701–29.

Cassidy, S. (2010). *The 'nappy curriculum' needs changing, minister says. The Independent*. Online at: independent.co.uk/news/education/education-news/the-nappy-curriculum-needs-changing-minister-says-2019182.html [Last accessed 31 July 2012].

Chapman, J. (2009). *Speak English in my Post Office or you're banned. Daily Express*. Online at: *dailyexpress.co.uk/posts/view/89956* [Last accessed 31 July 2012].

Clark, L. (2006). *One in five children unable to write their name or say alphabet. Daily Mail*. Online at: dailymail.co.uk/news/article-412816/One-children-unable-write-say-alphabet.html [Last accessed 10 Aug 2012].

CMPO and ESRC (2010). *Measuring Diversity*. Online at: measuringdiversity.org.uk [Last accessed 10 August 2012].

Connolly, P. (1998). *Racism, Gender Identities and Young Children: Social Relations in a Multi-ethnic, Inner-city Primary School*. London: Routledge.

—(2004). *Boys and Schooling in the Early Years*. London: RoutledgeFalmer.

Connolly, P. and Troyna, B. (1998). *Researching Racism in Education: Politics, Theory and Practice*. Buckingham: Open University Press.

Crenshaw, K. (1989). 'Demarginalizing the intersection of race and sex: A Black feminist critique of antidiscrimination doctrine, feminist theory and antiracist politics'. *University of Chicago Legal Forum*, 14, 538–54.

—(1991). 'Mapping the Margins: Intersectionality, identity politics and violence against women of color'. *Stanford Law Review*, 43 (6), 1241–99.

Crenshaw, K., Gotanda, N., Peller, G. and Thomas, K. (1995). *Critical Race Theory: The Key Writings that Formed the Movement.* New York: New York Press.

Crozier, G. (2000). *Parents and Schools: Partners or Protagonists?* Stoke-on-Trent: Trentham.

—(2005). 'Beyond the call of duty: the impact of racism on black parents' involvement in their children's education', in G. Crozier and D. Reay (eds) *Activating Participation: Parents and Teachers Working Towards Partnership.* Stoke-on-Trent: Trentham.

Curtis, P. (2009). *Nappy curriculum 'boosts basic skills'. The Guardian.* Online at: guardian. co.uk/education/2009/oct/14/nappy-curriculum-boosts-basic-skills [Last accessed 31 July 2012].

Dahlberg, G. and Moss, P. (2005). *Ethics and Politics in Early Childhood Education.* London: RoutledgeFalmer.

Dahlberg, G., Moss, P. and Pence, A. (2007). *Beyond Quality in Early Childhood Education and Care: Languages of Evaluation* (2nd edn). London: Routledge.

Davies, B. (1989). *Frogs and Snails and Feminist Tales: Preschool Children and Gender.* Sydney: Allen and Unwin.

—(1993). *Shards of Glass: Children Reading and Writing Beyond Gendered Identities.* Sydney: Allen and Unwin.

—(2006). 'Subjectification: The relevance of Butler's analysis for education'. *British Journal of Sociology of Education*, 27 (4), 425–38.

Davis, K. (2008). 'Intersectionality as buzzword: A sociology of science perspective on what makes a feminist theory successful'. *Feminist Theory*, 9 (1), 67–95.

DCSF (2007). *National Curriculum Assessment, GCSE and Equivalent Attainment and Post-16 Attainment by Pupil Characteristics, in England 2006/07.* Online at: dcsf.gov.uk/rsgateway/ DB/SFR/s000759/SFR38-2007.pdf [Last accessed 5 August 2010].

—(2008a). *Attainment by Pupil Characteristics, in England 2007/08 (Foundation Stage).* [Online at: education.gov.uk/rsgateway/DB/SFR/s000822/index.shtml [Last accessed 10 August 2012].

—(2008b). *Early Years Foundation Stage: Themes and Principles.* London: Department for Children, Schools and Families.

—(2008c). *London Families of Schools.* Online at: fos.dcsf.gov.uk/PDFDownloads/2009/ LondonDownloads.aspx [Last accessed 5 August 2010].

—(2009a). *Department Report 2009.* London: Department for Children, Schools and Families.

—(2009b). *The National Strategies: Early Years.* Online at: *nationalstrategies.standards.dcsf.gov. uk/node/83902?uc=force_uj* [Last accessed 22 September 2009].

—(2010a). *Early Years Foundation Stage Profile Results by Pupil Characteristics, 2008/09.* Online at: dcsf.gov.uk/rsgateway/DB/SFR/s000911/index.shtml [Last accessed 2 June 2010].

—(2010b). *National Curriculum Assessments at Key Stage 2 in England 2009.* London: Department for Children, Schools and Families.

DEEWR (2010). *Early Years Learning Framework, Australian Department of Education, Employment and Workplace Relations.* Online at: deewr.gov.au/EarlyChildhood/Policy_ Agenda/Quality/Pages/EarlyYearsLearningFramework.aspx [Last accessed 3 August 2010].

Delgado, R. (1995). *Critical Race Theory: The Cutting Edge.* Philadelphia: Temple University Press.

DES (2004). *Foundation Stage Profile 2003: National Results*. London: Department for Education and Skills.

—(2007). *Creating the Picture: Primary National Strategy Early Years document*. London: Department for Education and Skills.

DfE (2010a). *Development Matters for Birth – 11 months*. Online at: nationalstrategies. standards.dcsf.gov.uk/eyfs/taxonomy/33692/33699/0/46384 [Last accessed 30 July 2010].

—(2010b). *Early Years Foundation Stage Profile Attainment by Pupil Characteristics in England, 2009/10*. Online at: education.gov.uk/rsgateway/DB/SFR/s000979/index.shtml [Last accessed 21 January 2011].

—(2010c). *Month of Birth and Education*. London: Department for Education.

—(2010d). *National Strategies: Early Years Foundation Stage Profile*. Online at: nationalstrategies.standards.dcsf.gov.uk/node/83972 [Last accessed 30 July 2010].

—(2010e). *Provision for Children Under Five Years of Age in England: January 2010*. London: Department of Education.

—(2010f). *Review of the Early Years Foundation Stage*. Online at: education.gov.uk/ inthenews/inthenews/a0061485/review-of-early-years-foundation-stage [Last accessed 8 August 2012].

—(2010g). *The Importance of Teaching: Schools White Paper 2010*. [Online at: education.gov.uk/publications/eOrderingDownload/CM-7980.pdf [Last accessed 8 August 2012].

—(2011). *Early Years Foundation Stage Profile Results in England, 2010/11*. Online at: education.gov.uk/rsgateway/DB/SFR/s001033/sfr28-2011v2.pdf [Last accessed 8 August 2012].

—(2012a). *Early Years Foundation Stage (EYFS)*. Online at: education.gov.uk/ childrenandyoungpeople/earlylearningandchildcare/delivery/education/a0068102/ early-years-foundation-stage-eyfs [Last accessed 8 August 2012].

—(2012b). *Early Years Foundation Stage Profile Attainment by Pupil Characteristics, England 2010/11*. Online at: media.education.gov.uk/assets/files/pdf/m/main%20text%20 sfr292011.pdf [Last accessed 20 January 2012].

—(2012c). *Government sets out reform of early learning and children's centres*. Online at: education. gov.uk/childrenandyoungpeople/earlylearningandchildcare/a00191829/government-sets-out-reform-of-early-learning-and-childrens-centres [Last accessed 8 August 2012].

—(2012d). *New early years framework published*. Online at: education.gov.uk/inthenews/ inthenews/a00205838/eyfsframework [Last accessed 8 August 2012].

—(2012e). *Statutory Framework for the Early Years Foundation Stage*. London: Department for Education.

DfE (2012f). *EYFSP attainment by pupil characteristics in England 2011/12*. Online at: http:// www.education.gov.uk/researchandstatistics/statistics/a00215739/eyfsp-attainment-by-pupil-characteristics-england- [Last accessed 30 November 2012]

Dixson, A. and Rousseau, C. (2006). *Critical Race Theory in Education: All God's Children Got a Song*. New York: Taylor and Francis.

Donald, J. and Rattansi, A. (1992). *'Race', Culture and Difference*. London: Sage in association with the Open University.

Dreyfus, H. and Rabinow, P. (1983). *Beyond Structuralism and Hermeneutics*. Chicago: University of Chicago Press.

Dyson, A. H. (1997). *Writing Superheroes: Contemporary Childhood, Popular Culture, and Classroom Literacy*. New York: Teachers College Press.

Epstein, D., Ellwood, J., Hey, V. and Maw, J. (1998). *Failing Boys? Issues in Gender and Achievement*. Buckingham: Open University Press.

Exley, S. (2009). 'Emerging discourses within the English "choice advice" policy network'. *London Review of Education*, 7 (3), 249–60.

Fanon, F. (1967). *Black Skin, White Masks*. New York: Grove.

Farquhar, S. and Fitzsimons, P. (2008). *Philosophy of Early Childhood Education: Transforming Narratives*. Oxford: Blackwell.

Foucault, M. (1980). *Power/Knowledge: Selected Interviews and Other Writings, 1972–1977*. Brighton: Harvester Press.

—(1991). *Discipline and Punish: The Birth of the Prison*. Harmondsworth: Penguin.

Francis, B. and Skelton, C. (2005). *Reassessing Gender and Achievement: Questioning Contemporary Key Debates*. London: Routledge.

Gereluk, D. (2008). *Symbolic Clothing in Schools*. London: Continuum.

Gewirtz, S. (2001). 'Cloning the Blairs: New Labour's programme for the re-socialisation of working-class parents'. *Journal of Education Policy*, 16, 365–78.

Gewirtz, S., Ball, S. J. and Bowe, R. (1995). *Markets, Choice and Equity in Education*. Buckingham: Open University Press.

Gillborn, D. (1990). *'Race', Ethnicity and Education: Teaching and Learning in Multi-ethnic Schools*. London: Unwin Hyman.

—(1995). *Racism and Antiracism in Real Schools: Theory, Policy, Practice*. Buckingham: Open University Press.

—(2002). *Education and Institutional Racism*. London: Institute of Education University of London.

—(2006a). 'Critical Race Theory and education: Racism and anti-racism in educational theory and praxis'. *Discourse: Studies in the Cultural Politics of Education*, 27 (1), 11–32.

—(2006b). 'Critical Race Theory beyond North America: Towards a trans-Atlantic dialogue on racism and antiracism in educational theory and praxis'. In Dixson and Rousseau.

—(2006c). 'Rethinking White supremacy: Who counts in "WhiteWorld"'. *Ethnicities*, 6 (3), 318–40.

—(2008). *Racism and Education: Coincidence or Conspiracy?* London: Routledge.

—(2009). 'Education: The numbers game and the construction of White racial victimhood'. In K. Sveinsson (ed.), *Who Cares about the White Working Class?*. London: Runnymede Trust.

—(2010). 'The White working class, racism and respectability: Victims, degenerates and interest-convergence'. *British Journal of Educational Studies*, 58 (1), 3–25.

Gillborn, D. and Mirza, H. S. (2000). *Educational Inequality: Mapping Race, Class and Gender – A synthesis of research evidence*. London: Ofsted.

Gillborn, D. and Youdell, D. C. (2000). *Rationing Education: Policy, Practice, Reform and Equity*. Buckingham: Open University Press.

—(2009). 'Critical perspectives on race and schooling'. In J. Banks (ed.), *The Routledge International Companion to Multicultural Education*. New York: Routledge.

Glendinning, L. (2007). *Under-fives struggle with writing – report*. *The Guardian* Online at: guardian.co.uk/uk/2007/oct/12/earlyyearseducation.education [Last accessed 10 August 2012].

Graue, E. and Johnson, E. (2011). 'Reclaiming assessment through accountability that is "just right"'. *Teachers College Record*, 113 (8), 1827–62.

Guardian (2010). *At five, a third of poor boys cannot write their names, report says*. Online at: guardian.co.uk/education/2010/jan/28/poor-boys-cannot-write-names [Last accessed 3 November 2010].

Gulson, K. (2006). 'A white veneer: Education policy, space and "race" in the inner city'. *Discourse: Studies in the Cultural Politics of Education*, 27 (2), 259–74.

Gunaratnam, Y. (2003). *Researching 'Race' and Ethnicity: Methods, Knowledge and Power.* London: Sage.

Hargreaves, L. and Hopper, B. (2006). 'Early years, low status? Early years teachers' perceptions of their occupational status'. *Early Years,* 26 (2), 171–86.

Harris, C. (1993). 'Whiteness as property'. *Harvard Law Review,* 106 (8), 1707–91.

Hatch, J. A. (ed.) (2007). *Early Childhood Qualitative Research.* New York: Routledge.

Hultqvist, K. and Dahlberg, G. (2001). *Governing the Child in the New Millennium.* London: RoutledgeFalmer.

Ignatiev, N. (1995). *How the Irish Became White.* New York: Routledge.

Institute for Fiscal Studies (2009). *A Survey of Public Spending in the UK.* London: Institute for Fiscal Studies.

Jackson, C. (2006). '"Wild" girls? An exploration of "ladette" cultures in secondary schools'. *Gender and Education,* 18 (4), 339–60.

Jeffrey, B. and Woods, P. (1998). *Testing Teachers: The Effect of School Inspections on Primary Teachers.* London: Falmer Press.

Keddie, A. and Mills, M. (2007). 'Teaching for gender justice'. *Australian Journal of Education,* 51 (2), 205–19.

Kirkup, C., Sainsbury, M., Huddy, D., Adams, E., Burge, B. and Pyle, K. (2003). *The Introduction of the Foundation Stage Profile.* Slough: NFER.

Labaree, D. F. (2007). *Education, Markets, and the Public Good: The Selected Works of David F. Labaree.* London: Routledge.

Ladson-Billings, G. (2004). 'Just what is Critical Race Theory and what's it doing in a *nice* field like education?'. In G. Ladson-Billings and D. Gillborn (eds), *The RoutledgeFalmer Reader in Multicultural Education.* Abingdon: RoutledgeFalmer.

—(2006). 'Foreword: They're trying to wash us away – The adolescence of Critical Race Theory in education'. In Dixson and Rousseau.

Ladson-Billings, G. and Tate, W. (1995). 'Toward a critical race theory of education'. *Teachers College Record,* 97 (1), 47–68.

Lauder, H. and Hughes, D. (1999). *Trading in Futures: Why Markets in Education Don't Work.* Buckingham: Open University Press.

Leonardo, Z. (2004a). 'The color of supremacy: Beyond the discourse of "white privilege"'. *Educational Philosophy and Theory,* 36 (2), 137–52.

—(2004b). 'The souls of white folk: Critical pedagogy, whiteness studies, and globalization discourse'. In Ladson-Billings and Gilllborn.

—(2009). *Race, Whiteness and Education.* New York: Routledge.

—(2009). 'Race, class and imagining the urban'. In Z. Leonardo (ed.), *Race, Whiteness and Education.* New York: Routledge.

Lewis, G. (2000). 'Discursive histories, the pursuit of multiculturalism and social policy'. In G. Lewis, S. Gewirtz and J. Clarke (eds), *Rethinking Social Policy.* Buckingham: Open University Press.

Loveys, K. (2010). *One in six boys of five can't write their name after year of school. Daily Mail Online* at: dailymail.co.uk/news/article-1339275/One-boys-write-year-school.html [Last accessed 8 August 2012].

Loyd, A. (2009). *Helmand deaths cast fresh doubts on mission in Nato's bloodiest year. Times Online, 13 July 2009* [timesonline.co.uk/tol/news/uk/article6695650.ece].

Lupton, R. and Tunstall, R. (2008). 'Neighbourhood regeneration through mixed communities: A "social justice dilemma"?'. *Journal of Education Policy,* 23 (2), 105–17.

Mac an Ghaill, M. (1988). *Young, Gifted and Black: Student-Teacher Relations in the Schooling of Black Youth.* Milton Keynes: Open University Press.

MacNaughton, G. (2005). *Doing Foucault in Early Childhood Studies: Applying Poststructural Ideas*. London: Routledge.

Macpherson, W., Cook, T., Sentamu, J. and Stone, R. (1999). *The Stephen Lawrence Inquiry*. London: Stationery Office.

McCall, L. (2005). 'The complexity of intersectionality'. *Signs*, 30 (3), 1771–800.

McClintock, A. (1995). *Imperial Leather: Race, Gender, and Sexuality in the Colonial Conquest*. New York: Routledge.

McIntosh, P. (1992). 'White privilege and male privilege: A personal account of coming to see correspondences through work in women's studies'. In R. Delgado and J. Stefanic (eds), *Critical White Studies: Looking Behind the Mirror*. Philadelphia: Temple University Press.

Mirza, H. S. (1992). *Young, Female, and Black*. London: Routledge.

—(1998). 'Race, gender and IQ: The social consequence of a pseudo-scientific discourse'. *Race, Ethnicity and Education*, 1 (1), 109–26.

Mohanty, C. (1988). 'Under Western eyes: Feminist scholarship and colonial discourses'. *Feminist Review*, 30, 61–88.

Moss, G. (2007). *Literacy and Gender: Researching Texts, Contexts and Readers*. London: Routledge.

Moss, P. (2008). 'Meeting across the paradigmic divide'. In S. Farquhar and P. Fitzsimons (Eds), *Philosophy of early childhood education: transforming narratives* (pp. 7–23). Oxford: Blackwell.

Nayak, A. (2009). 'Beyond the pale: Chavs, youth and social class'. In K. P. Sveinsson (ed.), *Who cares about the White working class?* London: Runnymede Trust.

Nayak, A. and Kehily, M. J. (2006). 'Gender undone: Subversion, regulation and embodiment in the work of Judith Butler'. *British Journal of Sociology of Education*, 27 (4), 459–72.

Nutbrown, C. (2006). *Key Concepts in Early Childhood Education and Care*. London: Sage.

Oakley, A. (2005). *The Ann Oakley Reader: Gender, Women and Social Science*. Bristol: Policy Press.

Ofsted (2012). *The framework for school inspection from September 2012*. Online at: ofsted.gov.uk/resources/framework-for-school-inspection-january-2012 [Last accessed 8 August 2012].

Omi, M. and Winant, H. (2004). 'On the theoretical status of the concept of race'. In Ladson-Billings and Gillborn.

Osgood, J. (2006). 'Professionalism and Performativity: The feminist challenge facing early years practitioners'. *Early Years*, 26 (2), 187–99.

Paton, G. (2011). *Bureaucratic 'nappy curriculum' to be cut down*. *The Telegraph*. Available at: telegraph.co.uk/education/educationnews/8406667/Bureaucratic-nappy-curriculum-to-be-cut-down.html [Last accessed 31 October 2012].

—(2012). *Ofsted chief to tackle 'anti-school culture' in poor areas*. *The Telegraph*. Available at: telegraph.co.uk/education/educationnews/9331846/Ofsted-chief-to-tackle-anti-school-culture-in-poor-areas.html [Last accessed 8 August 2012].

Phoenix, A. (1996). 'Practising feminist research: The intersection of gender and race in the research process'. In M. Maynard and J. Purvis (eds), *Researching Women's Lives from a Feminist Perspective*. London: Taylor and Francis.

—(2009). 'De-colonising practices: Negotiating narratives from racialised and gendered experiences of education'. *Race, Ethnicity and Education*, 12 (1), 101–14.

Phoenix, A. and Pattynama, P. (2006). 'Editorial: Intersectionality'. *European Journal of Women's Studies*, 13 (3), 187–92.

QCA (2008). *The Early Years Foundation Stage Profile Handbook*. London: Qualifications and Curriculum Authority.

Radnofsky, L. (2007) *Translate less, councils are told. The Guardian.* Available at: guardian. co.uk/politics/2007/dec/07/localgovernment.uk [Last accessed 31 October 2012].

Rasmussen, M. L. and Harwood, V. (2003). 'Performativity, youth and injurious speech'. *Teaching Education,* 14 (1), 25–36.

Reay, D. (2001). 'The paradox of contemporary femininities in education: Combining fluidity with fixity'. In B. Francis and C. Skelton (eds), *Investigating Gender: Contemporary Perspectives in Education.* Buckingham: Open University Press.

Reay, D. and Mirza, H. S. (2005). 'Doing parental involvement differently: black women's participation as educators and mothers in black supplementary schooling'. In G. Crozier, D. Reay and C. Vincent (Eds), *Activating participation: parents and teachers working towards partnership* (pp. 177). Stoke on Trent: Trentham.

Renold, E. (2005). *Girls, Boys and Junior Sexualities: Exploring Children's Gender and Sexual Relations in the Primary School.* London: RoutledgeFalmer.

—(2006). '"They won't let us play ... unless you're going out with one of them": Girls, boys and Butler's "heterosexual matrix" in the primary years'. *British Journal of Sociology of Education,* 27 (4), 489–509.

Reuters (2009). *Troop deaths spiral in Afghanistan as debate rages. Reuters UK, 17 July 2009.* Reuters.com/article/idUKSP547451._CH_.2420.

Roediger, D. (1991). *The Wages of Whiteness: Race and the Making of the American Working Class.* New York: Verso.

Rollock, N. (2007). 'Legitimizing Black academic failure: Deconstructing staff discourses on academic success, appearance and behaviour'. *International Studies in the Sociology of Education,* 17 (3), 275–87.

Ross, T. (2006). *Under-fives too slow to catch on. TES.* Online at: tes.co.uk/article. aspx?storycode=2306035 [Last accessed 10 August 2012].

Said, E. W. (1978). *Orientalism.* London: Penguin.

Sewell, T. (1997). *Black Masculinities and Schooling: How Black Boys Survive Modern Schooling.* Stoke-on-Trent: Trentham.

Shain, F. (2003). *The Schooling and Identity of Asian Girls.* Stoke-on-Trent: Trentham.

—(2010). *The New Folk Devils: Muslim Boys and Education in England.* Stoke-on-Trent: Trentham.

Siraj-Blatchford, I. (1994). *The Early Years: Laying the Foundations for Racial Equality.* Stoke-on-Trent: Trentham.

Skelton, C. and Francis, B. (2009). *Feminism and 'The Schooling Scandal'.* London: Routledge.

Skelton, C., Francis, B. and Reiss, M. J. (2003). *Boys and Girls in the Primary Classroom.* Maidenhead: Open University Press.

Spivak, G. (1988). 'Can the subaltern speak?'. In P. Williams and L. Chrisman (eds), *Colonial Discourse and Post-colonial Theory: A Reader.* New York: Columbia University Press.

St.Pierre, E. A. and Pillow, W. S. (2000). *Working the Ruins: Feminist Poststructural Theory and Methods in Education.* London: Routledge.

Stobart, G. (2008). *Testing Times: The Uses and Abuses of Assessment.* London: Routledge.

Subedi, B. and Daza, S. (2008). 'The possibilities of postcolonial praxis in education'. *Race, Ethnicity and Education,* 11 (1), 1–10.

Tate, W. F. (1997). 'Critical Race Theory and education: History, theory and implications'. In M. W. Apple (ed.), *Review of Research in Education.* Washington, DC: American Educational Research Association.

Teachernet (2009). *Performance Management Process.* Online at: teachernet.gov.uk [Last accessed 27 July 2009].

Tickell, C. (2011). *The Early Years: Foundations for Life, Health and Learning.* Online at: media.education.gov.uk/MediaFiles/B/1/5/%7BB15EFF0D-A4DF-4294-93A1-1E1 B88C13F68%7DTickell%20review.pdf [Last accessed 20 January 2012].

Tikly, L., Haynes, J., Caballero, C., Hill, J. and Gillborn, D. (2006). *Aiming High: African Caribbean Achievement Project*. Nottingham: Department for Education and Skills.

Tobin, J. (1995). 'Post-structural research in early childhood education'. In J. Hatch (ed.), *Qualitative Research in Early Childhood Settings*. Westport: Praeger.

Troyna, B. (1995). 'Beyond reasonable doubt? Researching "race" in educational settings'. *Oxford Review of Education*, 21 (4), 395–408.

Vasagar, J. (2011). *Education chief identifies white working-class pupils as big challenge. The Guardian*. Online at: guardian.co.uk/education/2011/sep/23/education-chief-white-working-class-challenge [Last accessed 8 August 2012].

Verloo, M. (2006). 'Multiple inequalities, intersectionality and the European Union'. *European Journal of Women's Studies*, 13 (3), 211–28.

Vincent, C. and Ball, S. (2007). '"Making up" the middle-class child: Families, activities and class dispositions'. *Sociology*, 41 (6), 1061–77.

Viruru, R. (2005). 'The impact of postcolonial theory on early childhood education'. *Journal of Education*, 35, 7–29.

Walkerdine, V. (1990). *Schoolgirl Fictions*. London: Verso.

—(2003). 'Reclassifying upward mobility: Femininity and the neo-liberal subject'. *Gender and Education*, 15 (3), 237–48.

Walkerdine, V. and Ringrose, J. (2006). 'Femininities: Reclassifying upward mobility and the neo-liberal subject'. In C. Skelton, B. Francis and L. Smulyan (eds), *The Sage Handbook of Gender and Education*. London: Sage.

White House (2010). *Giving Every Child a World-Class Education*. Online at: whitehouse. gov/omb/factsheet_key_child_ed [Last accessed 10 August 2010].

Winnett, R. (2008). *Britain 'a soft touch for home grown terrorists'*. Online at: telegraph.co.uk/ news/uknews/1578785/Britain-a-soft-touch-for-home-grown-terrorists.html [Last accessed 3 November 2010].

Wood, E., Brooker, L., Pugh, G., Ball, S. and Vincent, C. (2008). *The Routledge Reader in Early Childhood Education*. London: Routledge.

Woodrow, C. and Press, F. (2008). '(Re)Positioning the child in the policy/politics of early childhood'. In S. Farquhar and P. Fitzsimons (Eds), *Philosophy of early childhood education: transforming narratives*. Oxford: Blackwell.

Woolf, M. (2010). *Broken homes 'damage infant brains', says Tory. Sunday Times,* 14 February 2010.

Wright, C. (1992). *Race Relations in the Primary School*. London: Fulton.

—(2000). *'Race', Class and Gender in Exclusion from School*. London: Falmer.

Yelland, N. (2005a). *Critical Issues in Early Childhood Education*. Maidenhead: Open University Press.

—(2005b). 'Series Editor's Introduction'. In M. Blaise (ed.), *Playing it Straight: Uncovering Gender Discourses in the Early Childhood Classroom*. New York: Routledge.

—(2007). 'Series Editor's Introduction'. In Hatch (2007).

—(ed.) (2010a), *Contemporary Perspectives on Early Childhood Education*. Maidenhead: Open University Press.

—(2010b). 'Extending possibilities and practices in early childhood education'. In Yelland (2010a).

Yelland, N., Lee, L., O'Rourke, M. and Harrison, C. (2008). *Rethinking Learning in Early Childhood Education*. Maidenhead: Open University Press.

Youdell, D. C. (2003). 'Identity traps or how black students fail: The interactions between biographical, sub-cultural and learner identities'. *British Journal of Sociology of Education*, 24 (1), 3–20.

—(2006a). 'Diversity, inequality, and a post-structural politics for education'. *Discourse: Studies in the Cultural Politics of Education*, 27 (1), 33–42.

—(2006b). *Impossible Bodies, Impossible Selves: Exclusions and Student Subjectivities*. Dordrecht: Springer.

—(2006c). 'Subjectivation and performative politics – Butler thinking Althusser and Foucault: Intelligibility, agency and the raced-nationed-religioned subjects of education'. *British Journal of Sociology of Education*, 27 (4) 511–28.

—(2007). 'Discourse, subjectivity and the margins: Students' constitutions of Shazas, Bazas and Dir'y 'ippies'. In M. J. Reiss, R. DePalma and E. Atkinson (eds), *Marginality and Difference in Education and Beyond*. Stoke-on-Trent: Trentham.

—(2010). 'Performativity: Making the subjects of education'. In Z. Leonardo (ed.), *Handbook of Cultural Politics in Education*. Rotterdam: Sense.

—(2011). *School Trouble: Identity, Power and Politics in Education*. London: Routledge.

Yuval-Davis, N. (2006). 'Intersectionality and feminist politics'. *European Journal of Women's Studies*, 13 (3), 193–209.

INDEX

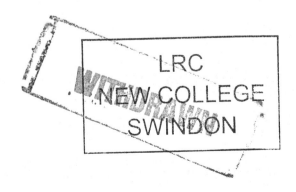

LRC
NEW COLLEGE
SWINDON

Taylor & Francis

eBooks

ORDER YOUR
FREE 30 DAY
INSTITUTIONAL
TRIAL TODAY!

FOR LIBRARIES

Over 23,000 eBook titles in the Humanities,
Social Sciences, STM and Law from some of the
world's leading imprints.

Choose from a range of subject packages or create your own!

▶ Free MARC records
▶ COUNTER-compliant usage statistics
▶ Flexible purchase and pricing options

▶ Off-site, anytime access via Athens or referring URL
▶ Print or copy pages or chapters
▶ Full content search
▶ Bookmark, highlight and annotate text
▶ Access to thousands of pages of quality research
  at the click of a button

For more information, pricing enquiries or to order
a free trial, contact your local online sales team.

UK and Rest of World: **online.sales@tandf.co.uk**

US, Canada and Latin America:
e-reference@taylorandfrancis.com

www.ebooksubscriptions.com

  Taylor & Francis eBooks
Taylor & Francis Group

A flexible and dynamic resource for teaching, learning and research.